P9-BUG-696

THEY
CALL ME
DIRTY

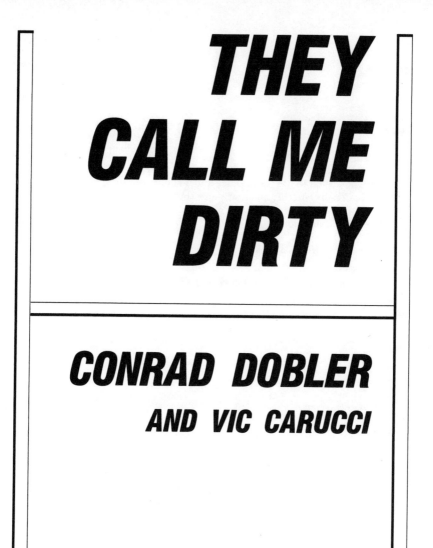

THEY CALL ME DIRTY

CONRAD DOBLER

AND VIC CARUCCI

G. P. Putnam's Sons ▪ New York

G. P. Putnam's Sons
Publishers Since 1838
200 Madison Avenue
New York, NY 10016

Copyright © 1988 by Conrad Dobler and Vic Carucci
All rights reserved. This book, or parts thereof,
may not be reproduced in any form without permission.
Published simultaneously in Canada

Library of Congress Cataloging-in-Publication Data

Dobler, Conrad.
They call me dirty / Conrad Dobler and Vic Carucci.—1st American ed.

p. cm.
1. Dobler, Conrad. 2. Football players—United States—Biography.
3. National Football League. 4. Violence in sports—United States.
I. Carucci, Vic. II. Title.
GV939.D63A3   1988
796.332'092'4—dc19
[B]

ISBN 0-399-13399-2   88-9775 CIP

Printed in the United States of America
1 2 3 4 5 6 7 8 9 10

To my former wife, Linda, who was there to give me the support, the strength and the love I needed throughout my NFL career—I only wish I could have reciprocated in equal proportion; to my children, Mark, Erin, Abbey, Holli Dai and Franco; and to Joy, for understanding this dedication.

—C.D.

To my wife, Rhonda, for believing in me, working with me, and staying behind me every step of the way; to my daughter, Kristen, for being her sweet, beautiful self, and to my mother, for all of those nights she helped me with my English homework.

—V.C.

ACKNOWLEDGMENTS

The authors wish to thank the following for their contributions to the production of this book: Rick Azar, Tom Banks, Richard Bennett, Marty Blackman, Michael Burke, Rhonda Carucci, Bill Dellamore, Dan Dierdorf, John and Clara Dobler, Larry Felser, Kent Goodman, Jerry Green, Jim Hanifan, Chuck Knox, Frank Luksa, Charles Mancuso, Bill Munson, Milt Northrop, Linda Ohler, Howard Smith, Phil Villapiano, Paul Zimmerman, the public relations departments of the St. Louis Cardinals, Buffalo Bills and New Orleans Saints, and the sports information office at the University of Wyoming.

We'd also like to give special thanks to our editor, Roger Scholl, for his hard work and patience, and to our agent, Basil Kane.

CONTENTS

Introduction

I wasn't feeling very thankful on Thanksgiving Day, 1977. My St. Louis Cardinal teammates and I were in the process of having our six-game winning streak, not to mention our dignity, obliterated by the Miami Dolphins. Television viewers throughout the country found themselves with at least two turkeys—the one in the oven and the one on the tube. By halftime, the Dolphins had scored twenty-eight of the fifty-five points they would produce that day, while we had scored seven—exactly half of our final total. I doubt very many people rushed from the dinner table for the start of the third quarter. I know most of the fifty thousand fans in cold, windy Busch Stadium didn't exactly hurry back to their seats—if they returned at all.

The Dolphins could do no wrong, especially their great quarterback, Bob Griese. He wound up throwing a club-record six touchdown passes, three to wide receiver Nat Moore, helping Miami produce 503 yards in total offense. On the other hand, we couldn't do a single thing right, which was quite a departure from the way we had been playing before the opening kickoff. We entered the game with a 7–3 record, second-best in the NFC East and third-best in the NFL. And those of us on the offensive line were on a pretty good roll of our own, having allowed an average of only one sack per game through those first ten weeks.

Miami's right defensive end, a rookie named A. J. Duhe, had been giving our veteran left tackle, Roger Finnie, a tough time all day long. Duhe would go on to become the league's Rookie of the Year, and I would imagine some of those votes came at Roger's expense. The left tackle usually protects the quarterback's blind side, so as he released the ball, Jim Hart often had no idea what hit him . . . until after he looked up from the artificial turf and saw the six-four, 235-pound Duhe standing there. Not that the rest of Jimmy's protection was anything to sing about. He was sacked twice and faced almost constant harassment. Our best all-around offensive lineman, right tackle Dan Dierdorf, was out with an injury and his replacement, Keith Wortman, was struggling. As the right guard, I had to work in sync with the right tackle, who lines up outside my right shoulder, and it was a hell of a lot more difficult with Wortman in there.

Hart finally was pulled, and with just under two minutes remaining, a youngster named Bill Donckers came in to guide us on what would prove to be the game's final offensive series. He drew a lot of strange looks in the huddle when he said, with a perfectly straight face, ''Come on, guys, we can still win this thing.''

Forty-one points down. A minute and forty-nine seconds left. Sorry, Bill, but your timing was off. Guys like myself, who had been on the field from the start, were in no mood to listen to another play being called, let alone a pep talk.

We were humiliated and frustrated and anxious for the clock to just put us out of our misery.

But Duhe—who also would get my vote for Loudmouth of the Year—thought we needed to be reminded we weren't playing worth a damn that day. "You guys are a bunch of dogs; I've played against high-school offensive lines that were better than you," he said, adding a few other wise-ass remarks aimed at the heart of our pride.

When we returned to the huddle, I told the rest of the boys on the offensive line, "Hey, let's shut that sucker up. Let's give him a welcome to the NFL he's never gonna forget."

What I meant was, the next time we put the ball in the air and Duhe turned around to pursue it, we would "pursue" Duhe. Maybe give him a shot to the ribs or a forearm to the chin—just a little something to remind him that he was a rookie and that he should think twice before mouthing off to a bunch of accomplished veterans.

I didn't mean what our crazy center, Tom Banks, thought I meant. After snapping the ball, he simply ignored the defensive tackle lined up in his face, took a five-yard running start, and drove his helmet right into the throat of Duhe, who was already down at the time. The momentum of Banks's spear took him to the ground, too, and as Duhe got up on one knee, it looked as if he was going to retaliate. So I sprinted away from my man and, before Duhe could get to his feet, I gave him another spear. I was just trying to protect my teammate by exercising a little first-strike capability. A. J. fell flat on his facemask, but got right back up and came after me. Banks and a couple of Miami players joined the scuffle, but order was restored quickly.

I'll be the first to admit my attack on Duhe was exactly that—an attack. It was flagrant and I should have been ejected right then and there. For reasons only the officials could explain, I wasn't.

But that doesn't mean I was sorry for what I had done. Not for a minute. First, I was looking out for one of my teammates. Second, Duhe had to pay for his insults. Two cold, hard facts in the violent world of professional football, where intimidation often is the most effective weapon a player can use. There are those who intimidate and those who are intimidated. And if you're the latter, you probably won't survive. Of course, I also was smart enough to realize at that point I had dodged a bullet that would have blown a sizable hole in my wallet. Ejections and the actions that lead to them usually result in hefty fines. I decided I would just cool down and keep my poise through the few remaining plays.

But I knew that wasn't going to be easy when, before the next snap, two linebackers—Bob Matheson and Kim Bokamper—positioned themselves right in front of me. When you play against a 3–4 defense like the one Miami uses, an offensive lineman usually has only one linebacker in front of him. I had a hunch, with the score being what it was and only fifty-seven seconds remaining, this wasn't part of some elaborate defensive front.

When Matheson started snarling and spitting on my helmet, I was certain of it.

"We're gonna kick your ass, Dobler," I heard Matheson growl as Donckers called the signals. Stay cool, I kept telling myself. Don't lose your poise. Don't start anything.

We had called a draw play, but Matheson and Bokamper forgot about the running back, Steve Jones, and just started beating on me. I tried to get away from them, tried to keep them at arm's length, but it was no use. They were out for revenge and they weren't going to settle for anything less. They finally got their arms around me, and as they were about to throw me to the ground, I grabbed both of them by their facemasks and pulled them down on top of me.

If I was going down, I wasn't going alone.

While we rolled around and punched each other, another fight broke out downfield. Then another. And another. Pretty soon, both benches emptied and we had one big donnybrook going.

This time, I was ejected, along with Matheson and Bokamper. Although I knew very well I should have been gone before then, I couldn't understand being thrown out after I had done my best to avoid the fight and only tried to protect myself. I wasn't going to leave the field without an argument, but the referee, Fred Wyant, didn't want to hear what I had to say. He just wanted me off the field—so much so that he started pushing me toward the sidelines. I shoved back and nearly knocked him right on his ass—a mortal sin in the eyes of the NFL. You're not even supposed to breathe on an official, let alone strike one on purpose. At least I had the good sense to grab him by the arm just before he hit the ground and brush off his pants.

Finally, reluctantly, I walked to the sidelines. I still had a lot of steam to vent, and since there wasn't anyone else to punch or shove, I pulled off my helmet and threw it about sixty feet in the air. How hard was that lovely artificial turf we played and practiced on in Busch Stadium? Hard enough that the helmet shattered like an eggshell on impact.

Don Coryell, our head coach, tried to calm me down. So did our offensive line coach, Jim Hanifan. He was wearing headphones and the wires ran down to a battery pack on his side. I didn't realize that, in all my ranting and raving, one of my arms had slid under the wires. And as I yanked that arm away, I pulled off the headphones and nearly decapitated poor Jim in the process. Thank God, his toupee stayed put. No punishment from the NFL could have matched the abuse I'd have gotten from Hanifan if his rug had come off.

What made that scene even more bizarre was the mail it generated. Hundreds of people throughout the country wrote to scold me for losing my temper to the point where I would punch one of my own coaches in the face. I guess all anyone saw on TV was me swinging my arm and Hanifan's head snapping back at the same time.

I also got letters from people who complained that, by throwing my helmet the way I did, I threatened the welfare of the fans sitting behind our bench. They probably were right. If the helmet itself didn't hurt somebody, I'm sure the fight over who got to keep it would have.

It took about twenty minutes for the officials to get everything under control. The final gun sounded, and as we walked into the dressing room, Tom Banks pulled me aside and suggested I not discuss the incident with reporters. Given my emotional state, it was good advice.

"I also think you better get away for a few days," Banks said. "Get away from the press, get away from everything until all this blows over."

So, for the first time in my career, I refused to grant any postgame interviews. And right after we got dressed, Tom drove me to the airport where I boarded a plane for Denver. I was going to have Thanksgiving dinner with my family at our off-season home in Laramie, Wyoming, which is about a three-hour drive from Denver.

I stayed in Wyoming through the following Monday, because we weren't due back to work until Tuesday morning. While I was out there, I read a newspaper account of the brawl. And I had to laugh when I came across a quotation from me that was supposed to have been obtained in an "exclusive" interview at my St. Louis home. How could anyone in St. Louis have quoted me when I had headed straight for the airport for my flight to Denver? The imagination of the press had scored again.

Don Shula, the Miami coach, and several Dolphin players had plenty to say to reporters. Shula called my play a "disgrace." Duhe accused me of "cheap-shotting" every time the ball was snapped, blocking after the whistle, and causing defensive end Vern Den Herder to suffer a season-ending knee injury.

"After a while, I don't even think Dobler was bothering to use any blocking techniques," Duhe said. "He was just trying to hurt people."

Linebacker Steve Towle said I was "sick" and that I had made myself a "marked man." Safety Tim Foley made the type of remark you'd expect from a leader in the Fellowship of Christian Athletes: "I really feel the guy needs to spend some time with himself, collect his thoughts, and realize where he's taking himself." As if he truly cared about me.

Nat Moore and offensive guard Bob Kuechenberg, neither of whom ever lined up across from me, made the most ignorant comments of all. They said they wanted me thrown out of the league.

"The NFL should show some guts now and give him the punishment he deserves," Moore said. "They can't continue to let this guy play."

But the fact was, if the NFL had thrown me out, it would have had to throw out just about every other player in the league. Because I wasn't being dirty for the sake of being dirty. Violence is the name of the game. Half the time I was just trying to hold my own. And no matter how hard I tried, I could never find a nonviolent way to hit a guy. The coaches were constantly on us, saying things like, "Kill the sonofabitches . . . Tear their heads off . . . Nail 'em where they breathe." And those same coaches, as they watched their own players receiving such treatment, would exclaim, "Oh, my! That's disgusting. How dare he do that sort of thing?"

Now, is that hypocritical or what?

In a sense, I patterned myself after football's old-timers, playing the game the way it's supposed to be played. And the way it's supposed to be played is, You and me and screw the rules. You want to kick my butt? You want to show me how bad you are? Let's forget the other twenty guys out here—you and me are going at it.

Pro football's basis is violence contained within a controlled atmosphere. That's why there are referees and those white out-of-bounds lines. As a player, as long as you're inside those white lines, you're expected to kick the other guy's ass. Period.

Sure, the quarterbacks don't loosen their ties and join the fun. But they're the white-collar workers of the game. The quarterbacks, receivers, and flashy running backs are the finesse players. Everybody else has to work for a living. And that means a lot of hard hitting. After all, violence is what the fans want. Why do you think so many people go to the Indianapolis 500 year after year? To watch the cars go around in a circle? They want the spinouts, the roll-overs, the crashes, the flames. They want that rush of adrenaline that comes from witnessing explosive action. What sells newspapers? What makes people watch the nightly news on television? What makes Rambo and Dirty Harry movies so popular? Violence and more violence.

Ninety-five percent of the population doesn't have a place or a method to release aggression. At least, not legally. And because we live in such a structured society, one reason people go to football games is to see all the things they know they'd never get away with in everyday life.

The thing I find so amusing is the NFL's reluctance to admit what its game is really all about. The NFL likes to think of itself as providing entertainment for the corporate set, for guys who go to work in three-piece suits but who show up at the stadium disguised in sweatshirts and Levi's. It forgets that the nucleus of its fans always has been and always will be the blue-collar workers. We're talking about a tough, dirty game. If you want sophistication, go to a tennis match.

Though even there the biggest draw is seeing John McEnroe smash his racket and scream at the umpire.

■   ■   ■

The day after I got back to St. Louis, I was told Pete Rozelle, the mighty commissioner of the NFL, wanted to see me in his office in New York. I'm sure Shula had a lot to do with that. As a leading member of the NFL's Competition Committee, he's like E. F. Hutton: When he sneezes, the NFL listens. Rozelle couldn't have kept his job all these years without playing the necessary politics. Shula's one guy who must be kept happy.

It just so happened our next game was against the Giants in East Rutherford, New Jersey. The decision was made to leave me behind after the game while the rest of the team returned to St. Louis Sunday night, so I could meet with Rozelle Monday morning in New York. I really didn't know what to expect, although I was somewhat relieved to know I'd be playing in the Giants game—at least I hadn't drawn an automatic suspension. The fines had yet to be levied, but I knew that, in addition to having my wallet lightened, I was in for a serious lecture.

The Giants, whom we had beaten in seven straight meetings, couldn't have picked a better time to play us. We were still reeling from the Miami game—physically and emotionally. Despite the fact they had only four wins and were coming off back-to-back defeats, the Giants gave us a 27–7 pounding. They held the ball for nearly forty minutes and outgained us, 318 yards to 252. They took a 10–7 halftime lead, and pretty much put the game away in the third quarter when cornerback Bill Bryant intercepted a Jim Hart pass and returned it fifty-four yards for a touchdown.

After the game, Giant offensive guard John Hicks invited me to join him and a number of his teammates at the Tittle-Tattle, a favorite hangout of sports celebrities on New York's East Side. You had to love Hicks. He was so big and round, at six-foot-two and 258 pounds, he looked like a black Pillsbury Doughboy.

We had been sitting at the bar for about an hour when, all of a sudden, Hicks and Jack Gregory, a defensive end for the Giants, started to argue. Gregory, who had been drinking vodka out of a malt-shaker, questioned Hicks's gender and lineage. Hicks, who was pretty tanked up with beer (and, judging from his weight, it obviously was not Miller Lite), said some things back to him. It wasn't long before the words turned into blows.

Timmy Secor, who owned the bar and was a good friend of both players, got them separated. But after taking a little breather, Hicks and Gregory went at it again, knocking over tables and bar stools and generally carrying on with their little disagreement. Secor stepped between them again, and this time he came away with a badly bruised left hand. Everybody wanted me to play peacemaker, but I had no desire to get involved. I figured I was already in enough trouble with the league. I also was having too good a time chatting up a pretty young stewardess. A guy has to have priorities.

Hicks wound up with a cut on his face and some loose teeth. Gregory sported a black eye. Talk about a little disagreement! I think that was one of the main reasons the Giants couldn't win in those days—too many of their players were showing their best moves *off* the field.

I didn't get out of there until about 4:30 A.M.—three and a half hours before my appointment with Rozelle. When I got back to the hotel, I didn't even bother to go to bed. I just jumped into the shower, put on my suit and tie, squeezed some Visine into my weary eyes, and began my walk over to league headquarters. I figured the walk would help me to sober up and the wind might blow off the aftereffects of a night on the town. Besides, I wasn't exactly in a hurry to get there.

As I sat in the waiting room outside Rozelle's office, his secretary offered me coffee. As I took my first few sips, I scanned the morning edition of the *New York Post*. My eyes immediately focused on a headline in the sports section: TWO GIANTS, DOBLER IN BARROOM FRACAS. I spit the coffee all over the paper.

The way the story came out, it sounded as if I was involved in the fight when I hadn't done a thing. An Associated Press story would make that clear a day later, but that morning, the only account was in the *Post*. And I could just picture Rozelle sitting in his office, reading that story and saying to himself, "Is this guy for real? Brawling in a bar the night before he's supposed to talk to me about brawling on the field?"

I know the Cardinals were pretty upset about my association with the Hicks-Gregory incident, because it drew attention to the fact I had remained in New York after the Giants game. They were trying to keep the meeting a secret, but when my name was mentioned in wire-service stories about the fight, reporters in St. Louis began to ask questions. A team spokesman said I stayed behind to "take care of matters concerning the making of a commercial." If only that had been true.

"The commissioner will see you now," Rozelle's secretary said.

I was carrying a briefcase that contained my defense—several newspaper clippings about the half-dozen or so starting quarterbacks in the NFL who had been sidelined that year with injuries. Jim Hart wasn't part of that group, and the point I was going to make was that I would do anything I could get away with to protect my quarterback. Hold. Trip. Tackle. Maim. Anything.

Keeping the quarterback healthy was the biggest part of my job. It was supposed to be the biggest part of every offensive lineman's job. Why should I be chastised just because I exercised more zeal than other players at my position? I figured I had two choices: Play the game the way I played it or have one of those poor, not-so-innocent defenders try their hand at body-sculpting with Jim Hart.

Rozelle has an aura of power. One look, and you know he's the commissioner—the number one man of the number one spectator sport in America. Still, I've always had a hard time trusting someone with a year-round tan who lives in New York.

I think I threw Rozelle for a loop by being so neatly dressed and sounding every bit as polished as he. We had never met before, so he was probably expecting a toothless Neanderthal with scars all over his face, wearing a Hawaiian shirt unbuttoned to the waist, shorts, and flip-flops.

"Having followed your career for the past six years, I knew it was only a matter of time before we would have this meeting," he said as I took a seat in front of his massive desk.

"And I'm glad we're having it," I said confidently. "I'd

like to explain some things about the way I feel the game should be played."

There was a little chitchat between us before Rozelle began. "Well, Conrad, there have been a few complaints about you. But I'm not going to get into that myself. I'm going to call in Art McNally, our director of officials."

That was Rozelle's way of telling me that, while the final decision on punishment would be his, he wasn't going to get into a debate over it with me. That was Art McNally's job. Executives never do their own explaining. The CEO of the Ford Motor Company doesn't discuss the reasons behind the design of a Mustang. He calls in his head designer. Rozelle has his staff of experts, too—including the person who follows him around each day with a sunlamp.

The three of us then headed for Rozelle's private screening room. With the commissioner walking on one side of me and McNally on the other, I felt like a defendant being led into court—the only thing missing was the handcuffs. The screening room turned out to be a minitheater, complete with rows of nicely cushioned seats. I knew the next thing I'd be seeing was a film clip of the Miami game.

Lights out. Projector on. Pass the popcorn, Pete.

The big eye in the sky had caught everything—the cheap shot I gave Duhe, the fight with Matheson and Bokamper, the shove I gave Wyant. (McNally said the only reason I wasn't suspended for pushing the referee was that he pushed me first and it was only natural for me to respond the way I did.) With the final scene from the Miami game, I figured the show was over.

Little did I know it was only beginning.

Attached to that film was what could best be described as Conrad Dobler Highlights. Or should I say Lowlights. The league office actually had gone through the films of every game I'd ever played in to splice together samples of the dirty tactics I had used through the first six years of my career. There were scenes of me punching guys, hitting them under the chin, hitting them out of bounds, hitting them in the knees, elbowing them in the throat, legwhipping (a form of tripping), kicking, kneeing, stepping on facemasks (with the faces still behind them), piling on, and, of course, holding. They had missed shots of me biting and eye-gouging, but I assume this was only because the photographers didn't use their zoom lenses.

With each scene, I sank lower and lower into my chair—to the point where I could barely see the screen over the seat back in front of me. My shirt was soaked with sweat. Except for the whir of the projector, there was dead silence in the room as McNally ran the film back and forth, back and forth . . .

After the lights came on, Rozelle said, "We just can't have this sort of thing in the NFL, Conrad."

"Well . . . but . . . uh . . ." I couldn't make any words come out. Then, finally, I regained my composure and said, "You could put together film clips like that of just about every player in the NFL. Everyone on the offensive and defensive lines uses tactics like that. Granted, their clips might not be as long as mine. But you could make them."

"Yes, we probably could," Rozelle said. "But we didn't. We only isolated on you."

I didn't even bother to defend my case at that point, because I knew it wasn't going to make a damn bit of difference. I figured I had one foot in the grave and the other on a banana peel—the best thing to do was keep my mouth shut and take my medicine.

While I'm sure Rozelle and McNally never would admit it, I'll bet that footage became part of the orientation for league officials before the start of each season. I can just picture McNally standing by a movie screen, pointer in hand, saying, "Gentlemen, these are the things we want to stop in the NFL," and the refs leaving the room saying, "We've got to stop Dobler."

I was too young and naive to understand that they were putting me on notice that day. Basically, Rozelle was saying, "If you don't clean up your act, Dobler, you're going to be out of the league."

I'd have gladly complied, except that the game wouldn't become any cleaner. And as long as it was a dirty game, I was going to remain a dirty player. The way I saw it, victory had to be achieved at all costs. So if I played it differently than everyone else, I would have been rendered ineffective. I was caught between a rock and a hard place.

Sorry, Pete. But my act was going to stay dirty. And my retirement was still five years away.

1

Keeping the Glamour Boys Glamorous

It was an amazing thing lining up next to Dobler for six years. Ten of us would be involved in a football game, and there would be Conrad, having his own private little war.

—Dan Dierdorf, ABC *Monday Night Football* analyst

*L*esson number one in the NFL is that you don't *play* so much as *survive*. Lesson number two is that if you don't grasp lesson number one quickly enough, you won't be around for lesson number three.

My understanding of lesson number one came at the end of my rookie training camp with the St. Louis Cardinals.

It came at roughly the same time I was informed of my failure to make the team.

Luckily, the Cardinals didn't throw away my telephone number when they placed me on waivers two days before their 1972 opener against Baltimore, because after the second game of the season, injuries had left them desperate for an offensive guard—desperate enough to give me a call. I checked my appointment book, saw I had nothing special planned the rest of my life, and headed back to St. Louis.

The next time around, I concentrated on being a survivor. The man across from me wasn't going to lay a finger on the quarterback. Period. The man across from me wasn't going to get anywhere near the running back. Period. The man I saw in the mirror every morning would stop at nothing to get his job done . . . and keep his spot on the roster.

Period.

I took that second opportunity and transformed it into a ten-year career, the last nine of which were spent as a regular starter. Before my retirement in 1982—after two seasons with the Buffalo Bills—I would appear in three consecutive Pro Bowls and five postseason games and would play a leading role on some of the most efficient pass-blocking units ever assembled in the NFL.

Along the way, I would employ a variety of tactics that didn't always come under the heading of "good sportsmanship." But as I discovered from the very start, "good sportsmanship" has almost nothing in common with the reality of the game.

I was no different from any other player in my never-ending quest to gain and maintain an edge over my opponent. I had to beat the other guy before he could beat me and annihilate the people I was paid to protect. If I was getting beat too often, the head coach—who was just as much of a survivor as any of his players (if not more so)—simply would find someone else to fill my position. Bob Hollway waived an average of two bodies per week during my first year with the Cardinals. The big joke was that the doors to our locker room should have been revolving instead of swinging.

Having already been cut once, I was too scared to laugh.

Football, no matter what anyone says or how many new rules are dreamed up, is still a game of controlled violence. You can't kill anyone . . . and that's about the *only* limit put on it. Regardless of how poised or professional you think you are, regardless of how many Bibles you carry to the stadium each Sunday, there will be a point in the game when you must get down and you must get dirty. It is unavoidable— unless you spend the entire sixty minutes on the bench, collecting splinters on your behind. And it is especially true for offensive linemen. I worked in the trenches; contact was the essence of my game. The glamour boys—the quarterbacks like Ken Stabler and the running backs like O. J. Simpson— usually didn't find contact until after it found them.

Offensive linemen are supposed to see to it that the glamour boys stay glamorous.

Consider the mentality of the people I had to block for ten years. Their idea of a good time was watching the man with the football stagger. Their idea of disappointment was if he did so with his head *still* attached to his body. So I had to be in the proper frame of mind to deal with these homicidal maniacs. I had to make myself tougher than they were. I had to make myself meaner than they were. I had to gain that edge.

I actually would spend an entire week building hatred for the guy who was going to line up across from me on Sunday. If he were a first-round draft pick, I'd hate him because I was only a fifth-round pick and I knew he thought he was so much better than me. If he had gone to a big school, like Michigan or Ohio State, I'd hate him because I had gone to a smaller school, Wyoming, and I knew he thought Wyoming's football program was a joke.

Or I might hate him because his wife had red hair and reminded me of a certain redhead I couldn't stand. Or because his number was similar to the one on the license plate of a car that had smashed into my car years ago. Or because, as in the case of Cincinnati Bengals defensive tackle Mike Reid, he played the piano and piano players just pissed me off. Or because he had freckles (and if he were really getting the better of me, I might have considered playing connect-the-dots on his face). Or because he was a Dallas Cowboy. I mean, how can you not hate someone from an organization that calls itself America's Team?

I'd look for any little thing I could find—a derogatory remark in the newspaper about me, one of my teammates, our team, our stadium, our city . . . life in general. In my later years, with the New Orleans Saints and Buffalo, I'd hate my opponent for having two good knees when both of mine were so bad. It didn't matter what the reason was. Just as long as I found it and used it to make myself the nastiest, most rotten sonofabitch I could possibly be on Game Day.

I know how ridiculous that might sound, but so was a head coach talking to his players as if they were hired killers. I'll never forget, when I was with the Bills, Chuck Knox telling us, "OK, men, we go to Cincinnati, we make the hit and leave town before anybody can finger us." I thought he was going to have us carry violin cases instead of duffel bags.

But Knox isn't the only NFL coach ever to encourage violence. Coaches and management throughout the league make no bones about wanting their players to show the kind of hostility on the field that, if displayed anywhere else, would lead to a prison stretch. They don't come right out and say it, of course. They use polite phrases such as, "The thing I like most about Larry Linebacker is that he has a good football temperament." Translation: It's likely he'll dismember somebody before the season's over.

The truth is, you can't play a sport like football by going out there and thinking it's only a game or it's only a job. You genuinely have to believe that you're on a field of combat and that each one-on-one confrontation is a war. A war within the war. After the game, you shake hands with your opponent, make small talk, maybe even buy him a beer. But inside those white lines, it's his ass or yours.

I always voted for his.

Offensive linemen such as Dierdorf and John Hannah of the New England Patriots were absolute technicians on the field. Almost everything they did was textbook-perfect. They were straight out of a football purist's dream. Me? I had great quickness, but I didn't possess the bulk and strength simply to overpower my opponents the way Dierdorf and Hannah could. Consequently, I played by my own set of rules. And if, on occasion, that meant cutting a defender's legs out from under him, so be it. I was straight out of a football purist's worst nightmare.

The intention wasn't so much to injure as it was to demoralize. Embarrass the guy in front of thousands of fans and, worse yet, his peers. Take away his game. Make him lose his poise. If an injury did occur along the way, it was by accident.

Usually.

My forte was pass protection. It was my ticket to all three Pro Bowls in which I played during my six years with the Cardinals. I wasn't as good at drive-blocking for the run, again because of my lack of bulk and strength. So I would do things in pass protection to make drive-blocking a little bit easier and a lot more effective. For instance, when I chopped a guy off his feet and put his face in the dirt on a pass, that would leave him with something to think about the next time we ran the ball. He'd be so pissed off, so bent on getting revenge, he'd just forget about making the tackle and concentrate on punishing me.

I know one little running back in St. Louis, Terry Metcalf, who really appreciated that. There were times when Chicago Bears defensive tackle Jim Osborne never even bothered to look at Terry because he was too busy pounding on the top of my helmet. I told him once, "I hope you're having fun, donkey, because the guy with the football just ran past you." Why would any defender expend so much time, energy, and emotion on someone who didn't have the ball? I've yet to see a statistic for number of punches landed on an offensive guard's helmet. But if such a category did exist, its all-time leader would be Jim Osborne. Fists down.

As time went on, the tactics I developed seemed to work better and better. Not only during games, but before them, too. I started to gain recognition and respect on a league-wide basis. So much so that opposing players started worrying about the things I was going to do to them well in advance of the opening kickoff. Any time you can make somebody think about something other than his own responsibilities, you've got most of the battle won. And let's face it, the majority of NFL players, particularly those on defense, don't have the capacity to handle more than one thought at a time.

Opposing coaches unknowingly aided my cause by warning their defenders during film review, "Conrad's going to be kicking you, he's going to be biting you, he's going to be punching you in the ribs." That's what the New York Jets coaches did with defensive tackle Abdul Salaam before one encounter with me when I was with the Bills. They actually had one of their offensive linemen spend a whole week of practice grabbing Salaam by the facemask, punching him, kicking him, holding him—all kinds of nasty things.

Now how was he supposed to play his game after spending all that time trying to learn how to deal with mine?

I may have mastered certain techniques, but I sure as hell didn't invent them. I may have gotten a lot of press for being the "meanest and dirtiest player in professional football," but I sure as hell wasn't the only one whose reputation struck fear in the hearts of the opposition. Green Bay Packers linebacker Ray Nitschke, Bears linebacker Dick Butkus, and Pittsburgh Steelers defensive tackle Mean Joe Greene are among the foremost intimidators the game has ever seen. They were responsible for the soiling and soaking of many a running back's pants—and I'm not talking about dirt and water. Then there were Raider defensive backs/assassins Jack Tatum and George Atkinson. They didn't merely cover wide receivers; they punished them. Tatum will always be remembered for the crushing hit in a 1978 preseason game that left Darryl Stingley of the Patriots a quadriplegic. Could wide receivers who faced the Oakland secondary after that truly devote full attention to running patterns and catching the football? I doubt it.

Lee Roy Jordan of the Dallas Cowboys said this about me when I was with the Cardinals: "You have to watch out for Conrad, especially after the whistle blows. If you hear something coming from the back, you tend to turn around in a hurry. He's usually there." Afterward, in a game against the Minnesota Vikings, we threw a pass and as I started to run downfield, one of their linebackers stopped running and yelled, "Watch out for him! Watch out for him!" He actually came to a complete halt in the middle of the play to warn his teammates about me. But that was part of the beauty of playing on the offensive line—the minute the ball went past the line of scrimmage, the defenders had to turn around and pursue it. And that was my cue to go on a search-and-destroy mission, which was when I settled a personal score or two, plus collected a few debts for other members of the offensive unit. The target might be the guy who had punched me in the chin or given me a shot to the back of the head. It might be the guy who had tried to decapitate our quarterback or crucify one of our running backs. Or it might just be the guy who had been giving me fits on the line all day and needed a little softening. If nothing else, I could send him back to the huddle too groggy to remember his assignment for the next play.

And the edge would be mine.

The most important part of an offensive lineman's job is pass protection. That's because the most important—and, when he's passing, the most vulnerable—man on the team is the starting quarterback. Since there tends to be a considerable talent gap between the starter and his understudy, a club's playoff hopes almost always depend upon the starter taking as many snaps as possible. I know the Cardinals wouldn't have played a single postseason game without Jim Hart. And the Bills, who had one of the worst backups of all time in Dan Manucci, certainly wouldn't have reached the playoffs without Joe Ferguson, who, as it was, got us there on one leg. Thus, the starter's health is a constant source of concern.

When the Steelers allowed Cleveland Browns defensive end Joe "Turkey" Jones to enter their backfield one Sunday in 1976, he picked up Terry Bradshaw, turned him upside down, and tried to use his head to drill for oil in the middle of Cleveland Stadium. And who could ever forget the horrifying sight of the Washington Redskins' Joe Theismann having his leg snapped under a pile of New York Giants on *Monday Night Football* in 1985? And what, besides sheer malice, could Packers linebacker Charles Martin have had in mind when he body-slammed Chicago's Jim McMahon, shoulder-first, long after he had released a pass in a 1986 game?

All it takes is for one defender to get past you, and if his hit causes the quarterback to leave the field on a stretcher, you might have just lit the match that causes your team's season to go up in smoke. It's a lonely feeling, standing over a crumpled mess that once was your QB—especially with thousands, even millions of people looking on. It's a feeling every offensive lineman prays he never has to experience. And it's a feeling I always had in mind before the snap on a pass play.

My pride just wouldn't allow me to believe pass protection was a simple case of blocking my opponent. Therefore, with few exceptions, the quarterbacks I was paid to protect for ten years stayed protected.

One of my more famous tactics was the legwhip. It was sort of like a karate kick. As I stood up straight to block on a pass play, I'd plant one foot, and, while going with the flow of my opponent's initial contact with me off the line, I'd swing the other foot around my back and smash my heel anywhere between his shins and thighs. Besides tripping him up, it also could be quite painful. Doug Sutherland of the Vikings said getting hit by me on the shins was worse than a catcher squatting in front of ten knuckleball pitchers. It could be quite painful for me, too. That's why I was one of the few players in the NFL who wore shinguards on the *back* of his legs.

At first, the referees didn't drop their flags when they saw the legwhip, because, I guess, they weren't certain it was a penalty. They eventually would determine it was, but I honestly thought they should have given me points for displaying the tremendous body control required for such a maneuver. It really was a thing of beauty. And I became so proficient at it, I would set defensive linemen up by letting them grab my shoulder pads and twist me around. They thought my momentum would take me out of their way, but what it really did was allow me to swing my leg around with greater force. And it didn't matter which way they turned me, because I was equally adept with either leg.

While I was with St. Louis, I helped influence two rule changes concerning the use of hands by offensive and defensive linemen. One of my favorite tactics to stop the momentum of a pass-rusher was to hit him under his chin and knock his head back. Try running with your head back sometime and you'll understand the effectiveness of this technique. George Allen, then head coach of the Redskins, understood. And that's why, at the league meetings one year, he proposed it be illegal for offensive linemen to strike to the head. Don Coryell, the head coach through my last five seasons with the Cardinals, said, "That's fine, George. But what about your defensive end Ron McDole using the headslap on offensive linemen? If offensive linemen can't strike to the head, defensive linemen shouldn't be allowed to, either." So both tactics became illegal, which was really too bad. Besides not being able to hit below the chin anymore, I also lost that free shot at the rib cage I had whenever a defensive lineman lifted his arm to headslap me. I'd say, "Go ahead, donkey, put your hand on my helmet. I'd just love a cut at those country ribs."

I also helped persuade the NFL to institute a no-taunting rule. The thinking was, if loudmouths like the Dolphins' A. J. Duhe weren't permitted to taunt, players like me wouldn't react with the kind of anger that might touch off a bench-clearing brawl like the one in the final moments of our humiliating Thanksgiving Day loss to Miami. So you can't say I didn't do my part to help improve the safety of the game.

Everybody used to make such a big fuss over my biting opponents. And I never could understand why. I always thought it was a fairly natural reaction when someone stuck his hand in your facemask and put his fingers in your mouth. Coryell made one of the funnier comments on the subject when he said, "Conrad bites, but he doesn't chew." To set the record straight, I didn't start biting until after *I* was bitten by Lee Roy Jordan, the Cowboys' All-Pro middle linebacker. He became a little upset when I tried to shove a cast, which I had worn for most of the 1974 season, through his facemask. So he took a healthy chunk out of my thumb and he probably would have gotten more if his dentures hadn't fallen out in the process. As I looked at my blood-covered cast, I thought, Hey, that's not a bad technique. I'm going to use it if I get a chance. Of course, with the ever-present fear of AIDS, I might think twice about sampling someone's flesh today. I've never known very many defensive players who practiced safe sex.

Although I have helped up a fallen referee in my time, I never believed in doing the same for my opponents. If you knocked me down and I was trying to get to my feet, you were wise to knock me down again. Because once I got back up, I was going to come looking for you. There's just no room for politeness during a war. Jim Pietrzak, a rookie defensive tackle with the Giants, found that out the hard way. There were about two seconds left in the 1974 season finale between the Giants and Cardinals, and all along the line of scrimmage, New York players began offering congratulatory handshakes for our 26–14 victory. When Pietrzak reached across to shake my hand, I punched him in the throat. He was totally stunned. Then, when the gun went off, I stuck out my hand and said, "Thanks." The game was officially over at that point. With two seconds left, the war was still in progress.

I'll bet that rookie never offered another premature handshake the rest of his career.

Not all of my intimidation was physical. Some of it was psychological. Quite a bit, in fact. Despite all the emphasis on athletic ability and X's and O's, football still comes down to one large head game. And getting into a defensive lineman's head doesn't take a Ph.D. in Freudian psychology. It's like scaring a three-year-old. Having minored in child psychology at Wyoming (where, incidentally, I maintained a B average and was an academic All-America), I was well prepared to deal with minds that weren't fully developed.

Believe it or not, my most effective psychological weapon was my smile. Opponents would start calling me all sorts of names and making all kinds of threats. And I wouldn't say a word. I'd just look at them and smile. It was my way of telling them, "It's all over, you dumb sonofabitch. You've already lost to me. I own you now." They thought that with all that screaming and yelling they would get me to lose my poise. But when my only response was a smile, it took a little of their poise away. They'd ask themselves, "What does he know that I don't?" During one game between Philadelphia and St. Louis, Eagles free safety Bill Bradley asked me when I was going to start playing like a professional. All I did was smile at him. And the more I smiled, the hotter he got. It was the same thing with Bill Bergey, the Eagles' outstanding middle linebacker. He'd give me his best shot and when the play was over, I'd just be grinning. I'm sure that was a real blow to the ego of a player of his caliber.

Pittsburgh defensive tackle Mean Joe Greene was one of

the few players on whom it was difficult for me to use any form of intimidation. Going into a game against a guy hostile enough to be called Mean Joe, I can't say that I didn't feel a little bit intimidated myself. During one of our confrontations, he jumped and raised his arms way over his head to try to knock down a pass. Unable to resist such a wide-open target, I hauled off and punched him right in the solar plexus. And when he came down, he yelled, "Dobler, you goddamn motherfucker! I'll kill you for that." I went back to the huddle and started thinking, Hey, this is Mean Joe Greene I'm messing with. This is a guy whose mental makeup isn't a whole lot different from mine.

But I wasn't completely convinced his threat was as serious as it sounded. I decided, if I got the chance, I'd try the technique one more time. Four plays later, we threw another pass and, sure enough, Greene was off his feet and stretching to get a paw on it. Once again, I was staring at that wide-open target. Once again, I hauled off with a punch. As I turned to walk away, he grabbed one of my shoulders and spun me around. I could tell, by his viselike grip, he was serious—very serious.

"What the hell's wrong with you, Conrad?" Greene yelled.

I looked at him and shrugged.

"I don't know what got into me, Joe. I guess I just lost my head."

He didn't say anything. He didn't do anything. He just stared at me with death in his eyes for a few seconds, then walked away.

Never knowing when to quit, I said, "You know, Joe, if you wouldn't keep jumping in the air, I wouldn't keep punching you in the stomach." He just shook his head, and the game proceeded without any further incidents. I guess Joe got the message.

Dierdorf always said I got so wrapped up in my one-on-one battles, I'd forget all about the rest of the game. Maybe so. But my focus sure as hell couldn't have been any narrower than that of Jackie Smith, our tight end in St. Louis, when he was on the same field as Philadelphia's Bill Bradley. Games between the Eagles and Cardinals were, as a rule, extra-chippy. But the friction between Smith and Bradley was on a personal level. They just flat-out despised each other. I'm sure part of it resulted from the fact Jackie was a big conservative guy from the South and Bradley was a wise-ass who wore his hair long and generally came off as a hippie. Bradley just didn't know when to keep his mouth shut, often telling Jackie he was a washed-up old man. You don't get away with saying something like that to an enormously proud veteran player. And Bradley never did. On more than one deep pass to a wide receiver, Jackie would run down-field looking only to smash an elbow into the head of a certain free safety. Bradley usually got his revenge when we tried extra points and field goals. Jackie had outside protection; Bradley rushed the outside gap. There were times Bradley wouldn't even try for the block and, instead, would go straight for Jackie's knees. There also were times when he tried to poke Jackie in the eyes. He tried to poke me in the eyes once, too.

And they called *me* dirty?

My use of psychology wasn't limited to intimidation. In fact, it played an even greater role in my pregame preparation. After a week of finding reasons to hate my opponent and feeling the normal anxiety that precedes each game, I was like a walking can of gasoline by the time Sunday arrived. And it wouldn't take a whole lot to set me off. I remember walking down the hallway of the Cardinals' hotel in Dallas early in the morning, about four-and-a-half hours before kickoff, and a blast of hot air hit me right in the side of the head. I immediately spun around and took a swing at one of my teammates who was behind me, just missing his face. Then, sheepishly, I looked up and saw that the hot air was coming from a vent in the wall. Conrad, I said to myself, I think you're ready for this game. My wide-eyed teammate seemed to agree.

I had a lot of little pregame quirks. For instance, there weren't many players in the league who covered themselves with more athletic tape than I did. Rumor has it Johnson & Johnson nearly went out of business after I retired. Let's put it this way: I used many more miles of tape than I ever ran in my ten-year career. And it had to be applied a certain way or I'd make the trainer cut it all off and start over. Needless to say, I drove a lot of trainers crazy. I always required between thirty-five and forty minutes for taping, whereas most players needed about ninety seconds. They'd have their ankles done and they were gone.

But the way I looked at it, an offensive lineman putting on his tape was like a knight putting on his armor. It was a ritual and it had to be performed exactly the same way every time. For instance, I wanted the four-inch tape for my arms overwrapped exactly two inches. If it was overwrapped, say, three-and-a-half inches, someone or something could rub against the edges and cause it to roll up on me. I did the fingers myself, because that was too delicate a job to entrust to a trainer in a rush. First, I'd wrap them all in elastic tape for flexibility. Then, over that, I'd apply each of the twenty little pieces of athletic tape that had been partially stuck to a wall in the trainer's room just for me. The smallest standard width was a half-inch, which was too wide to crisscross around the upper joints so I could still bend my fingertips. So the trainers had to special-order eighth-inch tape.

I always left my fingertips exposed. That way, I was able to really touch the material of my opponent's jersey. Just to see how it compared to that of other jerseys around the NFL. I always loved the feel of fine fabric.

Tape also helped me invent one hell of a weapon while I was with the Cardinals. I had broken a bone in my left hand early one season, and I wasn't going to let a little injury like that keep me on the sidelines. The only problem was, if I left the finger exposed during a game, I ran the risk of breaking it again. So I slipped the entire hand into a fiberglass shell—big enough so I could move my other fingers. Then, because of league rules, I had to soften the shell by wrapping it in half-inch-thick foam rubber. And when I covered the shell and foam rubber with several yards of tape—ta da!—my left hand became a club.

And defensive linemen had one more reason to worry when they faced me.

For instance, if they came rushing low, trying to drive me back into the quarterback's face, I'd swing that thing up under their chins and put them on their backs real quick. The cast also added about five inches to my thirty-seven-inch reach; when I extended my left arm into a defensive lineman's chest, it made it that much tougher for him to grab or headslap me. Not wanting to give up a good thing, I wore the cast long after the injury healed. Finally, a referee who had worked one of our games earlier in the season noticed I was still wearing it in the eighth or ninth week and said, "That's the longest-healing hand injury I've ever seen in my life. Isn't it about time you took that damn thing off?" So off it went.

But I would have cause to wear it again, again on my left hand, after being traded to New Orleans in 1978. I didn't leave it on very long then, because, for all of its advantages, it did have some big disadvantages. For one thing, it was very cumbersome. For another, it severely hampered my ability to compare jersey material around the league.

Before it was outlawed by the NFL, I was one of the few offensive linemen who covered his hands with stickum, the gluelike substance used primarily by running backs, receivers, and defensive backs to give them a better grip on the ball. If I did happen to get a fistful of a defender's jersey in the course of blocking him, I just wanted to make sure I wouldn't slip off. And there was always the chance I'd be in the vicinity of a fumble and would have to be able to pick up the ball and run with it. It was a slim chance, but, like a good Boy Scout, I always wanted to be prepared.

Despite the fact that offensive linemen tend to get penalized for holding much more often than defensive linemen, shirt-grabbing is a two-way street in the NFL. That's why I used to put double-stick carpet tape on my shoulder pads so my jersey would virtually mold itself around them and leave nothing for those donkeys to grab. I also had the equipment men tailor my jersey really tight. Besides leaving less material for defenders' paws, it made my arms look bigger and more intimidating, thus giving me a psychological edge.

Another of my pregame quirks was having to urinate just before I left the locker room for player introductions. It wouldn't matter if I had taken a leak two minutes earlier. When the coach said, "OK, let's take the field," I'd run right to the bathroom and take another leak. Never failed. I probably pissed a minimum of eight times before each game. I guess part of it also was wanting to hold my manhood one last time, in case someone succeeded in knocking if off—the way coaches instruct their players to do.

I'll be the first to admit I was frightened before each game

I played. Everyone goes into a game feeling scared. You have to have that fear, because fear is what makes you a champion. It's what makes you do your best work, no matter what field you're in. But I can honestly say that if, while we were lined up in the tunnel about to go onto the field, the coach told us, "Men, we're going to do it with knives and guns today," I'd have said, "Let's get on with it."

There were times, of course, when the contest seemed more like a gang war than a football game. Especially when the Cardinals played the Eagles. We were usually battling them for third place in the NFC East, while Dallas and Washington were fighting for first. And there were just a lot of hard feelings between their defense, which liked to intimidate, and our offense, which refused to be intimidated. When we clashed in St. Louis in 1976, a lot of that bad blood spilled. At one point, I wound up on the ground in a wrestling/punching match with Eagle defensive tackle Manny Sistrunk, who was a little peeved after I connected with a shot under his chin. This time, I avoided ejection. But our tight end J. V. Cain was thrown out for assaulting Bill Bradley after Bradley spit in his face. Bradley had spit in my face earlier in the season, so I got even with him that day. Right after he was beaten for a long touchdown pass and was face-down in the end zone, I ran all the way down the field, tapped him on the shoulder and as he rolled over, I spit in *his* face.

There was a lot of spitting and hitting going on that day. We left some people in the hospital, they left some people in the hospital. My kind of football.

A story by Rich Koster in the *St. Louis Globe-Democrat* the next morning, under the headline BLOODY SUNDAY, said: "The latest Cardinal-Eagle rumble on the riverfront produced its share of casualties and bitterness. Concussions and fractures. Stretchers and stitches. Brawls and bitter words. Anger and ejection.'' By the way, we won the game, 33–14.

Because Dallas and Washington were the teams to beat in our division—and because Dallas was Dallas—whenever I came up against a Cowboy or a Redskin, I'd take special pride in trying to humiliate him. Make that extra special.

In 1973, I caused a grown Redskin, defensive tackle Bill Brundige, to cry during a game. I've never seen anything like it in professional football. I don't think anybody from either team could believe his eyes. The Redskins were killing us on the scoreboard, but I was beating the stuffing out of Brundige—ramming my fist under his facemask, legwhipping him, kicking him while he was on the ground, anything I could possibly do to humiliate him. I even knocked him off the line legally on occasion. Then, all of a sudden, he dropped to his hands and knees and started weeping . . . right in the middle of RFK Stadium in Washington. ''Please, let me go,'' he begged. ''Please, quit doing that to me.''

I don't think I ever saw a player with a serious injury cry as much as Brundige did that day. And this was a big guy— six-foot-five, 270 pounds—who came into the league as a second-round draft pick from Colorado. What did that say for the drafting system of that organization? Our confrontation came down to simple pride—I was a fifth-round pick looking to show up a highly touted, better-paid second-rounder. And even though we were losing the game, I had every intention of winning my individual battle so I could at least look in the mirror the next morning and say I beat my man up and down, left and right, front and back. On the other hand, I doubt, even after his team's big win, Brundige felt very proud of himself when he crawled out of bed.

Another crybaby was Lee Roy Jordan. He suffered a

strained knee during a 1976 Cardinal victory over the Cowboys, and accused me of causing it by illegally tackling him from behind. He also threatened to call Pete Rozelle and demand the commissioner order an officiating crackdown on me. "The play was away from Dobler," Jordan told reporters the following day. "He was going down and dove into the back of my legs." What Lee Roy failed to point out was that, at the time of the contact, he was in an imaginary place on the line of scrimmage I liked to refer to as "No Man's Land." Its dimensions were roughly three yards from each side of the center, a yard and a half in front of him and a yard and a half behind him. The rules used to say almost anything could happen in that area. What happened when Jordan went through there was that I hit his leg while lunging forward out of control after missing my initial block.

"No Man's Land" was a World War I term used to describe the deadly territory between opposing trenches. Deadly, because those caught in the cross fire usually didn't live to talk about it. The football equivalent of cross fire between the trenches is bodies colliding, twisting, falling, and piling. Linemen weren't allowed to hold in "No Man's Land," but they could get away with just about anything else. After all, the officials couldn't call what, in all that jumbled humanity, they couldn't see. And I didn't know too many who were brave enough to try to get a closer view.

I would suffer a serious knee injury myself in "No Man's Land" later in my career, but I didn't complain. When you wandered through there, you expected the worst.

But Jordan was looking for a little sympathy and a lot of publicity. "It is unbelievable that I am able to walk today, that I am not in a cast or in a hospital being operated on," the poor thing was quoted as saying. "I just don't think that's the way the game's supposed to be played. If it was, we'd have a helluva lot of convicts who'd be great at it." Funny he never mentioned how, during the same game, a Dallas offensive tackle would stand up one of our defensive ends, John Zook, while a running back went after his knees. And what about the many times Cowboy defensive end Harvey Martin used both hands to try to ram an offensive tackle's chin up into his brain before taking a blind-side shot at the quarterback?

Or is it OK when members of America's Team do those things?

I will admit there was one Cowboy I truly respected—defensive tackle Jethro Pugh. I had some of the better games of my life against Jethro. Beat him every time we met. Maybe it was because I psyched him out with my reputation. Maybe it was because he was tall and lanky and that always allowed me to get good leverage on him. But it wasn't because he was a bad player. In fact, he was a great one. There were players I couldn't handle who didn't have half his ability. It's just that, occasionally, you get somebody's number and I had Jethro's and he knew it. He was one guy on whom every technique I used—clean or dirty—worked to perfection. I'd get on a roll and there was nothing he could do to beat me. There were games when he never once got near the quarterback. But I think the biggest ego-shattering moment for Jethro came when I managed to pull his jersey right over his helmet without being penalized.

I guess the officials just assumed it was his way of hiding from me.

One off-season, a bunch of players traveled to Puerto Rico together to take part in a football clinic sponsored by the NFL Players Association. During our spare time, we played volleyball and Jethro ended up being one of my teammates.

"Now, Conrad, I'm on *your* team this time," he reminded me. "So would you please leave my ass alone?"

Perhaps my most talked-about one-on-one matchup was against Merlin Olsen, the Los Angeles Rams' Hall-of-Fame defensive tackle, in 1976. First, a little background. Merlin and I had previously tangled in the Cardinals' playoff loss to the Rams after the 1975 season. I managed, through my aggressive style of play, to temper some of the joy he felt over advancing in the postseason tournament. As a perennial All-Pro, he simply wasn't used to the rugged treatment he had gotten from me that day in the Los Angeles Coliseum. But, hell, it was a playoff game—there was no tomorrow—and I was going to do everything in my power to help keep our season alive. That meant punching Olsen in the stomach. That meant legwhipping him in the vicinity of his crotch. That meant taking advantage of the fact he was ten years older and thoroughly manhandling him. He was so furious after the game, he told the press, "I won't send flowers if someone breaks Dobler's neck."

A month later, we would meet again, as NFC teammates for the Pro Bowl in New Orleans. I was in the trainer's room, getting my ankles taped for the first practice of the week, when in walked Olsen. Several other Rams had been in there screwing around, but the room suddenly became very quiet and very tense as they looked at him, then at me, then at him again. I thought, Oh, boy. Here comes the showdown. We were either going to talk or fight . . . or both. But whatever was going to happen, I wasn't going to back down, because I had a reputation and, more, my self-respect, to maintain. Even if Olsen was nearing the end of his career, there were some younger players in that room I'd have to face in the future and I couldn't lose whatever psychological edge I already had over them at that point.

Finally, Olsen broke the silence.

"You know that playoff game we had last month? I should have kicked you right in the nuts."

Now do you understand why taking that one last piss was so important to me?

"Well, Merlin," I said, "maybe we'll get to play against each other next season and you'll have that opportunity to kick me in the nuts. You wouldn't be the first to try and I'm sure you won't be the last. So grab a ticket and get in line. Your time will come."

Meanwhile, the trainer, who had been hurriedly working on my ankles, finished the tape job, thus giving me a perfect excuse to exit before anything could get started. We had a light, no-pads workout later that day. And as luck would have it, Olsen and I were squared off in one-on-one drills. Again, everybody around us got real quiet. Although we were only going through the motions, it was obvious we were both tensed up, each awaiting the false move that was never made. Which was fortunate, because that was neither the time nor the place to settle our differences.

Sure enough, the following season—which would prove to be the last of Olsen's fifteen-year career—we played the Rams, again in the L.A. Coliseum. As I got ready for that game, all I could think about was that little scene in the trainer's room at the Pro Bowl. I wanted to embarrass Olsen the way he had tried to embarrass me in front of his teammates. And I did.

But not before he almost gave me some of my own medicine. The same person who was always preaching against dirty tactics, "Mr. Goodie Two Cleats" himself, seemed to me to try to even the score in the first half with a play that would have taken my knees out. He grabbed my shoulder pads while Ram defensive end Jack Youngblood dove at my knees. But I saw Youngblood coming and stepped out of his way, and he went crashing into Olsen's legs. Then, while Youngblood was on the ground, I turned around and gave him a swift kick in the helmet.

The rest of the game, Olsen and I literally slugged it out. As Jim Murray of the *Los Angeles Times* wrote, what we did to each other "made a dock fight look like a square dance." CBS had a replay camera focused on us all afternoon, and I whipped Olsen's ass good for the whole country to see. He couldn't even get off the line of scrimmage, let alone within striking distance of Jim Hart or any of our ball-carriers. It was a perfect example of "victim-precipitated violence," a perfectly legitimate defense in a court of law. Olsen brought that punishment upon himself by saying what he said at the Pro Bowl and permitting Youngblood to take a shot at my knees.

I got him so pissed off and frustrated that he came charging toward our huddle after one play, pointed a finger at me, and said, "I'm gonna knock you out right now, Dobler!" Now was that any way for a future television-series priest to talk?

"Fuck you," I said. And he stopped, turned around, and walked back to his own side of the field.

Midway through the fourth quarter, Olsen realized that he had lost his poise, that he had played right into my hands. So he turned toward the Rams' bench, raised his arm, and took himself out of the game.

The only problem was he had a younger, taller, faster replacement in Mike Fanning, who had spent the previous three-and-a-half quarters resting. It suddenly dawned on me that maybe I should have been a little gentler with Merlin.

Today, the man makes more money than God. He shouldn't concern himself with what I did to him on the football field twelve years ago, but I'm still on his mind. During a graveyard scene in his since-canceled TV series, *Father Murphy*, he actually had the prop men place a tombstone on the set that said: HERE LIES CONRAD DOBLER . . . GONE BUT NOT FORGIVEN.

Nonetheless, his feelings have mellowed with time. My dad talked to him in San Diego when I was out there with the Bills, practicing for our game against the Chargers. Olsen was watching practice because he would be doing color commentary on the game for NBC.

"You don't like my son, do you?" my dad asked.

"Mr. Dobler, I really have kind of put that behind me," Merlin said. "As a matter of fact, at practice today, I shook hands with Conrad."

"You shook hands with my son?"

"Yeah."

My father looked at him and winked.

"Better count your fingers."

■   ■   ■

But I wasn't entirely unreasonable. Take, for example, one exhibition game between Cincinnati and St. Louis. I had just knocked my favorite music-man, defensive tackle Mike Reid, on his ass and I stood over him, grinning and challenging him to get up again. He didn't respond; he just sat there, staring up at me with sort of a blank expression. Then, as the quarterback was about to call the next play, we were all stunned when Reid came barging into our huddle and started yelling at me and punching me in the chest. Before the officials could intervene, Tom Banks threw him out of there and told him to get back to his own side of the line.

"What the hell did you do that for?" I asked Tommy.

"Are you kiddin'? The man was punching you and I came to your defense. What the hell's wrong with that?"

"I don't need you antagonizing the people I play against. That piano-playing sucker is going to try to pound a tune on my head, not yours, the next time. If he wants to come into our huddle, let him."

"You can't let someone from the other team come into our huddle, Conrad."

"Why not? It's only preseason."

I could be quite accommodating in the right circumstances.

I might be one of the few players in NFL history to be thrown out of a game after it was over. Not surprisingly, it followed a typical Cardinal-Eagle slugfest. We were leading by two or three touchdowns and had the ball at the Eagles' one-foot line with about two seconds left. We didn't need to score at that point and weren't really trying. Hart handed the ball off to Terry Metcalf, who was just supposed to fall on it. But we managed to open a pretty big hole and Terry simply walked into the end zone as time expired.

Eagles linebacker Bill Bergey started going berserk. "You motherfuckers!" he yelled. "You cocksuckers! You didn't need that touchdown!"

The end zone was on the end of the field closest to the tunnel that led to the locker rooms. Since I wasn't blocking for extra points at the time, I started walking off the field on my way to the tunnel. And as I trotted past Bergey, I said, "Quit your bellyaching." And I gave him a light backhand across the facemask. He jumped me and we started to fight. No time on the clock. Two feet from the mouth of the tunnel. It wound up costing us $250 each—the fine for being ejected—just to take a shower. Now was that stupid or what?

Bergey and I would have a couple of other memorable encounters. During my first year with New Orleans, he put me out of commission with a blow to my left knee. The injury was bad, but I made it worse through my own stupidity. I

told the trainer, "Just tape it up and I'll go back out there."
I already had torn some cartilage. By returning to the game,
I wound up tearing the cruciate ligament and needing an operation that would sideline me for the rest of the season and
contribute to more serious knee problems later on. But I
didn't want Bergey to think his hit had put me out of the
game.

My pride wouldn't allow it.

When the rest of the New Orleans players were introduced
in the Louisiana Superdome, they played "When the Saints
Go Marchin' In" over the public-address system. When it
came to me, they played "Macho Man." I guess I got carried
away with my image. And it cost me.

The following year, the NFL schedule-makers wound up
arranging a Superdome rematch between Bergey and me.
And I entered that game against the Eagles bent on dogging
him all afternoon. I constantly tried to cut his feet out from
under him; if, perchance, one of his knees were injured in
the process, well, those things happen. In fact, he did wind
up leaving the field with a knee injury—an injury that eventually would force him to retire. But it was more accidental
than intentional. I was pulling around end on an outside run,
and as I dove for Bergey's legs, he tried to jump over me. In
the process, he got one of his cleats caught in the artificial
turf and tore up his left knee. I don't think we even made
any contact, although I was indirectly responsible for what
happened.

I'll admit, I didn't give it much thought at the time, but
looking back, I'm not very proud of that because I had a lot
of respect for Bill. He was an outstanding linebacker. The
weird part about his injury was that it happened on the same
knee, at roughly the same spot on the field, with roughly the
same amount of time on the clock as mine had the year be-

fore. It also happened in the third week of the season, just as in 1978. No, I didn't plan it that way. A little *Twilight Zone* music, please.

■   ■   ■

Believe it or not, there were occasions on a football field when *I* was on the receiving end of intimidation. Many, in fact.

The Cardinals were playing San Diego and I was having a tough time with Louie Kelcher, the Chargers' six-foot-five, three-hundred-pound defensive tackle. Not that having a tough time with Kelcher was a unique experience for an offensive lineman. He is so big that when he lies on his stomach and opens his mouth, people mistake him for a coal mine. Hundreds of years from now, when archaeologists dig up his bones, they're going to wonder what the hell species he was. He truly fooled Mother Nature.

Anyway, we had a fourth and goal and Hart called a "Thirty Dive," a running play that would have me go straight at Kelcher. Having already convinced myself there was no way I was going to move him, I told Hart, "Look, if you want to go to the right of him, fine. If you want to go to the left of him, fine. But we can't go straight at him. No way." Hart called timeout and went to the sidelines to talk with the coaches. Meanwhile, all of my teammates on the field tried to pump air up my ass, telling me what a great ballplayer I was, telling me that I could make a molehill out of that mountain of a man. But it was no use. I knew I wasn't going to budge Kelcher an inch. Hart trotted back to the huddle and called a running play that had me make a cut-off block, where I would use my body as a screen between Kelcher and the ball-carrier as opposed to hitting him head-on. It was a very successful play, as we scored a touchdown, and very safe, as it kept me from falling into the "Kelcher Coal Mine." Like I always said, if you can't beat 'em, go around 'em.

One of the more humbling experiences of my career was the day I went up against another big Charger defensive lineman, Coy Bacon. I figured I would set things straight with old Coy right from the start. So the first play of the game, I came off the ball as hard as I've ever come off the ball in my life. Wham! He caught me right under the chin and dropped me to my knees. I went back to the huddle thinking, My God, that was my very best shot; I can't hit him any harder than that without using a brick.

And I've got four more hours of this guy?

I had a few snot-bubblers laid on me during my career. Snot-bubblers? Those are hits that are so fierce, they actually cause a little bubble of snot to form over one or both of your nostrils. Great for the sinuses. Terrible for the rest of the body.

One time I received a snot-bubbler from coming to the rescue of a teammate. The Patriots had a 250-pound linebacker named Sam Hunt, and Tom Banks was crab-blocking him, staying low and going for his legs. My man had already left me, so I didn't have anyone to block. I saw that big linebacker bending down to try to fend off Tommy and I figured, with a five-yard running start, I could help out by catching Hunt with a forearm to the helmet. That way, he'd be too busy trying to answer the telephone in his head to worry about Banks. I ran, I raised my forearm, but just as I was about to unload on him, he turned around and caught me with a forearm of his own that damn near knocked me out. He twisted my helmet around so that I was looking out one of the earholes.

After I straightened out my helmet and—as best I could—

my head, I looked at Tommy and said, "He's all yours, pal."
I decided charity should begin at home.

Another time, when the Cardinals were playing Chicago,
the Bears ran a tackle-tackle stunt in which the defensive
tackle lined up in front of me, Jim Osborne, took a hard inside rush, away from me, while Wally Chambers came loop-
ing around in my direction from right defensive tackle. I
expected Chambers to come in low, with his head down, because that's what pass-rushers usually do on stunts in order
to get good penetration and push you back into the quarterback's face. But he didn't; he came in high. And he came
in with a flying forearm that hit the bottom of my facemask
so hard, it drove the top of my helmet right down over my
eyes. Who turned off the lights?

During another game against the Bears, I talked Coryell
into letting Bob Young, our left guard, and me play on the
extra-point block team, because we'd been watching the snap
counts from the sidelines and we were fast off the ball and
we just knew we could get in there for the block.

Looking back, I wish I had just kept my mouth shut.

After the snap, one of Chicago's offensive guards, Noah
Jackson, dropped back his inside foot, leaving a big, beautiful gap to the kicker and holder. I took one look at that gap
and, tasting a blocked kick, came charging through as fast as
I could. And as I did, Jackson delivered an uppercut that
took me right off my feet and put me flat on my back. Young
wound up breaking his wrist on the same play. As we came
off the field, me holding my back and Bob holding his wrist,
we looked at each other and said, "Well, that's enough time
on defense for one career, don't you think?"

Probably the toughest overall defender I ever played
against was Kansas City Chiefs linebacker Willie Lanier. The

reason he was the toughest for me was that I rarely laid a lick on him. He was just so fast and had such great lateral movement that I could never get close enough to make any real contact. At the time I played against him, Willie was nearing the end of his career while I was a fairly young man. But that didn't matter. In addition to maintaining his great speed, he also had great knowledge of the game and would always take the fastest route to the point of attack. Because I was still in the learning stages, I had a hard time trying to find the right spot to make the cut-off block. But one time I did, bringing Willie to the ground. As we both were falling, he swung an elbow into my chest that I can still feel to this day.

"Willie, now why would a nice guy like you go and do a thing like that?" I asked.

He got up laughing.

"You just always seem to bring the worst out in me."

Guys like Kelcher and Bacon were tough because they would always claim that three feet of territory across the line and never give it up. Other defensive linemen, such as the Cowboys' Bob Lilly and the Vikings' Alan Page, were just very quick off the ball and would beat you that way. I remember how people always gushed about Page's incredible knack for knowing just when the ball was going to be snapped, how they said he must have had some sort of God-given alarm that told him precisely when to go. True, he did have great natural quickness. But one day, while watching films of Minnesota's defensive line, Tom Banks unlocked the *real* secret of Page's success. He noticed that every time the centers were about to snap the ball, they'd squeeze their thumbs. Page would see that and take off right in time with the snap. Like all NFL players, Page was a gambler. He was looking for the edge and he found it. Or so he thought.

During our next game against the Vikings, Tommy kept

squeezing his thumb without snapping the ball. Page must have jumped off-sides five times that day.

On the offensive line, more so than for any other position in the game, it is critical to know what the guy next to you is going to do. And when you play next to the same people over a period of time, you become comfortable with them. You know exactly how they operate and they know exactly how you operate. That was the situation we had in St. Louis, with Banks at center, me at right guard and Dierdorf at right tackle. The way Dierdorf and I worked, my back could be to him and I'd still know just when to rush forward to give him room to get by. If I hadn't we would have collided, fallen down, and probably suffered knee injuries. Same thing with Dan. He knew that if my man was coming in a certain way, I was going to put that guy on the ground. And just as I was getting ready to do so, Dan, without even looking, would move his leg out of the way.

We all had that sixth sense. That's one of the main reasons I would have preferred to finish my career in St. Louis, as part of one of the best offensive lines in NFL history: Roger Finnie at left tackle and All-Pros at left guard (Bob Young), center (Banks), right guard (myself), and right tackle (Dierdorf). Most of your great offensive lines stay together for a long time and have few injuries. I found out just how true that was after being traded to New Orleans. My first three months with the Saints were spent trying to dodge the hazards of other people's mistakes.

I never had any problem picking up all the stunting and switching defensive linemen do after the snap. I'd just step back and say to myself, One of you donkeys is going to come back to me sooner or later and when you do, I'm going to knock your head off. Dierdorf and I had a simple understanding: If you get the guy who makes the first move, no matter where he goes, I'll take the other guy. And it was almost that easy. We'd zone-block in some games, man-to-man block in others. We'd start out blocking man-to-man, then go to zone. Or we'd start out zone-blocking, then go to man-to-man. Opposing defensive coaches would watch us on film and scratch their heads. You could just hear them asking themselves, "Why did they go zone on this play? Why did they go man-to-man on that play? There must be a special technique involved. But what is it?"

The truth was, we usually didn't know what we were going to do until we did it, but we always had a pretty good idea of what was happening out there. Jim Hanifan, being the tremendous offensive line coach he was, taught us to think of the area in which we worked as a giant chessboard. "Just remember, you're always going to have a little square that needs to be filled," he would say. "If someone leaves your square, don't go chasing him because someone else is going to fill that square. If you go chase somebody, you're only going to create a big void in front of the quarterback." And give the defender an open invitation to mutilate.

Offensive guard is a lot like golf in one respect. In golf, you play the course, not your opponent. As a guard, you play your game, not your man. If the play calls for you to block the guy and turn him out, you can't get so mad that you try to run him over; you just take him wherever he wants to go. You don't ever get mad out there; you get even.

Most of my opponents never could understand that.

They always got mad.

I always got even.

2

"It's My Turn for a Crack at Dobler!"

When you play the brand of football I played, the consequences tend to be severe. I wasn't just another nameless, faceless blocker out there. I was number one on the hit list of almost every defensive donkey in the league. I was a problem that had to be eliminated.

I was a marked man.

John Madden, head coach of the Oakland Raiders, went so far as to put a bounty on my head. He offered a hundred bucks to any of his players who could knock me out of the game. Boy, did that piss me off. Not the idea of the bounty, but the price. I thought I was easily worth ten times what Madden was offering.

I had teammates who, during the the off-season, would do nothing but travel around the country and visit players from other teams. At training camp, they'd tell me that a lot of guys in the league were out to get me, out to hurt me. They'd tell me to watch myself.

I didn't go to a football stadium each Sunday; I went to

Dodge City. I sometimes felt like Wyatt Earp in a helmet and shoulder pads.

But once you give a cheap shot, even in retaliation, you'd better be ready to take one, too. I gave and, many more times than I care to admit, I received. My head still rattles from some of the blind-side hits I took during my career. After an interception, when the defense was out to block *me*, it could be downright frightening. As many as three guys would forget everyone else with a shot at the ball-carrier and come after me. It was as if they had radar in their helmets, because no matter where I was on the field, they always seemed to track me down.

They'd hit me high, they'd hit me low. Then, for good measure, they'd kick dirt in my face after I was down.

And if I made the tackle, I tried to do it as quickly as possible so no one would have that extra time to put my lights out. I didn't always succeed.

There was one interception, during a game between the Cardinals and Redskins at RFK Stadium, that I thought was going to cost me my life. Wide receiver Mel Gray and I gave chase to the defensive back, but we couldn't catch him and he scored a touchdown. As Gray got near the goal line, somebody knocked him down with a vicious clip. Several wooden folding chairs were set up behind the end zone and, much to my surprise, Mel grabbed one and swung it at the nearest Redskin. Needless to say, it wasn't long before he began to draw a crowd.

I decided to come to Mel's rescue, although considering I already had been blocked into the dirt twice myself, I don't know why. In the process of dragging one Washington player away from my teammate, I was pushed from behind by six others and sent crashing into the chairs. While I was on the ground, an angry mob of Redskins began kicking me and stomping on my chest. I thought, My God! They're not messing around. They're really out to kill me. So I grabbed a broken chair leg and began whacking at their toes and shins to keep them at bay until order was restored.

I was too scared to think about it at the time, but looking back, I find it kind of funny remembering those guys dancing like they were on hot coals and yelling, "Ooch! Ouch! Ah!" as I played Babe Ruth with the chair leg.

Although I don't regret it for one minute, I did pay an enormous price for playing the way I did. To borrow a line from former Kansas City Chiefs linebacker E. J. Holub, my knees look like they lost a knife fight with a midget. They have nine surgical scars between them, the ugliest of which is twelve inches long and runs along the outside of my left knee. Walking can be difficult, especially up and down stairs. If I stand or sit long enough, I can usually count on my knees to become very stiff.

There are times when I get out of bed these days that I hear a familiar moaning and groaning. I look around the room, expecting to see my father—then I realize those noises are coming from me. People often ask, "Do all ex–football players have bad knees?" And I say, "Most of the ones who played the game the way it's supposed to be played." If you play hard, your knees and every other part of your body are susceptible to serious injury. And I think most players from my era and from the 1960s and the 1950s would agree that that was a risk accepted for the sake of winning. We all looked at it as a given.

So who cares if there's enough metal in the bodies of former and current pro football players to build a 747? So what if we pick up radio stations with our knees?

If success doesn't motivate you to play hurt, fear usually will do the trick. Management and coaches always instill the belief that if you can't perform, you're out of a job. So you keep denying that the pain exists until you reach the point where, mentally, you're not putting on football gear each week—you're putting on a cape and a shirt with a big "S" on the front. You convince yourself it's always going to be the other guy who leaves the field on a stretcher, not you.

The soreness I felt after a victory actually gave me a strange sort of pleasure. It made me feel I had truly contributed to the outcome, regardless of our offensive statistics. On the other hand, the soreness I felt after a loss was always much worse, even if the injury wasn't. Still, in either case, it usually took from Monday to Wednesday to recover from an hour of pounding on Sunday. In my later years, I never really recovered at all—the aftereffects of one game just sort of blended into the next. The pills I swallowed to ease the throbbing and swelling in my joints helped to a certain extent, but I always felt my adrenaline was the best medicine of all. The pain was still there; I just didn't notice it for sixty minutes.

And there is nothing more personal than pain. I had to laugh when team doctors would ask, "How much pain are you feeling right now, Conrad?" Compared to what? Getting my leg cut off or getting my fingers slammed in a door? The pain I had might be crippling to some people; others might compare it to a hangnail. Even if I could put it into words, the doctors would never be able to understand. I felt like saying, "Here, Doc, let me break your jaw with my forearm— that might give you an idea of what my knee feels like."

I wore the bumps and the bruises and the scratch marks like red badges of courage. I still feel that way about the scars and other distortions on my body that resulted from ten seasons in the NFL. Bill Bergey of the Eagles gave me that foot-long scar on the outside of my left knee; there aren't enough pages in this book for me to list the names of those who, directly or indirectly, are responsible for the rest. My knees have been arthritic for years.

The huge lumps that protrude from my ankles and heels are calcium deposits. They're the result of ten years of leg-whipping. No matter what technique you use, you can't hit a guy and have it hurt him unless you hurt yourself a little bit, too. The legwhip could hurt the legwhipper a lot, particularly in cold weather. On one very frigid afternoon in Shea Stadium, I caught New York Jets defensive tackle Carl Barzilauskas (the guy was every bit as large as his name) with my calf, above the area protected by the shin guard, and I felt sharp pain followed by numbness from the knee down. Until I found out otherwise, I was certain he had snapped my leg right in two.

But when I legwhipped, I never thought about the pain I would feel. Nor did I worry about the consequences of anything else I did while trying to be the most effective blocker I could possibly be. Did Dick Butkus worry about the consequences? Did Mean Joe Greene? Jack Lambert? Jack Tatum?

With us, there was no middle ground. If we were playing, we were aggressive. Period.

■　　■　　■

Most opponents tried to get in their cheap shots when I was blocking for extra points. I was very vulnerable then because, unlike regular offensive line play, blocking for extra points requires a lineman to be stationary—a fact more and more players came to realize each year. So great was the opportunity to hurt me, there'd actually be arguments over who was going to line up in my face. The dialogue usually went something like this:

"Get the hell out of there, man. It's my turn for a crack at Dobler."

"Is not."

"Is so."

"Is not."

They'd go back and forth like a couple of little kids. My teammates couldn't help but laugh. My laughter, of course, was a little on the nervous side. After all, it was *my* hide they were fighting over.

One day, Don Coryell called me into his office to discuss the skirmishes that tended to occur around me whenever we tried an extra point.

"Connie, I've got to take you off the extra-point team," he said.

The moment I heard that, I smiled and my chest puffed with pride. I thought to myself, Well, Conrad, you've finally made it. You're such a valuable member of this team, the head coach is taking it upon himself to protect you.

"I can't tell you how much I appreciate your protecting me, Don," I said.

"It's not you I'm worried about. It's Tom Brahaney."

Brahaney was our backup center and long-snapper for extra points and field goals.

"Why are you taking me off the extra-point team if you're worried about Tom Brahaney?" I asked.

"Well, with all these guys trying to jump your ass, one of them might accidentally hit Tom's knees," Coryell said. "And if he gets hurt, we're in big trouble because we don't have anyone else who can snap the ball long. Do you know how hard it is to find a good long-snapper?"

The extra-point team wasn't the only place where my reputation caused me to be a disruptive force. Sometimes, during the huddle, there'd be so much yelling from across the line, we couldn't hear the quarterback give the play. I was called every name in the book. I was told to leave the field, the stadium, the town, the country, the planet. I was threatened with bodily harm—even death.

Dan Dierdorf, hearing those remarks, would start to laugh. Tom Banks, looking over all of those scowls and snarls on defense, would add, "I think you've really pissed them off now, ol' buddy." Banks and Dierdorf would laugh louder. And, finally, Jim Hart would explode, "Will you guys shut up so I can call the play?"

Another consequence of the way I played was the strange look I usually got from the defensive lineman I'd just punched and legwhipped for sixty minutes when, after the final gun, I'd extend my hand and say, "So, do you have time to grab a beer before you leave?"

They didn't understand that what I did in the game usually wasn't personal and always stayed in the game. When it was over, it was over . . . until the next kickoff. In the meantime, I saw no reason why we couldn't be civil toward each other. Whenever one of them wanted to fight me after the final gun, my standard reply was, "Sure. But first, you're going to have to write me a check, because I don't fight anyone for free. Fighting's part of my job, and right now I'm off duty."

Some people think my reputation as a dirty player was a product of the media. In particular, they point to the October 13, 1975, edition of ABC's *Monday Night Football.* The Cardinals were playing the Redskins and Alex Karras, a former defensive lineman for Detroit, was doing a more than slightly biased narration of a slow-motion replay of my pass protection.

"OK, folks, we're gonna zero in on Conrad Dobler, number

66, offensive right guard for St. Louis. Now you'll notice, folks, that he is going against Bill Brundige and right away he is doing something that is not legal. He is holding."

The camera faded out, then zoomed in again to show Brundige wrestling free and me sticking out my foot to trip him.

"Now, folks, you'll notice that he is tripping."

The camera faded out, then zoomed in again to show me kicking Brundige in the shin as he struggled to regain his balance.

"There you have it, folks. Holding, tripping, kicking. All on the *same* play. That's Conrad Dobler, folks. The dirtiest player in professional football."

I'm sure that influenced the opinions of at least a few people among the millions watching coast to coast. I know there weren't many conversations I had the rest of the year in which someone didn't seek a reaction to Karras's remarks. My standard reply to the controversy was: "Alex Karras has got a lot of class. And all of it is third."

I should point out that Karras himself hardly was recognized as one of the game's cleaner players. His frustration over the Lions' lost cause against Denver in an exhibition game prompted him to kick Broncos running back Cookie Gilchrist in the head and draw a penalty that led to a Denver touchdown. And there was the time he was beating the daylights out of a Chicago offensive lineman whose identity was a blur to him because of his bad eyes. He hammered away with fists and forearms before the guy finally said, "Hey, Alex, it's me . . . your brother, Ted. Go a little bit easier on me, would ya?"

Sportswriters and headline writers throughout the country contributed heavily to the popular, but highly inaccurate, notion that I was some sort of vicious monster.

Among the "reviews" my act on the field received:

We should all be thankful for the National Football League. If it weren't for pro football, the game's arch-villain, Conrad Dobler, surely would turn his wrath on the rest of society. Just imagine that big meanie—all 6-3, 255 pounds of him—loose on the streets. Heaven only knows the terror he'd cause, stealing candy from children, tying fair damsels to the railroad tracks, biting the ears off junkyard dogs. Anyone who follows pro football knows the legend of Count Conrad the Merciless. . . . Playing against Dobler, they say, is like grabbing onto the wrong end of a chainsaw. (Ray Didinger, *Philadelphia Bulletin*)

■ ■ ■

If Conrad Francis Dobler of the St. Louis Cardinals ever loses the ability to fire out on a run block or legwhip a blitzing linebacker, he can still have a lively career playing Chinese warlords in the movies or the guy standing guard at the gang hideout who says, "Just let me break one of his arms, huh, boss?" The troglodytic right guard of the Cards looks about like what you'd imagine Genghis Khan or Attila looked like. To say Dobler "plays" football is like saying the Gestapo "played" 20 Questions. It's like being in a pup tent with a grizzly. You couldn't call it a "game." The way he plays it, it would make more sense to call the rack a game. It's Dempsey-Firpo in facemasks. Dobler's tactics are right out of a "Take No Prisoners" manual. He could make a fortune in Central Park. (Jim Murray, *Los Angeles Times*. I'm sorry I never thought about Central Park; I'm sure it would have been far more lucrative than playing for the Cardinals.)

■ ■ ■

Lock the chicken house. Women, children and small pets inside. An armor suit and welder's goggles for John Dutton. Beware, he's coming back to town. It's Conrad Dobler. Mr. Vile. The master of mayhem. Dobler has been accused of more crimes against man and nature than Agent Orange: legwhips, eye-gouging, rabbit punches, spearing, clipping, late hits, swinging a tire tool and, at other times, something flagrantly illegal. . . . That Dobler can lift himself into the rank of a featured player—as a guard, yet—is testimony to his legend and left hook. (Frank Luksa, *Dallas Times-Herald*)

■ ■ ■

The reputation now precedes him everywhere he goes. When retold, his deeds grow dirtier. When described, he becomes more vile. He has emerged from the obscurity of the offensive line to a seat at the right of Lucifer. This is no average professional football player, this is legend. He is more than an offensive right guard; he is a villain. This is Conrad Dobler, hit man for the St. Louis Cardinals. (Tom Barnidge, *The Sporting News*)

■ ■ ■

At times all of that attention could be somewhat embarrassing. One time in Los Angeles, when the Cardinals were to face the Rams, most of the headlines about the game dealt with my upcoming confrontation with Merlin Olsen, rather than the fact the game was a key NFC showdown. This didn't go unnoticed by Coach Coryell. During his speech the night before the game, he said, "Well, men, we've got a real contest here tomorrow—Conrad Dobler against Merlin Olsen."

The room erupted with laughter. I just looked down at the floor, hoping he would quickly change the subject.

He didn't.

"Based on all the press clippings I've read, I'd say they know a hell of a lot about Dobler in this town," Coryell continued. "You forty-four other guys should be able to sneak up on them."

But I don't blame the media for my dirty label. I think, like so many other sports reputations, good and bad, mine was manufactured by the people I played against. They certainly had the right to speak their minds—those who had minds. Doug Sutherland, for example, bad-mouthed me to the media after a 1974 Monday-night game between St. Louis and Minnesota. The Vikings' defensive tackle told reporters he asked the team physician for a rabies shot at halftime because of a bite I had given him in the first half.

Of course, he might have also explained why his fingers were inside my facemask. I suppose he just wanted to stroke my mustache?

"What you need for Dobler is a string of garlic buds around your neck and a wooden stake," Sutherland said. "He must be the only guy in the league who sleeps in a casket."

Linebacker Lee Roy Jordan of the Cowboys was quoted as saying: "He'll hit and scratch and kick you. That's after he holds you and throws you down to start with." This from the man who taught *me* the finer points of "Fang Football."

Even my own teammates got into the act. Claimed Dierdorf: "Connie is so mean, he even hates himself."

Opponents weren't the only ones to express displeasure with my tactics. I received my share of negative feedback from their fans, too. When I entered a stadium on the road, my typical greeting was a banner that read, "Kill Dobler!" I never took them seriously . . . until an anonymous caller to San Diego's Jack Murphy Stadium threatened to assassinate me during a game between the Bills and the Chargers. I wasn't told of the call until after the game, so I had no idea why, every time I returned to the sidelines, a group of police officers would stand near me—I just thought they were trying to get a better look at the action. And what really pissed me off was that they were blocking my view of the cheerleaders.

When the game ended, Chuck Knox had all the other players gather around me so we could leave the field in a pack.

That way, if someone up there did have a gun, he'd have a hard time picking me out from the crowd. I made certain to walk close behind Phil Villapiano, my best friend on the team. If anyone was going to take a bullet in the heart for me, I wanted it to be Phil. After all, what are friends for?

Occasionally, going out in public would pose a problem for me. I'd be sitting in a barroom, minding my own business, and some drunk, having downed several shot glasses of courage, would stagger over wanting to find out just how tough I really was. I usually could avoid a fight by giving a look that said, "If you know what's good for you, you'll turn around and walk the other way." Or if I were out with a teammate like Banks, he'd step in front of the guy and tell him to get lost. Fortunately, I was smart enough to realize that barroom challengers, most of whom were pretty small (the smaller the body, the larger the mouth), had absolutely nothing to lose and everything to gain. If I punched them out, the story in the next day's paper would say: "Conrad Dobler, six-three, 255 pounds, reputed to be the dirtiest player in professional football, last night assaulted a defenseless citizen." If they punched me out, it would read: "The meanest and dirtiest player in professional football was no match for a 160-pound gentleman who was only trying to defend himself."

Either way, it would be one fight I'd never win.

Some people who saw me in public were afraid to approach me for an autograph because of my reputation as a player. And sometimes, just for fun, I'd play the part. I figured that was what people expected from me. They weren't looking for a calm, polite individual who could quote from the Bible. They wanted to meet the meanest player in professional football.

Those who weren't so shy wouldn't settle for a mere signature; they wanted me to bite the slip of paper after I signed it. Some even asked me to bite *them*. I'd usually oblige. And if they happened to be attractive females, I'd give them a bite on the neck, as well.

I always loved it when a fan complimented me for being such a great *defensive* lineman. I get the same comment to this day. I think it's because the aggressiveness with which I played is more commonly associated with defensive linemen than offensive linemen.

Off the field, I always tried to be nice to people who were nice to me. I could never understand a professional football player, or any pro athlete for that matter, refusing to sign autographs. To me, that was one way to give a little something back to the fans. I saw it as my duty, my responsibility. The fans are the customers and should be treated with the kind of respect with which customers of any business should be treated if you want to continue to receive their support. Without them, there wouldn't be professional sports— period. Unfortunately, a lot of players have a hard time understanding that.

I may have been the only offensive lineman in NFL history to consistently attract a crowd of reporters around his dressing stall after a game. Reporters, like fans, had certain expectations when they interviewed me for the first time. For one thing, it was one of the few times they ever talked to someone on offense who didn't throw, carry, or catch the football. And they were well aware of my nasty reputation. They prepared themselves for an earful of stone-age grunts and chest-thumping. I'd catch them completely off guard by answering their questions as articulately and with as much polish as a lot of quarterbacks, traditionally the most quotable players in the game. They'd say to themselves, "My God! He *is* human. He *can* talk."

As a result, I became one of the few offensive linemen ever to be featured on the cover of *Sports Illustrated*. Maybe what people say about "The S.I. Cover Jinx" is true, because that issue came out right before the 1977 season—a season the Cardinals would finish at 7–7 after three consecutive winning records. And the following year, I would be traded to New Orleans.

I was pleased with the way the article turned out, although in retrospect I shouldn't have been as candid as I was with some of my remarks. The most telling quotation seemed to sum up both my philosophy of life and my style of play. It had to do with people getting even with me, playing vindictively. Did that bother me?

My reply was, and remains, "Let 'em! After all, I've been playing dirty a lot longer than they have."

3

A Troublemaker
Is Born

*M*y parents claim I've been a troublemaker since October 1, 1950—the day I came into this world. I'm sure they're only exaggerating. A pussycat like me a lifelong troublemaker?

Nevertheless, my mother, Clara, still shakes her head whenever she thinks back to the arrival of the fourth of her seven children. On the way to Evangelical Hospital in Chicago, my father, John, was given a traffic ticket for failing to come to a complete stop at an intersection. Then, as he and my mother were rushing to the emergency room entrance, John fell on the sidewalk and injured his leg. Watching him limp inside, the nurse behind the desk thought he was seeking treatment for himself. Before he could explain he was there for my mother, Clara already was on a stretcher and being wheeled into an elevator. I apparently decided the elevator ride was taking too long, because I began to pop out between floors. As my mother tells it, there were no doctors or nurses with her at the time. Just a couple of very nervous orderlies . . . and a bouncing ten-pound baby boy named Conrad Francis Dobler.

When I was three years old, we moved to Twentynine Palms, California, a little town in the middle of the Mojave Desert. My older brother, Clifford, had a serious problem with asthma, so my parents figured it would be better for him if we left Chicago for a dry climate. You can't get much drier—or much more remote—than the middle of the Mojave Desert. In Chicago, my father was a milkman and my mother was a secretary. When they got to Twentynine Palms, they opened a milk distributorship that is still going strong today.

I guess you could say my earliest exposure to the art of intimidation came only minutes after we arrived at our new home. I was outside, minding my own business, when a six-year-old boy who lived next door threw a rock that hit me in the mouth and knocked out two of my front teeth. Welcome to the neighborhood!

Contrary to popular belief, the first living animal I ever bit in anger was not a defensive lineman. It wasn't even human. We had a dog named Princess that tried to take a chunk out of my leg when I was about four. So I turned around and grabbed old Princess and chomped down hard on her snout, tit for tat. What did the Old Testament say about an eye for an eye? She never flashed her teeth at me again.

My mother says I was a pretty mischievous kid. Again, I'm sure she's only exaggerating. But I suppose I may have done a few things to contribute to those migraines she always complained about. Like pulling nasty pranks on my second-youngest sister, Catherine. One time, my brothers and I tied her to a tree trunk, tossed some weeds around her feet and set them on fire. We had just seen the movie *Joan of Arc* on television, and decided to stage our own burning at the stake. We had no intention of really burning Catherine, but just as we were about to move the weeds away, my second-oldest sister, Cynthia, ran out of the house yelling and screaming. We panicked and scattered, leaving the fire to get a little bit out of control. Fortunately, Cynthia untied Catherine and got her away from the tree unharmed.

My dad's a big old man, about six-foot-one-and-a-half and three hundred pounds. And his hands represented the price you usually had to pay for being a wise-ass. He would get my two brothers and me out of bed at two in the morning to give us a licking. Of course, as soon as Mom sent Dad after us, we made sure we screamed as loud as we could, because we knew Mom would come running in and say, "Stop, John! You're killing them! You're killing them!" And Dad hadn't even laid a hand on us yet. But as big and as powerful as he was, it still was safer to have him do the beatings. When my mother did them, she'd get totally crazy. She'd grab anything within reach and hit you with it. A fly swatter. A wooden salt shaker. A yardstick. I suppose the pressures of raising three boys and four girls and running a business would be grounds for temporary insanity in anybody's book.

I'd use the same defense many times in the years ahead.

My father's parents lived with us, and my grandfather, who has since passed away, assumed the role of number three disciplinarian. He was a good man, I liked the hell out of him. But he was always yelling at my brothers and me. Sometimes, he'd take a lath from a garden fence, hit us on the ass with it and say, "That's just in case I don't catch you screwing off."

I went to a small Catholic grade school called Blessed Sacrament. It was so small, there were only four classrooms for eight grades. First and second were taught in one, third and fourth in another, and so on. The nuns who did the teaching were very tough and very, very mean—just the sight of their craggy faces, framed by those old-style habits, was enough to scare the devil out of you. Maybe that's why they looked that way. I'll never forget my first- and second-grade teacher, Sister Theresa, sitting behind her desk and yanking whiskers out of her chin. She reminded me of the wicked witch in *The Wizard of Oz*. Run, Toto, run.

If you got out of line with any of the nuns, they would immediately rap you on the palms with a ruler. Needless to say, I had my fair share of red palms. One day, a bunch of us were playing basketball during recess, and the ball went over the six-foot wall that surrounded the convent. No one wanted to get it, because there was a rule against climbing over the wall. Finally, I volunteered, figuring if I moved quickly enough, I wouldn't get caught. I worked my way to the top of that wall, jumped, and landed in the courtyard . . . right in the middle of where all the nuns were having lunch. I knew, right away, I was in trouble. So I just stuck out my palms and took my raps. Two things I learned about nuns: They don't like to be disturbed when they're praying or eating.

My eighth-grade graduating class consisted of eight students. And when we enrolled in Twentynine Palms High School, we were kind of like outcasts. Most of the other two hundred–plus freshmen had gone to public grammar schools together, so they thought we were a bunch of freaks.

I didn't play any organized sports while I was in grammar school, so the first time I was ever on an official football field was in ninth grade. Our season opener was against Hemet, and those guys were a lot bigger than we were. I was on the kickoff-receiving team, and this monster came charging downfield, screaming and yelling at the top of his lungs. I was supposed to block him, but just as he got in front of me, I stepped out of his way. I thought, Screw it. I'm not going to block him. He looks serious about this. The coach saw the whole thing and immediately chewed me out in front of everybody. It was very humiliating. From that day forward, I never stepped out of the way of anyone.

I played linebacker and halfback during my three years on the varsity squad, receiving all-league honors for offense and defense along the way. I never played on the offensive line, nor did I ever, in my wildest dreams, see myself playing there after high school. Still, at 205 pounds, I was pretty big for a halfback. I could run into defensive linemen, without anyone blocking for me (which was usually the case), and knock them on their can.

We were involved in some good contests as a team, but we always seemed to lose the big games. In the season opener of my senior year we played Beaumont, a school with about two thousand students—fourteen hundred more than we had at Twentynine Palms. We hadn't beaten Beaumont in twenty-three years. And there we were, holding a 6–0 lead with six seconds left on the clock. Our quarterback, Chris Floethe, a great baseball pitcher who already had a pro contract, took the snap. I was lined up at halfback and I didn't even bother to take a step, expecting him to just fall on the ball. Instead, Floethe tried a quarterback sneak and a linebacker pulled the ball right out of his hands. I let that guy run right past me, because I thought time had expired. I was on my way to the buses and I assumed he was, too. But when I turned around, I saw he was headed for the end zone. The extra point was good. Final score: Beaumont 7, Twentynine Palms 6.

In the last game of my high-school career, I tore up my knee badly enough to require surgery. That would mark the beginning of the knee problems that would plague me for the next fourteen years.

I was voted the Most Valuable Player of our varsity basketball team, despite fouling out of almost every game. I probably had more fouls than the second string had points (although I still managed to rank as one of our better scorers). I'd just drive right up a guy's chest if I had to, momentarily forgetting that neither of us was wearing helmets and shoulder pads. Basketball, in the 1960s, wasn't played the way it is now. In the sixties, if you just touched someone, it was a foul. Today, I'd never foul out.

I also was on the track team. Ran the 120-yard high hurdles in 14.1 seconds. Pole-vaulted thirteen-and-a-half feet. High-jumped six feet. Stayed away from the distance events.

My parents went to every single one of my football and basketball games. They'd work for sixteen hours, then get into the car and drive for another two or three to a game. I was amazed by my father. Although he played football and boxed in high school, he wasn't the type of guy to go outside and play a sport with you. But he'd go to any length to watch you perform.

The distributorship kept us all pretty busy year-round. We were on the payroll, just like regular employees. I usually got up at 5:30 each morning to load the trucks for our deliveries, most of which were to grocery stores and schools. On Saturdays, when other teenagers were out playing baseball and fooling around, we were working. You resented giving up the leisure time, but you also felt kind of proud that you had a job when most of the other kids didn't. And you just worked around the conflicts. For instance, if we had a home track meet on Saturday, I'd start my deliveries in the morning, go to the meet, change into my track gear in the back of the truck, run two or three races, do my pole-vaulting, do my high-jumping, get back in the truck, change back into my white milkman's uniform, sell four dozen Popsicles at the meet, finish up my route, and still beat most of the other drivers home by three hours.

During the week, I would drive a semi and deliver milk to about nine schools. Because it counted as "work experience," it was OK when I showed up for school an hour later than the rest of the students. Twentynine Palms High was my last stop and I had to drive up onto the sidewalk to get to the loading dock. The sidewalk was just high enough that, sitting in the cab, you could look right over a brick wall and into the girls' locker room. All my buddies wanted to come up into the cab. It was fun to sit there and watch the girls develop.

In addition to schools and stores, we also had some home deliveries. We were given keys by the customers, so we could just let ourselves in and put the milk in their refrigerators. In the desert heat, you can't leave milk in a little metal box on the porch and have it sit there for an hour or two—unless you like your milk naturally curly. I met a lot of housewives on my route. And, although I didn't know it at the time, I got hustled a lot. They'd answer their doors in negligees. Some even invited me in for coffee and cake. I'd go in and shoot the breeze with them for a little while, then leave. I had no idea what they were *really* after. What's so funny now is that I thought these women were old when they were twenty-eight, twenty-nine at the most. I can't believe the opportunities I passed up. I must have been pretty naive . . . or just plain stupid.

I wish my dad had sat me down and explained those things to me earlier in life.

If it had been up to my dad, we wouldn't have gotten a penny for our work, but my mother gave us twenty bucks a week (which I continued to receive even when I was in college and not working for the distributorship). We were not a rich family, but having twenty bucks in my wallet every week while I was in high school sure made me feel like a Rockefeller. Plus, my parents made sure we each had a car, and they paid for all of our gas and all of our insurance. I drove a Nash, a great car for dates because the front seats folded all the way down to the back seat. It was like having a built-in bed. God, I loved that car.

For the most part, I was fairly well-behaved as a teenager. It was kind of hard for any of us to go out and do a lot of carousing, because with the type of business my folks were in, everyone in town knew we were John and Clara's children. If you got in trouble at, say, the local Dairy Queen, my old man would hear about it the next day because we delivered milk there. Not that that ever stopped me from exploring Twentynine Palms after dark.

One night, when I was about sixteen, my parents went out and left strict orders that I was not to leave the house. Cynthia and her husband, Rick, a career Marine, were supposed to keep an eye on me, which, as far as I was concerned, meant I could do whatever I wanted. And what I wanted to do that night was go out.

"I'm watching you, Conrad, and I don't want you going anywhere," Cynthia said.

"Sorry, but I'm leaving anyway," I said.

She turned to Rick, and said, "Will you do something about this?"

Now, I liked Rick. But he was a little guy, about five-foot-eight and 145 pounds, and I knew he wasn't going to be able to stop me—not without his M16. I was six-foot-two and 198 pounds at the time, and could hold my own pretty well in a fight.

"You come near me," I warned him, "and I'll kick your ass."

He took one look at me and could see I was dead serious. Then he looked at my sister and said, "Hey, I think he's old enough to go out if he wants to." And I left.

Little did I know he would go on to become a crackerjack Marine, spend three tours of duty in Vietnam—and like it there. I was lucky he didn't kick *my* ass.

I dated a big-chested girl who lived in Yucca Valley, which is about twenty-five miles from Twentynine Palms. Yucca Valley was within our delivery territory, so almost every time I was about to leave the house to pick her up for a date, my father would load my car with whatever the driver going in that direction forgot to put on his truck. I'd have ten deliveries to make before I got to her house, so I was always late for our dates. The earliest I ever picked her up was forty-five minutes after I was supposed to get there. Sometimes, I'd pick her up and we'd have to make ten stops on the way to the movie theater.

I pretty much accepted it as being part of the responsibility that goes with working for the family business. However, there was one time when I strongly rebelled, and that touched off an inevitable showdown with my father. It was the Fourth of July after my senior year of high school. I had done all my day's work and I was ready to go see my girlfriend. I was really anxious to be with her, because I'd soon be leaving for Wyoming and I wanted to have one more night with that chest of hers.

"Take this stuff up to Yucca Valley," my dad said, matter-of-factly, as he began loading my car.

"No," I snapped. "I'm getting ready to go to college and I'm not going to be seeing her for a while. I just don't want to be late this time."

You'd think my dad would have understood where I was coming from. He was young once. Of course, after seven kids, maybe he just plain forgot what it was like.

"You're going to take this stuff with you!"

"No, I'm not."

He came charging at me and, instinctively, I gave him a shove—hard enough that he fell over a bunch of milk crates and landed flat on his back. Man, I ran out of there as fast as I could. I headed straight for my bedroom and started to pack my bags. My father got up and chased after me, with my younger brother, Christopher, running behind. Christopher was thirteen at the time and hardly big enough to do anything except watch.

"What the hell are you doing?" my dad yelled.

"You told me any time I wanted to leave here I could and you'd help me pack," I said. "Well, I want to leave, because you're just abusing me. You always want me to do this and do that . . . I don't have a life of my own."

My mother had taken the other kids to a fireworks display at the Marine base in town, so it was just the three of us. And as I was throwing clothes into a suitcase, my dad was taking them out.

"You can't leave now," he said.

"Why not?"

"Because your mother will kill both of us."

I never finished packing. For one thing, I really didn't have anywhere to go, because it still was too early to head for Wyoming. For another, I really didn't know what to do as I watched my father empty my suitcase. And I don't think he knew what he was going to do if I insisted on leaving.

I didn't realize it at the time, but that confrontation had an enormous impact on my father. There comes a point in every dad's life when he suddenly discovers the little boy he was looking at just the other day is a grown man—bigger and stronger than he ever imagined that little boy would be. And what probably hurt him the most was the realization that he wasn't the same authority figure he had been when I was younger.

The scene also underscored the fear he had of my mother. She ran everything—the business, the house. She was the glue that held it all together, and you had to love her for that. I know I did. She even put my father on a salary, just like the rest of us. He got a hundred bucks a week and that was *his* money. He wouldn't share it with anybody. He'd drive us to the show and when we'd ask him to buy our tickets, popcorn, and candy, he'd say, "Well, didn't your mother give you any money?" Or if I'd ask him to buy me new football shoes, he'd say, "Hey, that comes from your mother."

Not only wouldn't he spend any money on us, he wouldn't spend it on himself, either. He must have been carrying around three grand in hundred-dollar bills. You'd think that he would go out and buy himself a bottle of booze or something, but he didn't drink. In fact, I very seldom saw either of my parents have a drink at home. And it wasn't too often that they went out for cocktails or dinner, either. They really didn't care that much about entertaining themselves or buying new clothes for themselves or doing anything besides running their business and taking care of their family.

There was a lot of competition among the seven of us children, whether it came from striving for parental love and acceptance or peer acceptance in high school or anything else that was up for grabs. Looking back, I think the competitiveness interfered with us being really close as kids. And it seems, as adults, we've drifted even further apart. And that's really too bad. I mean, I love them and I know they love me, but that's as far as any of us will allow it to go.

My family wasn't big on displaying affection. In fact, it wasn't until the last five or six years that I can remember my folks actually telling me they loved me. I went back to see them recently after taping a Miller Lite reunion commercial. I hadn't been home in three years, and what kind of greeting do I get from my mother? A handshake. No hugs. No kisses. No tears. Just a cold, businesslike handshake. Now that's kind of sad. But I suppose, raising seven kids and running a business, she and my father were too involved with survival to offer a lot of affection. We knew we were loved. It just didn't seem like they had the time to show it. I don't even remember hearing them say "I love you" to each other that often. But I knew they did.

I will say this about John and Clara: They're probably the hardest-working people I've ever met in my life. They're also among the proudest. We were all very pride-oriented. It was always the Doblers against the world. I wonder if that had anything to do with the way I approached my athletic career?

■　■　■

I received scholarship offers for football from about twenty-five colleges. In addition to Wyoming, I heard from Arizona, Arizona State, Utah, Utah State, San Diego State, Cal Poly, Berkeley, and a whole bunch of smaller schools. I'd like to think the reason I got so many offers was that I was such a great talent. But I probably wouldn't have attracted any interest at all if it hadn't been for the tremendous efforts of my high-school coaches, Dick Trone and Al Peyton. They wrote countless letters and sent my game films all over the place.

I never thought of my dad as being particularly wise until it came time for me to sit down and decide which college to attend.

"Well, what do you think?" I said, with a whole bunch of letters and brochures scattered in front of me on a table.

"I have my preferences," he said. "But I'm not going to tell you what they are. If I pick the university you should go to and you find out you don't like it there or you get into a pissing contest with the coach or something, it would be very simple for you to quit because you could always say, 'I didn't want to go here, anyway. It was my dad's choice.' Wherever you go, you make or break it on your own. I'm staying out of this one. Make the decision like a man. Isn't it about time?"

He walked away and just left me sitting there. I was shocked. But looking back, it probably was the best advice he ever gave me in my life. It had to be my own decision, because I was the only one who would have to live with it. Smart man, my father.

The first thing that attracted me to Wyoming was that it was coming off a Sugar Bowl appearance. The Wyoming Cowboys had suffered a 20–13 loss to LSU, but their team seemed pretty strong and I had heard a lot of good things about the program from Coach Peyton, who was a Wyoming graduate. I really wanted to see the campus and would have to do so at my own expense, because Wyoming wasn't going to pay for my flight. My father, in one of the rare moments when he exposed the inside of his wallet to daylight, gave me the money.

Recruiting wasn't as aggressive then as it is now. I was put in a dorm with some football players, but they didn't do anything special for me. They didn't even try to get me laid. The next morning, the coaches took me to breakfast and made me a proposition: If I signed a Western Athletic Conference letter of intent—meaning the only WAC school I'd attend was Wyoming—they'd reimburse me for the air fare. So I signed. I knew, at the very least, my father would be pleased to get his $129 back.

Wyoming recruited me as a tight end, but I figured out right away I had two chances of playing at that position— slim and none. There was a quarterback from a high school in Billings, Montana, and it just so happened there was a tight end from the same high school. Some coincidence, huh? The so-called skill positions were filled long before we ever walked onto the field for our first practice, despite the coaches' insistence that every spot on the team was "wide open." I guess that was my first real exposure to athletic politics. There would be many others in the years ahead.

At six-foot-two and 205 pounds, I was considered a pretty large player for Wyoming's program. So the coaches decided to look at me as an offensive and defensive lineman and I wound up playing offensive tackle. It reminded me of when you were a kid and you would pick teams for sandlot football. You picked the quarterback, the running back, and the wide receivers. Then you threw everyone else on the line. I probably could have played tight end or running back, but I'd do so as a third-stringer. I figured, if I was going to be on the club and go to practice every day, I might as well start. And if I wanted to start, I'd have to play on the offensive line.

In those days, college coaches would just totally abuse people on the practice field. Mentally. Physically. They'd just try to break you. I figured the only way I could keep the coaches off me was to kick the behind of the guy across from me and have them get on *his* ass. But that approach had a catch: If you kicked too hard, as I usually did, the coaches would get even more pissed off than if you didn't kick hard enough. I understood their anger over my beating up one of their players in practice. But how could they say, "Hey, we wish you wouldn't do that," and really mean it?

After all, these were the same coaches who, in the second practice of my freshman year, had us take part in a drill designed to destroy our bodies. They set up a row of chutes, which were like cages with openings on two sides. Each chute was about four feet high, three-and-a-half feet wide and four-and-a-half feet long. Six-inch-wide boards were placed on the ground in the middle, forcing you to keep your feet apart as you ran through. On one side, they had some of us face the openings while kneeling on the boards and keeping our hands behind our backs. From the other side, guys would come running with their heads down, aiming straight for our chests. We weren't football players anymore; we were human blocking dummies. And we were extremely vulnerable. I remember saying to myself, I really need this scholarship. I can't afford to lose it by getting injured in something as absurd as this.

But they had a reason for putting us through that drill and it had nothing to do with making us better football players. There were 115 freshmen and they were trying to run people off. And they did. We lost about seventeen guys after the first day of workouts. By the end of the year, we would lose forty more.

Those of us who survived were part of one of the best and rowdiest freshman teams ever to hit that university. We were undefeated and uncontrollable. We were like a perpetual hurricane in the dorms—starting fires in wastebaskets, having women up in our rooms, beating up our floor proctors, crashing fraternity parties. We started food fights in the cafeteria and fistfights in the local taverns. Few days went by when one of us wasn't arrested for underage drinking. And none us took shit from anybody. We weren't even afraid of the varsity players, and they had just been to the Sugar Bowl.

I was one of fifteen players who were brought up to practice with the varsity after the freshman season, which ended earlier than the varsity's. At the time, the Cowboys had the top-ranked defense in the nation. They had a lot of outstanding players on that unit, some of whom went on to play professional football. They also had a pain-in-the-ass coach named Fritz Shurmur. He was a gruff, drill-sergeant type and everyone, including the other assistant coaches, feared him. The freshman offensive unit had to play the part of the opposition for the varsity defense. And before the first snap, I asked one of the assistant coaches, Burt Gustafson, how he wanted us to run the play.

"Just get out there and run the sonofabitch," he said.

"Yeah, but do you want us to come off the line easy, hard, or what?"

"Just run the goddamn play the way it's drawn up!"

Figuring he didn't care how we came off the line, I decided to do it my way. The guy in front of me was Larry Nels, Wyoming's best defensive tackle. I hit him twice, chest-high, with normal pass-protection technique. Then I chopped his legs out, putting him right on his face. Shurmur came running onto the field, mad as hell. He started kicking me in the helmet and kicking me in the ribs.

"You fucking punk," he yelled. "Don't you ever cut one of my defensive linemen again."

"Jesus Christ!" I said, not believing his outburst. "I

thought we were supposed to do whatever we had to do to hold them off.''

I thought wrong. What we were supposed to do was let those guys grab us, throw us in the dirt, and make us look like idiots. And I just wasn't going to stand for that. Meanwhile, Nels just sat there, rubbing his knees. He was the one who should have done the retaliating.

In spring practice after my freshman year, the coaches took a look at me on defense, as well as on offense, to see where they wanted me to play on the varsity squad. That meant I had to spend a half-hour each day working under Shurmur, who still hadn't forgiven me for chop-blocking one of his guys. He saw to it those thirty minutes felt like thirty hours when I was through. I wound up staying at offensive tackle. My preference would have been to move to defense, but I couldn't stand the thought of being tutored by Shurmur.

I learned how to legwhip from a guy named Tom Tatum, who was a graduate assistant coach of our freshman team. He was a former rodeo clown and one tough sonofabitch. He had to be tough to dodge all those charging bulls in the rodeo. One day, during a pass-blocking drill, I allowed a defensive lineman to blow right past me. Tatum was watching and he called me over. He told me an offensive lineman should never allow himself to get beat and he was going to show me something to reduce the chance of that happening very often in the future. He didn't actually call it a legwhip—I would give it that name in the NFL. He described it as a reverse body-block and demonstrated how it worked on a blocking dummy. "Any time you find yourself on the verge of getting beat, just throw your whole body around," Tatum explained. "Let the flow of the initial contact take you around and, at the same time, whip both of your legs around to knock the guy's feet out from under him." I thought it was a great tactic, which I would eventually modify by whipping one leg around while keeping the other planted. I caught the chemistry of it right away and it wasn't long before I became very, very good at it.

My first real understanding of the legwhip's effectiveness came during a practice in my junior year. A defensive end named Dan Fedore grabbed me by the shoulder pads and twisted me around. As he did, his head went down and when I swung my leg I caught him right in the facemask, cracking it and opening an eyebrow-to-eyebrow cut on his forehead. Shurmur came charging after me, again yelling and screaming and ready to place-kick my head. But this time Bill Baker, the offensive line coach, jumped in front of him and yelled, "I'll reprimand my own players, thank you. You just worry about your guys."

There was a lot of friction between Shurmur and Baker. Of course, there was a lot of friction between Shurmur and everybody. While they argued, Lloyd Eaton, the head coach, came over and told me to go jog. I guess that was his way of punishing me for what I had done to Fedore, but I think his bigger concern was to get me the hell out of there while two of his assistants were going at it. A head coach never wants his players to see dissension on his staff, a crack in the armor of the leadership. So I took off, once again having played the role of The Troublemaker.

I appreciated that Baker stood up for me. It only enhanced the great respect I already had for the man. Tatum might have introduced me to the legwhip, but it was Baker who taught me the fundamentals of pass protection. Things like balance, position, developing eyes in the back of my head, getting my hands up, and knocking the other guy's hands down. Those were techniques that would prove invaluable once I got to the NFL. However, when it came to drive-blocking for the run, Baker frankly wasn't much help at all. But that wasn't entirely his fault. The drive-blocking we did was a little bit different from the way it was done at, say, Michigan. In Michigan's wishbone offense, it was the old three-yards-and-a-cloud-of-dust approach. We were a lot smaller at Wyoming, so we had to use a lot of quick plays. We were always running away from defenses, and for the offensive linemen, that meant a lot of cut-off blocks. We never really tried to knock teams off the ball, because we couldn't. We had to rely on speed and finesse.

Eaton was an extremely conservative guy, a real straight arrow. He would always remind us we were much more than college football players—we were representatives of the state of Wyoming. Not just the university or its athletic department, but the entire state. And we were supposed to behave accordingly on and off the field, on and off the campus, on and off the planet. It was, to say the least, an awesome responsibility—especially for a bunch of young degenerates.

Before every team meal in a restaurant, Eaton gave detailed instructions on how he wanted us to conduct ourselves. He treated it with all the seriousness of a pregame speech. He'd say, "Now I don't want you acting like a bunch of goddamn hooligans. Sit straight. Keep your elbows off the table. And I don't want to see a single drop of food on the tablecloth when you're through." About the only things he didn't tell us were to eat all of our vegetables and to finish our milk. Not only did he dictate the way we were supposed to act, he also dictated the way we were supposed to look. That meant short hair and clean-shaven faces. Sideburns had to stay above the ears.

Eaton was a strict disciplinarian. If you broke his rules and were caught doing so, you paid dearly. Punishment ranged from running until you dropped to dismissal from the team. He wasn't very flexible when it came to his interpretation of right and wrong. And the most glaring and controversial example of his rigidness led to what will forever be known in the annals of Wyoming football as "The Black Fourteen" incident.

It all started four days before our home game against Brigham Young in 1969, the hundredth year of college football. Fourteen black members of the team approached Eaton to ask if it would be OK for all the players, whites included, to wear black armbands around their jersey sleeves to protest BYU's discriminatory policies. Eaton said no.

"The way to protest is to go out there and kick BYU's ass," he told them. "And I'm warning you: Any player who shows up wearing an armband is off the team."

It should be pointed out Eaton had a long-standing rule against protesting or demonstrating, regardless of the cause. His standard explanation was that no Wyoming football player could be a competent student and an excellent athlete and still devote himself to such actions as political and social movements. So if you were seen taking part in a peace march or a sit-in or a rally and the coaching staff found out about it, you were history. Period.

The fourteen black players, who were being prodded by the university's Black Students Alliance, wouldn't quit. They approached Eaton two days later, this time asking him to permit only the fourteen of them to wear the armbands. Eaton started losing his temper.

"I told you, no!" he said. "And I don't want to see you wearing them around campus, either."

The next morning, with kickoff a little more than twenty-four hours away, they showed up in Eaton's office for a third time . . . wearing the armbands. "I warned you," he said.

"Now you're gone." They were immediately dismissed from the team for the balance of the season, which, counting the BYU game, had six weeks remaining. The action received the approval of the school's board of trustees, but not until after an all-night emergency meeting with the coaching staff and the athletes in question.

One of "The Black Fourteen," defensive back Jerry Berry, gave a reporter this version of the final meeting with Eaton: "As soon as we went into his office, Eaton said he could save us a lot of words. He told us we had made our bid and from now on we were off the team. All we heard ninety-five percent of the time was, 'Shut up.' We didn't even get a chance to explain our purpose to him."

A number of black students picketed the practice that followed the dismissal. In their eyes, our continuing to prepare for the game meant we opposed their cause. They called us whities, honkies, racists, you name it. I didn't think that was really fair on their part, because we had absolutely no say in the matter. My feeling was if they wanted to wear the armbands, fine, let them. I'd have worn one, too. I didn't consider myself a racist. I was never brought up to think that way. I never even heard the word "nigger" until I was in college. I'm sure the isolation of Twentynine Palms had something to do with that, but the biggest reason was my folks just didn't use such terms around our house. There were blacks and Mexicans working for the distributorship and to me they were equals.

Still, when we were out there practicing and the black students were yelling at us, we couldn't help but get a little defensive and use the whole situation as a rallying point.

"We'll show those fourteen guys we can win without them," we said. "We don't need them."

And, for two games, we didn't. We pounded Brigham

Young, 40–7. The following week we defeated San Jose State, 16–7, to improve our record to 6–0. The BYU victory was critical for Eaton, because it helped deflect some of the heat he was getting from various factions on campus. Chants of "We love Eaton! We love Eaton!" could be heard among the crowd of fifteen thousand. But after the game, there were reports of professors threatening to resign if the players were not reinstated. The Casper, Wyoming, Quarterback Club responded by offering to pay the moving expenses of any faculty members opposing Eaton's decision. Now that's what I call support.

Eaton also received a number of supportive telegrams from throughout the country. One was signed Paul "Bear" Bryant.

After the San Jose State game, we began to feel the effects of losing fourteen players, five of whom had been starters. The combination of that and a rash of injuries left us pretty thin. We were so desperate for bodies, we suited up our equipment manager and a male cheerleader. We ended up losing our last four games. As if that weren't painful enough, I broke my wrist in our season finale, a 41–14 loss to the University of Houston, and I had to undergo a postseason knee operation. A very memorable year, to say the least.

Some of "The Black Fourteen" with eligibility remaining transferred to other schools. But there were three who applied for reinstatement just before spring practice in 1970. Eaton, who had had his fill of controversy for one lifetime, wanted absolutely no part of that decision. So he turned it over to a vote of his white players. He told the three black guys to present their cases during a team meeting with no coaches present.

I felt sorry for them, having to stand up there, one at a

time, and be grilled by us. All they wanted to do was get back on the team, save their scholarships, play some football, and get their educations.

I said, "If it's a vote Eaton wants, then I say we vote to bring you back."

Everyone else agreed and they were reinstated. Years after I left Wyoming, I was shocked to find out "The Black Fourteen" were under some very intense pressure to do what they did. One of them told me he actually received a death threat from a black organization pushing them to wear the armbands. He said he carried a gun with him for two weeks.

I had my own encounter with Eaton's wrath at the end of my sophomore year, just before I was ready to leave for home. I finished classes on a Friday, but I had to stick around until the following Monday to attend a steak fry for the football team. After my last class on Friday, I figured, since I was going home for the summer, I might as well let my sideburns grow to the bottom of my ears. I had every intention of shaving them back to the Eaton-imposed length before returning for preseason practice.

By Monday, they were still very much in the stubbly stage. But as I stood on line for food at the steak fry, Eaton walked up to me and he didn't look happy. He asked if he could see my ceramic plate, which was empty. I gave it to him and he proceeded to hit me right over the head with it. The plate didn't break, but for a brief moment, I wasn't too sure about my skull.

"Now get your ass back to your dorm room and cut those damn sideburns off," Eaton yelled. "Then I want to see you back here when they're gone."

I shaved them off and when I returned, Eaton said, "You know the rules, Conrad. That'll cost you your book money and fees for one year.'' Which was no big deal, aside from the minor hassle of having my friends get the books for me. Maybe I should have staged my own personal protest.

Our 0–4 finish in 1969 turned out to be a preview of the disaster that was to follow. We went 1–9 in 1970, Wyoming's worst record since going 1–8–1 in 1946 and Eaton's worst since replacing Bob Devaney as head coach in 1962. We were pathetic, scoring only 110 points to our opponents' 314. The only thing that preserved a little bit of dignity for us was beating Colorado State, our biggest rival. But it was obvious neither Eaton nor the program had recovered from the previous year's turmoil. Eaton couldn't recruit black players, because if they hadn't already heard about ''The Black Fourteen'' incident for themselves, coaches from other schools made damn certain they were brought up to date. The whole thing, in my opinion, destroyed him as a coach and a man. He resigned after the 1970 season.

In my senior year, the dormitory room I shared with our tight end, Ken Hustad, doubled as a cocktail lounge after home games. During the summer, Ken had constructed a five-foot-long, L-shaped bar that we stocked with all kinds of booze, mixes, and beer. The coaches always had postgame cocktail parties at their homes, so we decided we were entitled to the same luxury—and a little profit to boot. We charged a buck a head and a buck a drink. Our parties would always start with a small group in the room, then spill into the hall, then into other rooms, then all the way down to the lobby. We'd have close to a hundred people, including the dorm director. And after we closed, we'd take the money and spend it on the additional drinking and partying we did the rest of the night.

Things were going pretty good between Ken and me until I started dating his sister, Carla, a tall blonde who was absolutely gorgeous. She was a freshman, and Ken wasn't the least bit happy about her having a relationship with an older man—especially this older man. He eventually broke us up by handing her a piece of paper on which he had listed all my good and bad points.

The bad outnumbered the good ten to one.

As luck would have it, my senior year Fritz Shurmur was promoted to replace Eaton as head coach. To no one's surprise, Bill Baker promptly quit the staff. Of course, even if Baker had stayed, I wouldn't have had very much to do with him because Shurmur moved me to defensive tackle and Baker still would have been coaching the offensive line. Despite my feelings toward Shurmur, now the defensive coordinator of the Los Angeles Rams, I actually felt a lot of pride in being switched because I knew his philosophy was to use the best athletes he had on defense. I was up to 230 pounds, twenty-five heavier than my freshman year, and quicker and more agile than ever. I also felt, deep down, my temperament probably was better suited for the defensive line than the offensive line. And maybe I was right. I wasn't named defensive MVP that year for being passive. I wouldn't have had eight tackles behind the line of scrimmage, either, if I hadn't been good at my new position. On the other hand, the move may have cost me two or three rounds in the NFL draft—not to mention a lot of money—because the scouts couldn't be certain about what position I'd play.

Another costly factor as far as the draft was concerned was my failure to appear in any college all-star games. I remember all the hard work my high-school coaches did to get me scholarship offers. But when applications for the Senior Bowl, Blue-Gray Classic, and East-West Shrine Game were sent to Shurmur so he could recommend players from his squad, he didn't even bother to fill them out. Instead, he called me and a linebacker named Mick Carter into his office, threw the applications in front of us and said, "If you want to play in these games, fill out the applications."

Now how were we supposed to recommend ourselves? We filled them out, but we knew, with no kind words from our own head coach, we didn't have a chance of being selected. And we weren't. Shurmur's feeling was, "You gave us four years. I'm doing something else now. Get the hell out of here."

For the first time in my athletic life, I didn't feel like a person. I felt like a machine—a piece of equipment that no longer was useful, that was being wheeled out to make room for a newer model.

Little did I know I would witness and experience the same thing, day in and day out, over the next ten years.

4

From the Waiver Wire to the Pro Bowl

"The St. Louis Cardinals?" I said, after hearing on the radio they had just made me their fifth-round draft choice. "Why would a baseball team want to pick me?"

That should give you a pretty good idea of how closely I had followed professional football up to that point. It was 1972, yet the only football Cardinals I knew of were located in Chicago. Nobody told me they had moved to St. Louis twelve years earlier. What can I say? I loved to play the games; I just wasn't all that crazy about watching them. If I happened to flip through the sports section of the newspaper, it usually was during a search for the comics—unless, of course, I came across a story about myself. Would you believe it wasn't until my third NFL season that I could name all the teams in the National and American conferences?

When I finally figured out who the Cardinals were and where St. Louis was, I was excited. But I didn't get the impression the Cardinals felt the same about acquiring me. It wasn't until ten days after the draft that they called to officially welcome me to the organization and arrange for my trip to St. Louis to begin contract talks. When I didn't hear from them for a week—and saw television interviews with other draftees throughout the league—I started wondering if they had changed their minds.

Of course, I almost gave them a reason to while driving to the airport to catch my flight to St. Louis. The roads were icy and Mick Carter, who was in the car along with each of our girlfriends, kept telling me to slow down.

"Naw," I said, "it's no fun to drive slow."

The next thing I knew, I was skidding into the back of a pickup truck that was stopped at a red light. The impact pushed the car's hood right over the top of the windshield, but fortunately no one was hurt.

"Boy, Conrad," Mick said, "now that's what I call fun."

The first thing I received when I walked into the Cardinals' executive offices was a tie tack with the team's logo on it. The second thing I received was an insult from the team's owner, Bill Bidwill, as we sat down to discuss my contract (Bill handled contract signings himself in those days). He wrote his initial offer on a piece of paper—a base salary of $14,000 with a bonus of $1,000—and slid it across his desk. I took one look at it and said, "I really don't know what I'm supposed to make, Mr. Bidwill, but I sure as hell thought it was going to be more than this."

When all the negotiating was complete, I wound up with a base salary of $17,500 and a signing bonus of $5,000, which, at first, made me feel fabulously rich. I couldn't decide whether my first investment should be a sports car or a yacht. But after taxes gobbled up nearly half of the bonus, I suddenly returned to earth.

I weighed 230 pounds after my final year at Wyoming—far too light for an NFL lineman. I knew that to have any hope of surviving the Cardinals' training camp, I would have to bulk up in a hurry. So I went back to Twentynine Palms and ate just about everything in sight, especially ice cream; I consumed no less than a gallon a day. By the time I was ready to report to camp at Lake Forest, Illinois, I had gained about twenty pounds. I also had this almost uncontrollable urge to cover myself with chocolate syrup and whipped cream and wear a cherry on my head.

All NFL players must undergo physical examinations before they can take part in preseason drills. And the one the Cardinals' medical staff gave me was incredibly thorough. They checked me from the top of my scalp to the soles of my feet, poking and probing parts of my body I didn't know even existed. But I had no doubts, despite the injuries I had suffered in high school and college, they would conclude I was in perfect health.

Then came the results of my blood test.

They showed an extremely high cholesterol count. Even though I knew it was from eating all of that ice cream—and I pointed that out to the doctors—I wouldn't be allowed to practice until I got it down via a low-cholesterol diet. Then one of the doctors started listening to my heart. He kept listening and listening, moving the stethoscope all over my chest. It was obvious he was concerned about something.

"Just lie there for a minute," he said. "I'm going to get a second opinion on this."

He called over another doctor, who put his stethoscope to my chest and said, "Breathe." He, too, wore a look of concern as he listened and listened. Then they walked to a corner of the room and started speaking in hushed tones. When they finished, they called in a third doctor. The third doctor put his stethoscope to my chest and said, "OK, now breathe normally."

That was the last straw.

"How am I supposed to breathe normally?" I snapped. "You guys have got me so goddamn scared, I don't even know what breathing normally means anymore. Now tell me, what's going on here? Am I going to live? Am I going to die? Somebody please tell me what this is all about!" They explained they had found a heart murmur, which I never knew existed, and that I would have to go to St. Louis for additional testing. But there would be nothing to find. I was in great shape, having trained for four years in the high altitude of Wyoming.

I think I set a record on the treadmill in the doctor's office in St. Louis, staying on for twenty minutes and still running at the eighth elevation. Once the ice cream passed through my system, my cholesterol count plummeted.

Still, I wound up being a spectator for the first ten days of camp, and that was something I'd regret for quite a long time. There were only a half-dozen or so offensive linemen to begin with, and as the only rookie member of the unit, I was viewed with contempt by the others long before I ever showed up. That I wasn't practicing only made matters worse. When you can't practice or play in the NFL because of injury or illness, you're like the walking dead. You become invisible to the coaches and, most of all, your teammates. They don't care what the doctors say. Until you prove otherwise, they dismiss you as a pussy who's only trying to avoid contact.

There's an old saying in the NFL: "You can't make the club when you're sittin' in the tub." And that's exactly what Bob Hollway, the Cards' head coach at the time, said when he saw about twenty players seeking relief for their aches and pains in the whirlpool tubs one day in camp. Shaking his head in disgust, he turned to our trainer, Johnny Omohundro, and roared, "I want all these guys healed by tomorrow!"

"What the hell am I supposed to do?" Omohundro said. "Call Oral Roberts?"

I fell way behind in the learning process, which is much more critical on the offensive line than almost any other position. I could stand there and watch practice, but that really didn't provide me with a whole lot of knowledge. You physically have to take part in the plays and run them again and again before you understand precisely what you're supposed to do on each one. Repetition is the teacher in football, and the only thing I had repeated through those first ten days was a question to the trainers: "When can I practice?"

By the time I received medical clearance, thirty percent of the offense already had been covered. When I asked a question, the coaches would say, "Hell, Dobler, we put that play in two weeks ago. Just go out there and run it the way it's diagramed." But looking at things from down in your stance and staring at a bunch of X's and O's on a piece of paper are quite a bit different. The biggest difference is that X's and O's never move. Therefore, I made a lot of mistakes. I blew assignments, missed blocks, blocked the wrong guys, and quite frequently jumped off-sides. It's said that an offensive lineman should never jump off-sides, because he knows the snap count. But I was so caught up with what I was supposed to do, I'd forget to listen for the snap count in the huddle.

My first offensive line coach with the Cardinals was Bill Austin, who was a notorious rookie-hater (a philosophy he acquired while coaching for the Washington Redskins, first from Vince Lombardi and then from George Allen). He had a policy that if one guy screwed up, everybody had to suffer for it. Needless to say, my linemates did a lot of suffering. And I became less popular with each practice.

Dan Dierdorf and Tom Banks, both of whom had joined the team a year earlier, did everything they could to make my rookie season as miserable as possible. It's amazing how close the three of us eventually became, because at the time, I thought they were the biggest bozos I'd ever met in my life. They would steal my playbook so that I wouldn't have it during meetings. They'd say, "Well, you'd better tell the coach that you lost it," when I knew damn well they had the thing the whole time. And when the meetings were over, they'd *miraculously* discover where it was. In practice, they'd feed me false information and when it caused me to make a mistake, they'd tell Austin, "Damn it, Coach, we told him not to do it that way." Or, when I'd ask them who I was supposed to block on a particular play, they'd pretend they couldn't hear me and not answer. They were just constantly setting me up for embarrassment. Which I'd have understood if they were defensive players, because defensive players are jerks, by definition. But these were two of my line-mates—guys I was supposed to be working with as part of a unit, guys I was supposed to be able to look to for a little help and direction.

I had to ask myself, Is this what camaraderie in the NFL is all about?

I reached the height of my hatred for Dierdorf and Banks the one day I spent practicing on the defensive line. We were short of bodies over there, and since I had played defensive tackle in my senior year of college, the coaches were curious about my ability to play the position in the NFL. I had beaten Dierdorf twice on pass rushes, so before our third encounter, he and Banks quietly arranged to trap-block me. They even got the consent of Austin, because, as I said, he despised rookies. In a trap block, an offensive lineman tries to lure a particular defensive lineman across the line by moving away from him when the ball is snapped, hoping the defensive lineman will think he has a clear path to the backfield and come charging through. As he does, another offensive lineman or a tight end will come from the opposite side and blindside him. Sure enough, I took the bait from Dan and Tommy came flying out from nowhere to knock me flat on my ass. I just sat there for a minute, shaking my head and wondering, Why are they doing this to me? Why don't they trap a real defensive lineman instead of one of their own guys?

When Dierdorf and Banks weren't trying to make me look bad, veteran defensive linemen such as Fred Heron were. The first time I went up against him in practice, he whispered to me across the line, "Listen, kid, this is just a little hut-and-butt play, so go easy." And I said to myself, He's a veteran, I'm a rookie, he must know better than I do how it's supposed to be done. I also wanted to change the approach I had taken in college and try to do things to gain the acceptance of my peers rather than alienate them. So, when the ball was snapped, I came off the line easy—easy enough for Heron, who had come off as hard as he could, to trample me into the dirt. The next time, I came off hard and he became really indignant. "Man, I told you this isn't a fast drill," he reminded me. So I came off easy again and, sure enough, he knocked me down again. This happened about five or six times before I finally caught on to his game.

Who said I was a fast learner?

I received my share of hazing, too. I don't mean the nonsense Dierdorf and Banks pulled, but the standard stuff that all rookies go through. Like having to sing for my supper. Most of the veterans showed up late for dinner in the cafeteria, because they usually stopped for a few beers after practice. The rookies knew this and would try to get to the cafeteria as early as possible so they could eat and get out before the abuse started. But I always said, The hell with it! I'm going to go out and drink some beer and show up late for dinner, too. I'm not going to be intimidated. Thus, I wound up singing just about every night. Not that I was all that devastated by it. I'm a terrible singer, and if they wanted to listen to me, fine, that was their problem.

I had an aunt and uncle who owned a couple of grocery stores in Chicago. Since our training camp wasn't too far away, I drove over to see them on a few of the days we had off. During one of my visits, we talked about my chances of making the team and they began to wonder aloud about what they might be able to do to help improve my odds.

"Pro football is just another form of business," they concluded. "And the Cardinals are in business to fill seats."

So they got together a whole bunch of postcards that said things like, "We want to see a lot more of Conrad Dobler on the field during the regular season than we did during the preseason," and, "Conrad Dobler is number 66 in your program, but number one in our heart." They had stacks of them in their grocery stores and at several nearby barrooms and other businesses.

The Cardinals wound up receiving about five thousand of them. I found out when Austin put every single one into a cardboard box and dumped the whole batch inside my dressing stall one day. Embarrassed the daylights out of me.

Even without the postcard-writing campaign, I was confident I had performed well enough to make a favorable impression on the team's brain trust. I didn't think I had won a starting job, but I felt I had displayed quite a bit of potential and was certainly no worse than any of the older backup offensive linemen in camp. The only thing I lacked was experience, but I figured, for the time being, my enthusiasm and whatever natural ability I had would make up for that.

Little did I know it was going to be necessary to far exceed the minimum requirements in order to bump a veteran off the roster. Just as in boxing—a challenger rarely dethrones the champion on a decision; he has to knock him out.

Almost all of my action came on the practice field, because Bob Hollway didn't like the idea of playing mistake-prone rookies, even during the preseason. In those days coaches tried to win exhibition games. Coming off a 4–9–1 season, Hollway was bent on getting as many victories as he could, regardless of whether they counted. That was far more important to him than evaluating his young talent. So I was a spectator for our preseason-opening triumph over Buffalo and remained one for our loss to Kansas City the following week, our victory over Denver the week after that, and our defeat against Houston in week four.

As I had been a starter throughout high school and college, it was quite an adjustment. But I rationalized that watching in uniform from the sidelines was still a whole lot better than watching in street clothes from the stands.

I saw spot duty in our final two exhibition games, wins over the Packers and Bears. Not enough really to get into the flow of either game, but I set out to keep my mistakes to a minimum and I thought I at least succeeded at that.

I probably did less carousing in that first training camp than any other in my career, because I was too preoccupied with making the team to worry about making half the female population of Lake Forest, Illinois. But one highlight of that summer was the beautiful girl in Chicago I met through one of my cousins who lived there. She was dating the captain of the University of Wisconsin football team at the same time she was seeing me—I guess she wanted the best of both the collegiate and professional worlds. Quite a few heads turned when she visited me at practice. My bigger-name teammates would go up to her and say, "Why would a gorgeous creature like you waste your time with some nobody offensive guard from Wyoming?"

But that was only because they wanted her for themselves.

■   ■   ■

Two days before the first regular-season game of 1972, Bill Austin told me Hollway wanted to see me. Usually, guys start to sweat bullets when their position coaches tell them in the preseason they have an appointment with the head man. That's because, usually, they come back with a one-way ticket home. One of my training-camp roommates that year, a linebacker named Kent Carter, would hide in the closet every time there was a knock on the door late at night—as if that was going to prevent him from being cut. He eventually was found . . . and sent packing.

But I wasn't the least bit concerned about meeting Hollway at that point. In fact, I couldn't have been happier. I knew I had had a strong training camp, for as little as I played, and was already living in an apartment in St. Louis with a couple of fellow rookies. I figured the head coach wanted to congratulate me personally for making the team, then tell me I'd be starting in the opener against the Colts.

Instead, the first words out of his mouth were, "Sorry, Conrad." I didn't need to hear the rest, but he proceeded to tell me I got caught up in numbers and he had to let me go. At first, I thought to myself, Caught up in numbers? That can't be possible. I counted all the players myself at practice this morning and there were exactly forty-six—the prescribed forty on the active roster and six on the taxi squad. Then, it suddenly dawned on me: I had counted everyone except a certain offensive guard wearing number 66.

It was one of the few moments in my life I was left speechless. I was just totally shocked.

"We'd like to bring you back and we will if we run into any injury problems," Hollway said. "We also made calls to five or six other teams to let them know you were out there in case they were looking for a good, young guard."

I knew he was only saying that to appease me. I didn't hold out a lot of hope for being brought back and I held out even less for another team picking me up. At that point, every club in the NFL had determined its final forty-six. And if one were in dire need of help, it would take an unemployed veteran player, who probably could adapt to its system right away, over some rookie reject who barely knew the system he had spent an entire summer trying to learn.

When I finally gained enough composure to speak, I told Hollway I thought he was making a big mistake. I told him his decision would come back to haunt him.

"I'm going to play in this league someday," I said. "And when I get to play against this team, I'm gonna kick a few asses. You'll be sorry."

I stormed out of his office and down to the locker room to pick up my personal belongings, which the equipment man already had stuffed into a plastic garbage bag. Now is that symbolic or what? Then I headed for my apartment to pack. The next day, while the rest of the team was getting ready to leave for Baltimore, I was driving to Chicago. There, I would receive some badly needed consolation from my lady friend in the Windy City. I also would hook up with a bunch of my relatives and enlist their help in spending the nine hundred dollars I had in my pocket. I just wanted to drink and party my troubles away.

I later found out that, after learning of my release, Dierdorf and Banks did quite a bit of drinking and partying themselves. Suffice it to say they weren't drowning their sorrows.

I was twenty-one years old and didn't have the slightest idea what my next move was going to be. Go back to school? Get a *real* job? I really wasn't prepared to address any questions that required me to think beyond twenty-four hours.

Ron Gwynn, a good friend of mine who was a real estate broker in Wyoming, called to tell me that whether I played football again or not, he'd have some sort of work for me if I were interested. That was comforting. Ron, who has since passed away, and I had remained close ever since we ran into each other one night while sneaking out of the women's dormitory at the University of Wyoming. What was so great was that Ron was nearly forty at the time. And he wasn't even a part-time student.

My decision-making ended a little over a week later with one phone call from the Cardinals. "We need you back right away," the team official said. He proceeded to explain that the offensive line had been hit hard by injuries through the first two games, a victory over Baltimore and a loss to Washington, and that Chuck Hutchison, a third-year veteran guard, was among the wounded. "Gee, that's too bad about Hutch," I said, wearing a grin from ear to ear. I reported for duty the Monday after the Redskins game.

Upon my return, I promised myself I was never going to give the Cardinals a reason to cut me a second time. That meant doing everything possible—legally and illegally—to keep opposing defensive linemen and linebackers from invading my space. That also meant having to scuffle with teammates who didn't always appreciate the highly aggressive, survival-oriented approach I was taking. But as far as I was concerned, the coaches were scrutinizing me more closely than anyone else on the squad. I felt I was always one mistake away from being told, once again, to pack my bags and go home. I also felt I had to prove something to the guys on the team.

I made up my mind that whenever I wore my helmet and shoulder pads I was playing for keeps. As a result, I got into a fight in just about every practice. I was taking on one defender after another—sometimes two or three in the same workout. It wasn't long before members of the defensive unit started using my photograph as a dart board in their meeting room.

I had been re-signed to a taxi-squad contract, which paid me $500 a week to be an inactive member of the club. It wasn't a whole lot different from the injured-reserve list, although the chances of being activated were slightly better. The primary function of the taxi-squadders was to help in the preparation of the "real" team by playing the part of opposing offenses and defenses in practice. Which, besides fighting with my teammates, was all I did through my first two weeks back. Meanwhile, the "real" players suffered a loss to Pittsburgh and squeaked a 19–17 win over Minnesota. As much as I hate to admit it, I'd be less than honest if I said I wasn't a little happy to see us lose the Pittsburgh game. On the taxi squad, your entire focus is on being activated. Every loss—or injury—puts you a step closer to playing.

My big chance finally came when I was put on special teams for our fifth game, our second meeting with Washington. We got our asses kicked, 33–3, but the coaches were impressed with what they saw of me. They must have been, because in week six, four days before we were to face the Giants, I was informed of my promotion to the starting lineup, though I'd still have to play special teams.

I'll admit, I was more than a little nervous. In addition to what we covered in meetings, I spent hours studying film of my opponent, defensive tackle John Mendenhall. I was determined to familiarize myself with everything about him—his strengths and, most important, his weaknesses. The first thing I noticed about the guy was that he was pretty short for his position, which meant I would have to get even lower than he was in order to get good leverage. The second thing I noticed was that he made up for his lack of height through extreme aggressiveness.

I was going to have my hands full.

The game was played in Yankee Stadium, the Giants' home field before they moved to the Meadowlands. As I said, I wasn't much of a sports fan growing up. But I did know this much about Yankee Stadium: It wasn't just any old ballpark; it was the place where baseball legends such as Babe Ruth, Yogi Berra, and Mickey Mantle, and football greats such as Y. A. Tittle, Sam Huff, and Frank Gifford had played. I couldn't help but think about that as I looked around our locker room before the opening kickoff. It was, I knew, the stuff of dreams.

It was an especially memorable day for me. In the second quarter, as Giant punter Tom Blanchard went back to punt, I charged through a gaping hole in the protection with my arms extended, my eyes the size of silver dollars. The ball banged off the end of Blanchard's foot and, just as quickly, deflected off my fingertips. "All right!" I yelled. Then I looked down, and saw the ball rolling in front of my feet at the Giants' fifteen-yard line. Oh-oh, I said to myself, I've got to pick this thing up now. I really didn't want to pick it up, because the instant I did, I was going to have a whole bunch of Giants trying to squash me into those hallowed grounds. Nevertheless, I picked up the ball and ran.

Sure enough, hands instantly appeared from nowhere and started grabbing at my arms. Much to my surprise, they belonged to our toothless veteran defensive back, Larry Wilson. "Give me the ball so I can run with it," he screamed. I pretended not to hear him, figuring if he fumbled, I'd get the blame. I could just picture him giving the same type of explanation Dierdorf and Banks had offered in training camp: "Damn it, Coach, I *told* him not to give the ball to me." If I learned nothing else in the preseason, I learned that veterans couldn't be trusted.

So I clutched the ball tighter and kept running. I started to think how much fun I was having, how long it had been since my high-school days, when I carried the ball on just about every play. And just about the time I decided to ask Hollway to switch me to fullback, my momentum came to a sudden stop as a whole bunch of Giants pounced on me at the eight-yard line.

Next time, I said to myself at the bottom of the pile, I think I'll let Wilson have all the fun. He has no teeth; I'd like to keep mine a little longer.

Two plays later, Johnny Roland ran for a one-yard touchdown to put us ahead, 21–7. We wound up pissing away the lead and losing, 27–21. But, still, I had a few reasons to feel satisfied: One, I blocked a punt in my NFL debut at Yankee Stadium. Two, I had a hell of a game against Mendenhall, which would set the tone for most of our future confrontations. Three, Dierdorf and Banks actually showed signs of humanity by going up to Bill Austin at halftime to try to convince him to remove me from special teams in the second half. "Hey, Dobler's playing a hell of a game out there, but he's dying because you've got him on every one of the special teams," they said. "He's a starter now. He should be treated like one." I remained on all of the bomb squads the rest of the game, but I appreciated their efforts. I finally felt like I was part of the unit.

We would continue to go winless through the next six weeks, losing to Chicago, 27–10, then playing to a 6–6 tie with Philadelphia and suffering losses to Dallas (33–24), the Giants (13–7), Miami (31–10), and Dallas again (27–6). Before the Miami game, which was played on a Monday night, my mother got a call from one of her friends in Twentynine Palms, California, who wanted to know what number I'd be wearing so she could watch me on television. "Sixty-six, and he'll be playing on the offensive line," my mother said. Shortly after the game, the woman called again. "You never told me your son was black," she said, sounding a bit startled.

She had been watching the Dolphins' number 66, offensive guard Larry Little.

I guess she wasn't paying attention when Howard Cosell said I bore a striking resemblance to a prominent ex–college football player in Florida by the name of Burt Reynolds. *Cosmopolitan* magazine would have asked me to pose for a risqué photograph, just as Reynolds did, but there was one problem: My hands were too small.

We finally snapped our eight-game winless streak, beating the Los Angeles Rams, 24–14, in the second-to-last game of the season. A couple of bizarre occurrences made that an unforgettable day in Busch Stadium. First, our quarterback, Jim Hart, and a rookie wide receiver named Bobby Moore combined for a ninety-eight-yard completion and a dubious honor—the longest non–touchdown play from scrimmage in NFL history. It happened on the first snap after we took over on a goal-line stand at our own one-yard line. Hart threw a ten-yard pass to Moore, who simply ran out of gas on the way to the end zone and was caught from behind at the Rams' one. We scored a touchdown two plays later, but it was an extremely cold day and everybody else on offense bitched at Bobby for making us stay out there for two more plays when we could have been keeping warm on the sidelines.

Bobby went on to have a very distinguished career in the NFL. If the name doesn't ring a bell, it's because, after his rookie season, he changed it to Ahmad Rashad.

The other crazy thing I remember about that game is the Cardinals' use, or shall I say misuse, of a chemical to melt the ice that had formed on the artificial turf. I think about it every time I see the scars on my legs left behind by chemical burns. A number of players from both teams experienced the same thing all over their bodies, some more than others. Afterward, the shower room was like a torture chamber with guys screaming in agony as soap and hot water hit their open wounds. We later found out how lucky we all were not to have been blinded by the stuff.

We closed the season on a high note, beating the Eagles, 24–23. That gave Hollway his second consecutive 4–9–1 record and, much to the relief of most everyone on the team, Bidwill promptly gave him the boot. In fact, I heard about the firing on my car radio as I drove home from the stadium.

It made the trip a bit more pleasurable.

All in all, I thought I had a pretty good rookie year. I thought I left the opponents I'd be facing over the next several seasons with a little something to think about: guys like John Mendenhall of the Giants, Jim Osborne of the Bears, Jethro Pugh of the Cowboys, Manny Fernandez of the Dolphins, and Merlin Olsen of the Rams. There were times when I dominated, times when they dominated me, and times when we fought to a draw.

I felt I played well enough to remain a starter the following year. But when we reported to minicamp in 1973, I was moved back to second string while Chuck Hutchison, having recovered from his knee injury, returned to the starting lineup. Hollway's replacement as head coach, Don Coryell, had a policy that starting positions could not be lost through injury. I didn't like it. And I liked it even less at training camp as it became increasingly obvious, with each practice, I was the better player. Then one day Jim Hanifan, Austin's replacement as the offensive line coach, took me aside and said, "Be patient, Connie. First chance I get to put you in there with the starting unit, I will."

Five days before our first exhibition game, we were scrimmaging Minnesota. Hutchison ran onto the field for the first offensive series, then suddenly turned around and headed back to the sidelines. "Anyone got a chinstrap?" he yelled. "I forgot mine." Before a replacement could be produced, Hanifan turned to me and said, "Dobler, get in there! Hutchison, you're out!" From that point on, I was the Cardinals' starting right offensive guard. And I always made certain to carry an extra chinstrap on the field.

■   ■   ■

Even before Hanifan made me a starter, I was feeling very good about myself at that second training camp. I knew I had arrived, that I was a part of the team. I no longer felt like an outsider. I began to get the respect from my teammates and coaches that I so desperately wanted as a rookie.

Thanks to Hanifan's tutelage, I could see a vast improvement in my entire game. Because we were a throwing team, he worked particularly hard at helping me perfect my pass-blocking technique. He taught me to rely more on finesse than muscle. For instance, I was doing a much better job of preventing defenders from getting their hands on me and throwing me off balance than I ever did as a rookie because Hanifan showed me how to use my hands to keep their hands away. He also enhanced my drive-blocking for the run by putting a twelve-inch-wide board on the ground and making me straddle it while working against a blocking dummy. That forced me to keep my feet apart and, therefore, maintain the good, wide base necessary in order to get that push off the ball. Austin never showed us any of those things; he operated under the incorrect presumption that all of his players were seasoned pros who knew everything there was to know. He told us only what to do, not how to do it.

I also did some improvising to enhance my game. I started using the legwhip, which was introduced to me as a reverse body-block in my freshman year of college. Instead of throwing my entire body at an oncoming defensive lineman, I began planting one foot, swinging the other around my back, karate-style, and connecting with thighs, knees, shins, and so forth. Another little trick I started to employ was ramming my fists under my opponents' chinstraps, driving their heads back and stopping them dead in their tracks. Worked every time.

The NFL would eventually outlaw both tactics. But not before I had established myself as one of the more intimidating players in the game.

We began the 1973 season with a 34–23 victory over Philadelphia, followed by a 34–27 win over Washington. Counting the final two games of 1972, the Cardinals had their longest winning streak going since they had won four straight early in 1970.

But Dallas burst our bubble with a vengeance, pounding us, 45–10. We proceeded to lose to Oakland, Philadelphia, and Washington before rebounding with a 35–27 victory over the Giants. In those days you could usually count on the Giants to be your "get-well" opponent.

But our health improved only to a point. We played to a

17–17 tie with Denver the following week. After that, we lost to Green Bay, the Giants, Cincinnati, and Detroit. I let my rapidly developing warrior instincts get the better of me during the Detroit game. I suffered a partial dislocation of my right shoulder, but instead of going to the sidelines, I bit down hard on my lip and played the rest of the series. There hasn't been an offensive lineman born who can block with one shoulder, and I was no exception. And the times I made contact with my injured shoulder I saw stars and nearly passed out. But the most serious consequence of my decision to stay on the field was my allowing my man to come free to sack Jim Hart and knock him out of the game with a shoulder injury.

I learned the hard way I wasn't as indestructible as I thought.

The injury caused me to miss our final two contests, a victory over a pretty good Falcons team in Atlanta, and a 30–3 loss to America's Team at St. Louis, for which we were booed off the field. Our 4–9–1 finish marked the third year in a row and fourth time in five seasons the Cardinals posted the same record. I'd say the fans were entitled to do a little booing. But the predominant feeling among the players was that we were a far better 4–9–1 team than we had been the year before. We were more competitive and much more unified. We had faith that Don Coryell, with his intense, highly energetic approach, would build us into a winner.

■　■　■

The 1974 players' strike, which began at the start of the preseason, created a pretty tense atmosphere at our Illinois State University training camp. The Cardinals were scheduled to face the Bills in the Hall of Fame Game in Canton,

Ohio, traditionally the first contest of the preseason. But with most of the regulars on the picket line, including yours truly, both teams had to field scab squads composed mostly of rookies and any other warm bodies they could find.

The league was so fearful of a strike-related incident erupting at the game that it had both replacement teams arrive, without notice, at a secret airport only hours before kickoff. Greyhound buses met them right on the Tarmac so the players could board quickly and avoid any possible confrontation in the terminal building. Not that we were planning a confrontation with them, but there's another example of the power of intimidation.

We set up a picket line, along with our fellow NFLPA members from Buffalo, outside the stadium. The buses came roaring through the back gate and pulled up within six inches of the doors to each dressing room so the players could disembark without being seen. As it turned out, we were the ones who needed shielding. A group of gray-haired men, representing the players who had been in the NFL before 1959 but were left out when the union negotiated the original player pension fund, began to picket us. Those old guys were really pissed off, and I couldn't blame them. They had been forgotten by the NFLPA because remembering them would have meant less pension money for those who played after 1959 (the Pre-'59ers, as they were called, wouldn't finally be remembered until March of 1987, when the NFL owners voted unanimously to create a special fund for them).

Management used all sorts of little games to try to get us to defect from the union, to turn against our own teammates and come back to work while they continued to stay out and lose money. They didn't give a hoot about maintaining the cohesion necessary for success on the field. The bottom line was collecting the television, radio, and gate revenues that would have been lost if they didn't keep teeing it up as scheduled.

Don Coryell was really pissed off at us while we were on the picket line. It wasn't that he was antiunion. It was just that he was so completely devoted to football, he refused to accept that we would place anything ahead of the game. He didn't have the slightest interest in the details of our dispute. All he knew was that *our* strike was interfering with *his* training camp. Because it is during training camp that all NFL coaches look for the right ingredients for a winning season. They like to think of themselves as mad scientists, hoping to create a bunch of Frankensteins that will go out and terrorize the rest of the league.

But as angry as Coryell was, he didn't hold any grudges when we did return to work. Doing so, in his view, would have taken time and energy away from the business at hand, which was getting us ready for the regular season. Don made his stance clear when he began our first team meeting with one simple phrase: "Let's get after it!"

We did.

■　　■　　■

The good feelings we had at the end of the 1973 season didn't evaporate during the strike. We were still unified, still excited. We had one goal and that was to get to the Super Bowl.

For the first time since I joined the Cardinals, there were no questions in anyone's mind about who was going to play what position. As a result, all of us were able to concentrate more on becoming better football players rather than just making the team. And those of us on the offensive line were blending into a quality unit. We knew each other's strengths and weaknesses. We began to develop that sixth sense that allowed each of us to anticipate what everyone else on the line would do on a particular play.

But as dominant as we thought we were going to be on offense, scoring points was like squeezing blood from a stone in our first two regular-season games. We barely slipped past Philadelphia, 7–3, in the opener, our lone score coming on a four-yard Jim Hart to Donny Anderson touchdown pass. The following week, we nipped the Redskins, 17–10, at Washington, the offense's only touchdown coming from a seventy-five-yard TD run by Terry Metcalf. The rest came on a seventy-one-yard fumble return for a touchdown by defensive end Ron Yankowski and a forty-six-yard Jim Bakken field goal. Defense and special teams provided another fourteen points in our 29–7 win over Cleveland.

Meanwhile, I sustained a broken bone in my left hand. No problem. I just created my clublike cast—from a fiberglass shell, foam rubber, and athletic tape—and kept playing. That became a useful tool . . . until one day when a referee finally made me take it off.

We improved our record to 4–0 by pounding the '49ers, 34–9. In four weeks we had equaled the number of victories we'd won in fourteen weeks in each of the previous two seasons. We were excited, but everyone—the players, the coaches, the fans, the media—was wondering, "When is our bubble going to burst?" As much as we tried, we just couldn't put those 4–9–1 seasons behind us. We had never won three consecutive games before, let alone four.

In week five, we beat Dallas, 31–28, at St. Louis to end a four-year losing streak to the Cowboys. We held leads of 21–14 at halftime and 28–14 early in the third quarter, but the Cowboys came back to tie the game on a pair of one-yard touchdown runs in the fourth. They had been kicking off short all day to keep the ball away from Metcalf, one of the league's most dangerous return men. But for some reason, after Roger Staubach's tying TD, Efren Herrera booted it long. Metcalf returned it fifty-seven yards, to the Dallas thirty-four, to help set up Bakken's winning thirty-one-yard field goal with 1:02 left.

Our 31–27 victory over Houston gave us a 6–0 record and the Cardinals their best start in the franchise's history. But there was nothing sweeter than our seventh straight win, 23–20, over Washington at Busch Stadium. Besides ranking as the lone undefeated team in the NFL at the time, we also became the first club to defeat the George Allen–coached Redskins twice in the same season. We built a 16–0 lead in the second quarter, but the Redskins cut the margin to 16–10 before halftime on a forty-eight-yard field goal by Mark Moseley and a two-yard touchdown pass from Sonny Jurgensen to Larry Brown. They pulled to within three on a field goal in the third quarter, but we came right back with a seventeen-yard TD pass from Hart to Anderson. Jurgensen threw a thirteen-yard scoring pass to make it 23–20 with 6:13 left in the game, but we controlled the ball with four first downs and ran out the clock.

Through that seven-game stretch, our passing attack became recognized as one of the most explosive in the league. And a major reason for that was the performance of our offensive line, which had allowed only two sacks up to that point. We had so much confidence that, regardless of whom we faced, none of us ever expected to be beaten for a sack.

The end to our winning streak finally came in week eight, when we lost, 17–14, to the Cowboys. Not coincidentally, Hart was sacked three times in that game, which the Cowboys won on a twenty-yard field goal with four seconds left. As a young team that had been riding so high, we took the defeat very hard. The horrible taste it left in our mouths was a vivid reminder of a time we all hoped was dead and buried. It was only one game, but many of us couldn't help asking ourselves, Is this it? Is this as far as it goes?

Those questions intensified the following week when, in a Monday-night game at St. Louis, we were defeated by Minnesota, 28–24. Hart had a brilliant performance, completing twenty-eight of forty-three passes for 353 yards and two touchdowns. I think I picked up a few Pro Bowl votes with ABC's cameras isolating on me as I kept defensive tackle Doug Sutherland away from the football (that also was the night I bit Sutherland's fingers and he asked the Vikings' physician for a rabies shot). But we killed ourselves with two first-quarter fumbles, which led to fourteen Viking points.

We beat Philadelphia in the next game, and in week eleven we faced the Giants at the Yale Bowl in New Haven, Connecticut, one of their temporary homes while Giants Stadium was being built. Because the Giants were an NFC Eastern Division neighbor, a win would put us in position to do something no other Cardinal team had done since 1948—win a divisional crown. The Giants had us down, 14–6, midway through the third quarter, but Hart and that trusty arm of his put us in front, 20–14, with a pair of touchdown passes. New York moved ahead again, on a seventeen-yard TD pass from Craig Morton to Walker Gillette with 1:16 remaining in the game. However, we took the kickoff and marched quickly upfield to set up Bakken's winning thirty-six-yard field goal with three seconds left, to give us a 23–21 win.

I swear, Bakken had ice water running through his veins.

At 9–2, we needed only one victory to clinch a division championship. Our final three opponents were Kansas City, New Orleans, and the Giants. With three such pushovers, we figured on a three-game sweep.

But the Chiefs had other plans, beating us, 17–13, in a sloppy, turnover-filled game played under wintry conditions at Busch Stadium. The Saints also were spoilers, handing us our first shutout since 1971, 14–0, and dropping us into a tie with the Redskins for first place in the NFC East. The offensive line had its worst day of the season, allowing Hart to be sacked four times and giving our running backs almost no room to operate.

We were determined to save face in our season finale against the Giants. The division championship we'd fought so hard for lay in the balance. Yet, before we knew what hit us, we were trailing at halftime, 14–0. On our way to the dressing room, we reminded ourselves and each other of what we were playing for. We just couldn't permit the lowly Giants, a team going nowhere, to screw up the finest season in Cardinal history.

That proved to be all of the motivation we needed, because in the second half our defense came up with four interceptions and our offense turned three of them into touchdowns. Final score: St. Louis 26, New York 14. Final record: 10–4. Final sack count: sixteen, lowest in the NFL.

We were division champs and headed for the playoffs.

■   ■   ■

The divisional round of the postseason tournament put us in a rematch with Minnesota. It also prompted us to become more businesslike than I've ever seen us before a game. All of a sudden, everybody was attending meetings with the intensity of graduate students cramming for final exams. Those of us on the offensive line even carried notebooks into our skull sessions in order not to forget anything. To tell the truth, we couldn't believe our own eyes. The only thing we had ever used notebooks for previously was to keep the phone numbers of our favorite female acquaintances.

We didn't really have an official meeting room because in football, offensive linemen are treated like second-class citizens. The Cardinals put us in what could best be described as a concrete closet—a cold little spot whose lone redeeming quality was that it was next to a bathroom. The rest of the team had larger, nicer facilities. Cardinal management couldn't even spare us a movie screen. Jim Hanifan had to show the game films on the wall.

We wanted to get ourselves as thoroughly prepared as possible for the Vikings, because we knew we couldn't afford to make any mental mistakes. With their vast playoff experience, they sure as hell were going to keep any blunders to a minimum. Plus, we were going up against the Purple People Eaters—Carl Eller, Alan Page, Jim Marshall, and Doug Sutherland. I'd be lying if I said we weren't a bit intimidated by their reputation, but we felt they had a little something to worry about, too. After all, we were the best pass-blocking unit in the NFL.

My opponent was Sutherland, a hard-nosed, straight-ahead, bull-type pass-rusher, a guy who relied heavily upon strength, as opposed to Page, who was extremely quick and spent little time wrestling with blockers. Sutherland was built low to the ground, so getting good leverage on him wasn't easy. And on a frozen field in Metropolitan Stadium in Bloomington, Minnesota, I knew I wouldn't be able to get enough traction to counter his muscle with my muscle. I'd have to rely mainly on the tactics that, at that point, were starting to gain league-wide notoriety.

Temperatures were well below freezing and light snow began to fall as the first quarter ended in a 0–0 standoff. Then,

9:55 into the second quarter, Jim Hart connected with Earl Thomas for a thirteen-yard touchdown pass to give us a 7–0 lead. We had about four minutes to feel good about our chances of avenging that close loss to the Vikings during the regular season. That was all the time that expired before Fran Tarkenton, doing his usual Fred Astaire routine to avoid pressure, hooked up with John Gilliam for a sixteen-yard TD pass to make it 7–7.

The offensive line was holding its own against the Purple People Eaters, and linemen from both teams held on to each other for dear life to keep from falling on the slick turf. It was the closest I've ever come to knowing what it's like to play ice hockey. Of course, if that had been the sport that day, my "goonish" treatment of Sutherland probably would have caused me to spend plenty of time in the penalty box. You might say I did a little bit of tripping, slashing, and cross-checking, in addition to a whole lot of roughing.

Although we saw no shame in being deadlocked with the defending NFC champions, we were still, as a team, as tight as could be. We'd find out just how tight with six seconds left in the second quarter when our kicker, Jim Bakken, did the unthinkable in sending a twenty-three-yard field goal wide left. The tie stood at halftime.

Early in the third quarter, we did a little more gagging as Minnesota safety Jeff Wright intercepted Hart to set up a thirty-seven-yard Fred Cox field goal. Two plays into the very next series, Terry Metcalf fumbled on a hit by Eller, and cornerback Nate Wright recovered and returned the ball twenty yards for a touchdown to give the Vikings a 17–7 lead. A few minutes later, Tarkenton found Gilliam for another scoring pass, this time from thirty-eight yards, and we found ourselves staring up from the bottom of a sixteen-point hole at the end of the third quarter.

The hole became a grave a few minutes into the fourth period when Chuck Foreman banged his way into the end zone from four yards to give the Vikings a 30–7 lead on their way to a 30–14 victory. We had tried our best to close the experience gap. Maybe we tried too hard.

Afterward, most of us sat in front of our lockers in a daze, still wearing our uniforms and pads. We couldn't accept that our season had just come to an end (the Vikings would go on to a second straight Super Bowl appearance, against Pittsburgh, only to lose for the second year in a row).

■　■　■

The off-season seemed to last an eternity. I'm sure it moved just as slowly for my teammates and the coaching staff. We all felt we had something to prove—that what we did in 1974 was no fluke. That we were good enough to go all the way.

The offensive line, I felt, was reaching its peak. We had been together for three years, and there was almost nothing we didn't know about ourselves or our opponents. My mental files on the guys I played against were as thick as an unabridged dictionary. In those days, it was common for teams to keep a little black book containing the names of players with whom they had a score to settle—ours was pretty thick, too. For instance, if someone had given Roger Finnie a cheap shot and none of us got a chance to retaliate in the same game, that player would be in the black book. Then, if the schedule had us playing his team again, we'd just look him up and settle the account, so to speak. We believed the punishment should fit the crime.

We began defense of the NFC Eastern Division championship with a 23–20 victory over Atlanta. That was exciting, coming down to a Bakken field goal in the final two seconds. But our clash with Dallas the following week turned into an emotional roller-coaster ride I'll never forget. This was one time I felt more like part of a show than part of a war. This was pro-football entertainment at its very finest.

After a scoreless first quarter, we took a 3–0 second-period lead on a twenty-eight-yard Bakken field goal. The Cowboys then moved in front 14–3 on a pair of Roger Staubach touchdown passes. We cut the margin to 14–10 on a twenty-three-yard Hart-to-Gray scoring pass, but the Cowboys responded with a one-yard touchdown run. Hart and Thomas combined on an eighty-yard scoring play to make it 21–17 in the third. But Hollywood Henderson, a fast linebacker with an equally fast mouth, returned the ensuing kickoff ninety-seven yards for a TD to put the Cowboys in front, 28–17. That closed the third-period scoring.

Dallas increased its lead on a forty-yard Tony Fritsch field goal in the fourth quarter. But Hart came back with a thirty-five-yard touchdown pass to Jackie Smith and a thirty-seven-yard TD throw to Gray to tie the game at 31–31 with forty-six seconds left. Time expired, and we found ourselves in the first overtime game in Cardinal history.

We won the coin toss for the extra period, took the kickoff, and drove all the way to the Cowboys' twenty-six yard line. It looked as if we had the game in our back pocket. But an otherwise sterling afternoon for Hart (fifteen of thirty-two for 314 yards, 292 in the second half, and four touchdowns) was spoiled when he put up a pass that Lee Roy Jordan intercepted and returned thirty-eight yards. Shortly afterward, Staubach connected with Billy Joe DuPree for a three-yard touchdown to end the game.

As much as I despised the Cowboys, I can honestly say I was not all that bitter about the loss. After all, the thing we're paid to do is entertain the fans. When I looked up into that crowd in Texas Stadium from time to time, it was obvious the people felt they were getting their money's worth. I know it was the most exciting game I'd ever seen.

"Sorry you guys lost," said defensive tackle Jethro Pugh, whom I had dominated for most of the day, as we walked off the field.

"There's nothing to be sorry about," I said. "This was a great game, no matter which team came out on top."

We rebounded the following week with a 26-14 victory over the Giants. Terry Metcalf and Jim Otis rushed for 109 and 101 yards, the first time two Cardinals gained more than a hundred yards in the same game. Who said pass-blocking was our only strength?

Our first disappointment that season came in our next game, a 27-17 loss to Washington on a Monday night in D.C. We came from behind three times to tie the score—but the Redskins scored ten unanswered points in the fourth quarter, and we were stopped twice by interceptions.

After the game, we all gave ourselves a little pep talk: "Hey, we're a good team; this shouldn't be happening to us. Let's get it together. Let's stop thinking about what we're supposed to do and just go out there and do it."

That little attitude adjustment worked wonders. We pounded the Eagles, and boosted our record to 4-2 with a win over the Giants at Shea Stadium (their second temporary home before moving to East Rutherford, New Jersey). The following week, we defeated New England, 24-17, to move into a three-way tie, along with the Cowboys and Redskins, for first place in the NFC East.

Because of our knack for winning—or losing—in the final minute, we became known as the "Cardiac Cardinals." A perfect example was our 24-23 triumph over Philadelphia in week eight. We fell behind, 23-7, with 7:38 to go in the third quarter. But touchdowns on our next two possessions re-duced the margin to 23–21. We got the ball again with 7:48 remaining in the game and mounted a sixty-six-yard drive that ended with a thirty-yard Bakken field goal as the clock ran out.

Last-minute heroics also were the order of the day in our 20–17 overtime win against the Redskins to give us our fifth consecutive victory and sole possession of first place in the division. As we trailed 17–10 with 1:43 left in the fourth quarter, Metcalf returned a punt nineteen yards to put us on Washington's thirty-nine yard line. We advanced to the six, from where Hart threw a desperation pass into the end zone to Gray, tying the score at 17–17 and forcing the game into overtime. After winning the coin toss, we drove fifty-five yards to set up Bakken's third winning field goal of the year.

We did make things a little easier by running our string of victories to six games, beating the New York Jets, 37–6, before getting complacent and allowing Buffalo to beat us, 32–14, on Thanksgiving Day. It was one of our sloppiest games ever, with seven turnovers. The only bright spot was Metcalf, who set a Cardinal record with 280 all-purpose yards.

However, we quickly regrouped, winning our final three games in fairly easy fashion—31–17 over the Cowboys (who would go on to become Pittsburgh's second Super Bowl victim), 34–20 over the Bears, and 24–13 over the Lions. We finished with an 11–3 record and our second consecutive NFC East crown. Along the way, the offensive line tied a league standard by allowing only eight sacks. As two of them resulted from running backs failing to pick up blitzers and one came on a botched field-goal attempt, as an offensive line, we really gave up only five sacks that year.

Our great pass protection had a lot to do with Hart's completing 53 percent of his attempts for 2,507 yards and nineteen touchdowns. We also did a good job running the ball.

Above left: *At age 3, posing with my older brother, Clifford. (author's collection)*

Above right: *The Doblers invade Mexico. In front of my mother, from the left, my sister, Corrine; my brother, Clifford; and my sister, Cynthia. That's me in my father's arms. (author's collection)*

Just your average, clean-cut, All-American teenager. (author's collection)

Diving for that extra yard as a high school running back in Twentynine Palms, Calif. (author's collection)

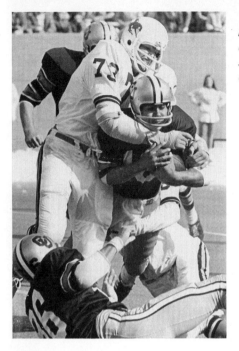

That's me, No. 73, abusing a running back from the University of Colorado, who happened to be 5′2″ —my kind of running back. (University of Wyoming)

Displaying my lightning-quick speed while pulling around to block for Terry Metcalf. (Paul Fine/NFL Photos)

No NFL team has fielded a better offensive line than this rowdy bunch. From left, Roger Finnie, in back, backup lineman Greg Kindle, Bob Young, Tom ''Wolfman'' Banks, yours truly and Dan Dierdorf, the game's greatest—and hairiest—offensive lineman. (Herb Weitman/NFL Photos)

Banks, yours truly, Dierdorf, and offensive line coach Jim Hanifan, getting ready for war. (Herb Weitman/NFL Photos)

Well, can you guess?
(Herb Weitman/NFL Photos)

Just checking to see if Philadelphia
Eagles' defensive end Manny Sistrunk
brushed his teeth before kickoff.
(Herb Weitman/NFL Photos)

This is one reason Merlin Olsen, the Hall-of-Fame defensive
tackle for the Los Angeles Rams, said he wouldn't send flowers
if someone broke my neck. (Herb Weitman/NFL Photos)

Now this is what I call hands-on experience. (David Boss/NFL Photos)

Another typical fracas, with yours truly center stage. And all I'd said was, "Less filling!" (NFL Photos)

I managed to put myself on my butt with this legwhip. But I also took a couple of Cowboys with me. (Jack Fahland)

Wearing the cast that I doctored into a lethal weapon— they said I carried a six pack in it. (Erby Aucoin)

Merlin Olsen, with the infamous tombstone, used as a prop for an episode of Father Murphy. (Wide World Photos)

Phil Villapiano, my wacky teammate in Buffalo, and I were rebels in more ways than one. (author's collection)

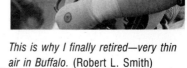

*Protecting quarterback Archie Manning,
after I'd joined the Saints.* (Erby Aucoin)

*This is why I finally retired—very thin
air in Buffalo.* (Robert L. Smith)

*An aging warrior sizes
up his opponent.*
(Robert L. Smith)

No, I haven't lost my game face in retirement. I just use a different kind of club.
(Robert L. Smith)

The next generation. That's Mark in the football gear, and on the right, counterclockwise from the top, Erin, Abbey, Holli, and Franco. (author's collection)

Opponents were so preoccupied with beating us for sacks that they didn't put all that much emphasis on stopping the run. As a result, Jim Otis, a power fullback built more for short duty than big plays, finished as the NFC's leading rusher with a club-record 1,076 yards. And Metcalf produced 816 rushing yards on the way to setting an NFL record with 2,462 all-purpose yards.

■　　■　　■

As good as we were in 1974, we felt we were even better in 1975. Not just one game better, as the record indicated, but vastly improved in every respect. And our playoff experience, although not extensive, gave us a comfortable feeling as we approached our postseason encounter with the Los Angeles Rams at the L.A. Coliseum.

We were much more relaxed than we were before that Viking game the year before. We didn't think there was any way the Rams, despite winning the NFC Western Division championship with a 12–2 record, were going to beat us. We respected their defense and I expected to have my hands full with Merlin Olsen. But we knew their offense wasn't nearly as potent as ours, and we were confident they wouldn't be able to outscore us.

The Rams had other ideas, however. They took the opening kickoff and promptly drove to our five yard line, from where quarterback Ron Jaworski ran for a touchdown. No problem, we thought. We knew we'd reply with a quick TD of our own. That's how it had gone for us all season long—you score, we score, you score, we score. The first points in one of our games were about as significant as the first points on a basketball court. Five of our victories had come in the last sixty seconds. We were the "Cardiac Cardinals." Comebacks were our specialty.

But on the second play of our opening possession, a freaky thing happened that severely rattled our confidence. Hart, attempting to hit Otis with a little flare pass, had the ball tipped by defensive end Jack Youngblood, who caught it and returned it forty-seven yards for a touchdown. Before we even knew what hit us, we were down, 14–0, with only seven minutes gone. Two plays, and we were already fighting for our postseason lives. Outscoring the Rams' offense was one thing. We weren't expecting to have to outscore their defense, too.

Youngblood, who possessed great upfield quickness, had lined up across from Dierdorf. The best way for an offensive lineman to protect on a flare pass is to cut the legs out from under the defensive lineman, thus preventing him from getting his hands up between the quarterback and the receiver. Dan had tried, but Youngblood, sniffing out the screen, slipped away and made the tip on Hart's pass, which was a little low. Those things happen.

But after that play, Dan became uptight and began to overcompensate for Youngblood's speed off the ball. Instead of taking him on at the line, he started dropping off a couple of yards to keep Youngblood from beating him to the outside. After about two or three plays, Jack said to himself, "If he wants to take the outside away from me, fine. Because he's leaving the inside wide open." Youngblood then started repeatedly beating Dan inside, knocking the stuffing out of Hart a few times after he released the ball and sacking him once.

Hart turned to me in the huddle and said, "Would you please talk to Dan and calm him down? I'm getting killed."

So I turned to Dierdorf and said, "Just take it easy, man. You can beat Youngblood. You outweigh him. You're a better football player. You can knock the shit out of him. Forget about what happened before. You own this guy.''

Dan's eyes were as big as silver dollars. There was panic in his voice.

"Yeah, yeah, yeah,'' he said, the words coming rapid-fire. "I know what I'm doing wrong, I'll get it straightened out. Yeah, yeah, yeah.''

I turned to Banks and, out of the corner of my mouth, said, "I think Hart's in a lot of trouble.'' Actually, Dan would eventually return to his normal self and contain Youngblood the rest of the way.

But that's what the finality of a playoff game does to a player. It's totally different from the regular season. If you make a mistake that costs you a victory during the regular season, you usually have another game to redeem yourself. But if you miss a block or miss a tackle or throw an interception or drop a pass in a playoff game, that could be the one play that ends the entire season. It's like death, as opposed to just having pneumonia.

The Rams took a 21–0 lead at the start of the second quarter when safety Bill Simpson intercepted a Hart pass and returned it sixty-five yards for a touchdown. Our first visit to the end zone finally came at the 4:07 mark of the second period when Otis ran three yards for a TD. But we knew it wasn't meant to be for us that day when Bakken's extra-point try was blocked by—who else?—Youngblood.

And on the very next play after Cullen Bryant returned the kickoff to the Rams' thirty-four yard line, Jaworski heaved a sixty-six-yard scoring bomb to Harold Jackson. A twenty-nine-yard Bakken field goal made it 28–9 at halftime.

We cut the lead to twelve points with Hart's eleven-yard touchdown pass to Gray in the third quarter. But the Rams came right back in the fourth, on another freaky play. Running back Lawrence McCutcheon fumbled at our four yard line on a hit by Larry Stallings. Wide receiver Ron Jessie picked up the ball at the two and carried it across the goal line to put Los Angeles up, 35–16. A three-yard TD run by Steve Jones made the final a not-so-respectable 35–23.

My only satisfaction that day came from upsetting Olsen to the point where he said all kinds of unpleasant things about me to the media after the game. Another classic example of gaining the edge. Instead of savoring the victory, like all of his teammates, Olsen still was thinking about the aggressive tactics I had used on him during the game. Our next encounter as opponents wouldn't come for another eleven months. And I already had him beat.

Losing to the Rams was humbling, but I can't say I was as devastated as I was after our defeat to Minnesota, probably because I was one of nine Cardinals selected to play in the Pro Bowl in New Orleans. The others were offensive teammates Dierdorf, Banks, Hart, Gray, Metcalf, and Otis, as well as Bakken and cornerback Roger Wehrli. Having one more game to play helped offset some of the frustration of missing a second consecutive chance to get a Super Bowl ring.

Making that first Pro Bowl was one of the most thrilling moments of my career. It meant I had arrived as a professional football player. It meant I was regarded as one of the very best at my job. In those days, voting was done strictly by coaches (players would later be included in the process), so there was a sense of pride that the men who ultimately decided who played in the league and who didn't included me among the cream of the crop.

Dan was the only member of our offensive line to be picked to the NFC squad after the 1974 season. That three of us made it the following year was a good reflection of how well we had played as a unit, but not good enough. Roger Finnie and Bob Young should have been there with us. Five men tied the NFL record for allowing the fewest sacks in a season, not three.

Part of the Pro Bowl reward is spending a week of leisure in the town where the game is played (it was just my luck that the last three Pro Bowls during my career were held in Hawaii, and I didn't make any of them). For the most part, players expend more energy in their nightly partying than in daily practicing. It wasn't until game day that I remembered the primary purpose of our trip.

I must say it was nice being a part of the NFC's 23–20 victory over the AFC under the Louisiana Superdome. It was even nicer to see four Cardinals contribute to the scoring—Bakken with a forty-two-yard field goal and two extra points, Hart with a four-yard touchdown pass to Minnesota's Chuck Foreman, Metcalf with a fourteen-yard TD reception from Philadelphia quarterback Mike Boryla and Gray with the winning, eight-yard TD catch from Boryla.

■ ■ ■

The 1976 season was my first real taste of what it was like to be a marked man. I was part of one of the greatest offensive lines in NFL history, I was a Pro Bowl guard, and I was developing a reputation as the dirtiest, meanest player in professional football. Three good reasons for my opponents to want to separate my head from my shoulders like never before.

I had to be more mentally disciplined that year than any of the previous four; I couldn't afford to be anything less than fully prepared each week. No one was going to take the day off against me.

Our opening day opponent in 1976 was the Seattle Seahawks, playing the first regular-season game in the franchise's history, before fifty-eight-thousand Kingdome fans. We spoiled their debut, 30–24, but not before safety Mike Sensibaugh killed a final Seattle scoring threat with an end-zone interception as time expired. For the second time in Cardinal history, two runners surpassed the hundred-yard mark in the same game, as Otis and Metcalf gained 140 and 113 yards.

Our 29–0 victory over Green Bay in week two marked the Cardinals' first shutout win since 1970. I thought Bakken's foot was going to fall off that day, as he kicked five consecutive field goals for our first fifteen points.

At 2–0 and with fifty-nine points in our first two games, we were flying high before facing the Chargers at San Diego—high enough to be brought down hard, 43–24. We bounced back a week later with a 27–21 victory over the Giants, followed by wins over Philadelphia (33–14) and Dallas (21–17) to move into a tie with the Cowboys for first in the NFC East.

Our three-game winning streak and first-place standing ended with a 20–10 defeat at Washington. But we put together another 3–0 stretch with victories against the '49ers (23–20 in overtime), Eagles (17–14), and Rams (30–28) to improve our record to 8–2. In typical "Cardiac Cardinals" fashion, we rallied from a 21–6 third-quarter deficit to beat the Rams. That was the day I physically conquered Olsen and enraged him to the point that he made a finger-pointing visit to our huddle. He finally took himself out of the game in the fourth quarter and was replaced by Mike Fanning.

Maintaining our up-and-down form that year, we proceeded to suffer critical back-to-back division losses to Washington, 16–10, at home, and Dallas, 19–14, on Thanksgiving Day at Texas Stadium. The loss to the Cowboys was the most bitter of the season, because it crushed our chances of capturing a third consecutive NFC East title. It also was the most controversial. After falling behind, 19–7, midway through the fourth quarter, we drove sixty-eight yards for a touchdown, which came on a nineteen-yard, fourth-down pass from Hart to Gray. Then, with 1:23 left, we got the ball back at our own thirty-seven yard line and marched to a first down at the Dallas thirteen. After three incompletions, Hart finally connected—but for only a five-yard gain that proved too little too late. We protested that the Cowboys had interfered on two of those final pass attempts, but the officials didn't want to hear it.

We kept our hopes for a wild-card playoff berth alive with a 24–17 victory over Baltimore in the second-to-last week of the season. Then we beat the Giants, 17–14, on the road to finish with a 10–4 record.

All we needed was for Washington to lose to Dallas (which had already clinched the division title) later in the day, and we'd beat out the Redskins for one of two NFC wild-card spots. But if the Redskins won, they'd be a wild card, and we'd be packing for the off-season.

On the plane ride back to St. Louis, we were all feeling very good about our playoff prospects. We figured there was no way the Cowboys would allow themselves to be beaten in their own back yard. But with an hour left in the flight, the pilot opened his microphone, cleared his throat, and gave us the bad news: "I hate to tell you this, gentlemen, but we've just been informed the Redskins have defeated the Cowboys, 27–14." Hardly a word was spoken during those final sixty minutes; our season was over.

We became the first 10–4 club in NFC history not to play a postseason game. Once again, we had been a great clutch team, winning eight games by seven points or less. Once again, we had allowed fewer sacks (seventeen) than anyone else in the league. But it was all for naught.

In fact, the frustration of missing the playoffs despite such a great record even took some of the satisfaction out of being selected to my second straight Pro Bowl. I'm sure the six other Cardinals who were picked—Dierdorf, Banks, Hart, Gray, Bakken, and Wehrli—felt the same way.

The Pro Bowl game that year was played in Seattle, but our practices the week before were held in San Diego. One night, a bunch of us were sitting around having a few beers, and one of my NFC linemates, Ed White, who was playing for Minnesota at the time, said, "You know, Conrad, offensive linemen don't get a lot of recognition. But because of you, everybody's starting to notice us a little bit more. I'm not saying you're not an asshole, because you are. But I have to admit, it's kind of nice when people recognize you *before* you introduce yourself. Thanks."

■　　■　　■

My most frustrating and disappointing year in St. Louis was my last, 1977. Things actually began to turn sour during the off-season when I heard whispers that Don Coryell, the best coach I ever played for, was on his way out because of steadily growing friction between him and management. Don's relationship with the front office was never the same after the college draft that year. He felt the team needed immediate help on defense and wanted to trade our number one choice for an experienced, top-notch defensive player. Not only did the player-personnel brain trust refuse to make such a deal, it also used three of its first four picks on offensive players, including a quarterback (Steve Pisarkiewicz) on the first round and a running back (George Franklin) on the second. Coryell was left out of the drafting completely.

The players had a beef of their own with management going into the 1977 season. We were tired of Bill Bidwill's cheapness when it came to our salaries. After taking the franchise to its first two playoff appearances in ages and generating thirty-one wins over the previous three seasons, most of us felt we were entitled to some sort of financial reward. I sure as hell thought, as a two-time Pro Bowler, I was worth more than fifty thousand dollars a year, but the Cardinals refused to compensate me accordingly. Nor did they want to give raises to the several other players who were recognized as being among the league's best.

Our 1–3 start confirmed my worst fears—we weren't the same team we had been from 1974 to 1976. We opened with a 7–0 loss to Denver (our first shutout since 1974), scored a 16–13 victory over Chicago, then lost to Washington (24–14) and Dallas (30–24). The Cowboys game was particularly frustrating, because we blew a 24–16 third-quarter lead.

We did manage to put together a six-game winning streak. It began with a 21–17 victory over Philadelphia—once again, we built a big advantage, 21–3 in the second half, but this time we hung on to it. The following week, we produced the most points by a Cardinal team since 1965 in beating New Orleans, 49–31. Terry Metcalf was virtually a one-man team that day, accounting for 286 yards: 99 on kickoff returns, 78 on rushing attempts, 62 on pass receptions, 29 on punt returns, and 18 on two pass completions on option plays.

We bettered our record to 4–3 by shutting out the Giants, 28–0, on *Monday Night Football.* That game will always stand out in my mind for two reasons—one, I scored the first and only touchdown of my pro career; two, I did it while battling one of the worst hangovers of my life.

Mick Carter, a former college teammate, had just gotten married, and he and his new bride stopped in St. Louis on the way to their honeymoon. I couldn't make the wedding, so I took them to dinner the night before the game. With kickoff a good twenty-four hours away, I decided to celebrate through the night. I probably drank more wine than the five hundred guests at their reception put together. Thank God it was a night game, because I was still hanging on to the porcelain pony by late that afternoon.

I finally managed to pick myself up and drive to Busch Stadium. My head pounded the entire way and would continue doing so through the balance of the evening. Nonetheless, I wound up having one of my best games ever. I know, having spent all that time throwing up, I was as quick as ever because I was so light. As one New York sportswriter put it, I blocked John Mendenhall "right off the prime-time television screen." My added quickness also played a key role in allowing me to pounce on the end-zone fumble of our fullback, Wayne Morris, to give us a 14–0 lead late in the first half.

Most people score a touchdown and spike the ball. In my case, it was someone's head that got spiked. As I was on the ground, Giants linebacker Brian Kelley started to grab for the ball. It's rare for an offensive lineman to score a touchdown, and I wasn't going to let Kelley spoil this chance of a lifetime. So I lifted my leg and his crotch just happened to collide with my foot. Then he started kicking me, and that infuriated Dierdorf to no end. The next thing I knew, Dan got Kelley in a bear hug, hoisted him right off the ground, carried him about ten yards, and shishkebobbed him, headfirst, into the goal post. I had to laugh at how Dierdorf explained his actions to the press afterward: "Well, Conrad was in kind of a helpless position, so I thought I'd just get that guy off him. We start running together, and pretty soon his head's banging into the goal post. Just one of those things."

Chalk up another one for The Troublemaker.

I did manage to elicit a little sympathy from reporters who wondered why I looked so pale and drawn after the game. I told them I had the flu . . . and that I had probably caught it from a dirty wineglass. They seemed to buy it.

We proceeded to win our next three games—27–7 over Minnesota (giving the Vikings their worst home defeat in nine seasons), 24–17 over Dallas (giving the Cowboys their first loss of the season) and 21–16 over Philadelphia. We were at our "Cardiac Cardinals" best against the Eagles, rallying from a 16–0 third-quarter deficit and winning in the final thirty-eight seconds. All things considered, we were flying pretty high at 7–3.

Then the bottom fell out.

First came the 55–14 Thanksgiving Day Massacre against Miami. For at least one Dolphin, rookie defensive end A. J. Duhe, it wasn't enough that his team was making franchise history that day for most points scored in a game. He thought we needed to hear some insults to boot, which led to the monumental bench-clearing brawl in the final seconds. After that, we were beaten by the Giants (27–7) and Redskins (26–20) before closing the season with the embarrassment to end all embarrassments—a 17–7 loss to Tampa Bay. Thanks to us, the Buccaneers, who would have had to struggle to compete on the junior-college level at the time, finished the year with a grand total of two victories—their first two since their birth in 1976.

With a 7–7 record, we wound up in third place in the division. We were playoff spectators for the second time in as many seasons.

After our four previous season-ending games, Coryell had finished his address to the team with something to the effect of, "Have a good off-season, keep yourselves safe, and get prepared for next year. Because we're going to come back and kick some ass!'' He made no such remarks after the Tampa Bay game. All he said, in a somber voice, was, ''Sorry it had to end this way.''

Coryell wasn't referring to the game or the season. He was referring to his employment with the Cardinals, which would officially terminate during the off-season. Four weeks into the 1978 campaign, he replaced Tommy Prothro as head coach of the Chargers. Gene Klein, the Chargers' owner, had to give the Cardinals a third-round draft choice for the right to sign Coryell. As Klein would say later, ''It was more than I wanted to give them, but less than they could have gotten from me.''

I made some remarks to the press that probably convinced Joe Sullivan, the St. Louis general manager, I was too much trouble to keep around. I complained openly about my contract and about the way the Cardinals did business. And after Coryell left, I told reporters, ''Well, he's the winningest coach the Cardinals ever had since they came to St. Louis and it wasn't right for them to treat him the way they did, to just say, 'Go ahead and leave.' If they could do that to him, they'll probably trade me, too.'' The headlines the next day said, DOBLER ASKS TO BE TRADED, when I never really said anything of the sort. But Sullivan saw that and said, ''If he feels that strongly about it, let's appease him.''

While I was in Tampa, preparing for my third Pro Bowl, my agent, Richard Bennett, called to tell me a trade was being worked out that would send me and wide receiver Ike Harris to New Orleans in exchange for offensive guard Terry Stieve and defensive end Bob Pollard.

I didn't play the politics right, because I never believed it was necessary for me to play them at all. I thought my ability to perform on the field meant more than how well I played the game within the game, and I was dead wrong. But I didn't regret what I had told the press, because I had tremendous respect for Coryell. The man deserved that kind of respect, regardless of his differences with the team's administration. Other players, like Hart, publicly accused Coryell of abandoning ship, of walking out on us to satisfy his own career interests. Of course, Sullivan and Bidwill loved those comments. Ate them right up.

But the way I saw it, it wasn't Coryell's fault he was unhappy in St. Louis; it was the fault of the front office for not trying to make him happy. He was driven away by having his power diminished when it came to the draft. And when he tried to convince management to loosen its purse strings with us for the sake of team morale, he was told to mind his own business.

It was an awkward feeling to play in the Pro Bowl as a representative of the Cardinals when, in fact, I was about to become a member of the Saints. But I guess, religiously speaking, I had to be pleased with my promotion.

I had been elevated from Cardinal to Saint.

5

The Saint Who Got Buffaloed

Joe Sullivan and the rest of the Cardinal brain trust took a lot of flak for getting rid of me. It was obvious they underestimated the strong following I had developed in and around St. Louis. While addressing a meeting of the St. Louis Rotary Club, Sullivan said, "I trade Conrad Dobler, and all of a sudden the town turns upside down. Before that, they said we should do anything for a pass-rusher. I make the trade, and they say, 'What did you do that for?'" The deal met the disapproval of more than two-thirds of the readers who responded to a poll conducted by the *St. Louis Post-Dispatch*. As one man commented in casting his negative vote, "Bidwill would trade a horse for a jackass."

Tom Banks was so upset, he wanted to be traded, too. He even asked me how he could convince the Cardinals to ship his ass out. I told him, "It didn't take much for me, just a little by-the-way comment about Coryell. And I'm kind of conservative-looking, Tommy. You've got that big ol' beard, you've got long hair, you wear Levi's all the time and are kind of a hippie. I don't think you'll have to say much of anything.'' So Banks dog-cussed the organization for days and days, but they just ignored him. Then he said, "I'm so confused now, Conrad, I don't know what to do. They won't trade me; they won't even reprimand me. I wish they'd fire me or something.'' He wound up staying with the Cardinals until his release in 1980.

I couldn't have been happier about my contract with the Saints. Counting the signing bonus of $60,000 (very modest by today's standards, but a lot of bread for an offensive lineman at the time), the $175,000 I made in that first year with New Orleans was more than I had made in six with St. Louis. The Cardinals never would have come across with that kind of money, no matter how many Pro Bowls I made. Still, it was hard to leave behind the friends I had had since 1972. I don't know if there ever was or will be a more tightly knit group than that offensive line. It wasn't just on the field; it was off, too. And it wasn't just the players. Jim Hanifan was as much a part of us as anybody. We were the best offensive line in the league at one time.

And that's not something you easily forget.

■   ■   ■

I tried to bring the unity we had in St. Louis to New Orleans and, later, to Buffalo. I tried to be a leader, employing the same methods that did so much to create the incredible bonding we had—such as the fine system, which required members of the offensive line to throw five dollars into a kitty for each sack they allowed or assignment they missed. At the end of the season, we'd use the money to give ourselves a party. We hoped there wouldn't be enough for anything more elaborate than a night at Burger King. If we were able to finance a major blowout, I'm sure the coaches would have seen to it that it was our last supper as Cardinals.

As it turned out, the fine system was as big a success in New Orleans and Buffalo as it was in St. Louis. That's because the greatest pain for the average professional athlete, no matter how much money he has, is reaching for his wallet. He'd prefer a broken leg any day.

I thought a big part of my job was to make the other guys on the line believe in themselves. I'd get all the boys together and say, "Look, we're the people who control this game and we're going to get as much publicity as everyone else. And the way we're going to get it is to not let the guys on the other side of the line touch the quarterback. What we're saying to them is, 'Come get us, sumbitches, 'cause we ain't movin'.' And if one of us gets into a fight with a defensive guy, in a game or even on the practice field, don't ever let me see another offensive lineman try to restrain him. Grab that defensive donkey and let your teammate get two or three more shots in. Let another defender worry about pulling away our man. And if any of you tries to grab me when I'm in a fight, I'm going to kick your ass after I finish with the defensive guy."

I'd also talk to the quarterback, telling him, "Look, when you get in trouble, man, don't just take the sack. Throw that goddamn ball away. If you do your part to keep the sack total down, that'll help build our confidence. And the greater our confidence, the healthier you're gonna stay."

I never sensed the other offensive linemen or quarterbacks I played with resented my self-appointed leadership role. Consider this comment from Saints center John Hill: "Conrad has a certain persona about him that emanates. Everyone picks it up, the way he talks, the way he acts . . . it's a tough, aggressive attitude. It takes off on other people who may have it but don't express it." And this from Saints quarterback Archie Manning: "I'll admit it, I'm a Conrad Dobler fan. There is something special about the guy. Wherever he's been, he's made a contribution. I know I've never been so inspired by another football player. Conrad is the only man I ever met who wears his game face 365 days a year."

I'm not saying it was all because of me, but I don't think it was mere coincidence that each team I played for in the NFL became significantly better between the time I arrived and the time I left. The Cardinals went from 4-9-1 to 11-3 and two division championships. The Saints, despite the handicap of having Dick Nolan as their head coach, went from 3-11 in 1977 to 7-9 in 1978 to 8-8 in 1979, their best record until 1987. The Bills went from 7-9 in 1979 to 11-5 and a division championship in 1980. They were 10-6 in 1981, but reached the playoffs as a wild-card team and advanced to the divisional round. It also should be pointed out that in 1979, the Saints allowed only seventeen sacks—twenty fewer than the previous season and the second-lowest league total that year—and the Bills gave up the fewest sacks in the NFL in both 1980 (twenty, after permitting forty-three the season before) and 1981 (sixteen).

What happened to those three "Doblerized" clubs after I left? The Cardinals won no more than six games in each of the four years I played in the NFL after my departure and they went from allowing fifteen sacks, the league's second-lowest total, in 1977, to twenty-two in 1978. The Saints became the 1-15 "Aint's" in 1980, giving up forty-five sacks along the way. The Bills haven't had a winning season since my retirement in 1982.

The first thing about the Saints that caught my attention was their training camp. Coming from the Cardinals, I was conditioned not to expect much in the way of luxury from training-camp sites. I always felt more like a POW than a football player at our various summer addresses. You get what you pay for, and Bidwill tried to pay as little as possible—which probably explained why we moved so much. But with Saints' owner John Mecom, it was spare no expense. He had us based in Dodgertown, the spring training facility of the Los Angeles Dodgers at Vero Beach, Florida. The place was like a country club, complete with a swimming pool, conference rooms, and a fancy restaurant. I couldn't believe my eyes the first time I sat down to dinner. Beautiful linen napkins. Fine china. A filled glass of ice water, complete with a lemon slice, at each setting. I suddenly felt very under-dressed in the standard training-camp garb of T-shirt, shorts, and sandals. There even were times when we ate by candle-light.

With the Cardinals, we considered ourselves fortunate when our meals were as hot as our dormitory rooms.

But the posh surroundings of Dodgertown account for the only pleasant memory I have of that first year with the Saints.

Not long after I arrived at Vero Beach, I was sent back to New Orleans for surgery to repair a ligament tear in the ring finger of my left hand suffered during a scrimmage. I returned a short while later, wearing the same type of protective "club" I had worn in St. Louis.

We began the regular season by defeating Minnesota, 31–24. That gave the Saints their first opening-day win since the franchise's inception in 1967 and first regular-season triumph since the tenth week of their 3–11 campaign the year before. But the euphoria was short-lived, as we proceeded to suffer consecutive losses to Green Bay (28–17) at Milwaukee and Philadelphia (24–17) in the Superdome.

I had removed my "club" after the Green Bay game. I only wish I had been wearing something to protect my left knee against the Eagles, because I tore it to shreds that day. Philadelphia's Bill Bergey did the initial damage, but I made it much more severe by returning to the field after convincing the Saints' medical staff that all I needed was a little tape around it. I was operated on later, then sidelined for the rest of the year. My knee would never be the same.

I can't begin to describe how miserable I felt through the rest of that season. Not so much because of the knee itself as because of the walking-dead label I automatically assumed as an injured player. When you can't play and you can't practice, you're no longer a part of the team. Someone else is doing your job and life goes on without you. The healthy players treat you as if you have something terribly contagious, as if getting too close might cause them to get struck by lightning from the dark cloud over your head. And Dick Nolan didn't improve matters any by having those of us on the injured-reserve list show up for treatment each day at 6:00 A.M., so we could leave before the "real players," as he called them, came in to be taped for practice.

Therefore, I felt like an outsider through the remaining thirteen games. As if I wasn't entitled to share in the joy of our 10–3 upset of the Rams, giving the Saints their first-ever win at the L.A. Coliseum. Or our 24–13 victory over San Francisco, marking the first time any New Orleans team had won six games in a season. Or our year-ending, 17–10 triumph over the Buccaneers to give us a 7–9 record, best in franchise history at the time. Or Archie Manning's becoming the NFC's Player of the Year with a league-high completion percentage of 61.8 for 3,416 yards and seventeen touchdowns.

There was a little comic relief, however, before the Tampa

Bay game when it was discovered there was no film to watch of the Saints' 33–14 loss to the Bucs the year before. Hank Stram, who Nolan had replaced as head coach after the 1977 season, had burned it. I guess he didn't want any visual evidence that his team had become the very first victim of what, at the time, was the worst club in professional football.

■   ■   ■

While rehabilitating my knee, I spent the entire off-season commuting between Laramie, Wyoming, and New Orleans. I was held out of spring minicamp, and didn't do very much after reporting to training camp at Vero Beach. It wasn't until warmups before our second preseason game, against Chicago in the Superdome, that I actually ran for the first time. I wasn't going to play that day; the medical staff just wanted to see how I felt running on artificial turf again (we practiced on grass fields at Vero Beach). And I felt strange as hell. I had returned to the scene of the crime, so to speak, and my main concern was avoiding reinjury. I found myself comparing notes with Emanuel Zanders, another offensive guard, who had injured his knee in the same Philadelphia game and was also running for the first time that day.

We both stepped very high and very carefully, as if we were walking on eggs.

My only playing time in the 1979 preseason came in the second half of our final exhibition game, a 10–7 victory over the Oilers. Although I wasn't moving with the same tentativeness as before, I never felt the knee was 100 percent healed when I started playing on it. I wish I'd had another year of rehabilitation, but the desire to get back into the lineup, as well as the pressure put on me to do so from the coaches and administration, made that impossible.

The Saints seemed headed right back to their incompetent ways as we got off to an 0–3 start in the regular season. Atlanta beat us in the opener, 40–34, in overtime, then we lost to the Packers and Eagles. During the Eagles game, I was determined to get back at Bill Bergey for what he had done to my left knee the year before. So I shadowed him from our very first possession, trying to cut his legs out from under him at every turn. He wound up tearing his left knee to shreds when, while hurdling me in pursuit of a ball-carrier, he caught his foot in the artificial turf.

We broke out of our losing streak and our offensive slump the next week, beating San Francisco, 30–21, and producing a club-record 514 yards in the process. After that, we beat the Giants, but suffered a quick return to reality with a 35–17 loss to the Rams. Manning was intercepted five times, and I think, with all of those defensive ball-carriers running around, I was our leading tackler.

In week seven, we pounded Tampa Bay, 42–14, and we then scored victories over Detroit (17–7) and Washington (14–10) to boost our record to 5–4 and move into first place in the NFC West. The only other time the Saints had ever led the division was when we won our opener in 1978. But the Redskins game touched off a schizophrenic stretch as we lost to Denver the following week, beat San Francisco, lost to Seattle, and beat Atlanta. Our next game was a Monday-night encounter with Oakland.

The Raiders somehow always seem to win on *Monday Night Football*. And in week fourteen, we fell victim to their Monday Night Magic, allowing them to rally from a 35–14 deficit in the third quarter to score a 42–35 victory. The most amazing thing about that game was the performance of Raider quarterback Ken Stabler. He set up two of our four second-quarter touchdowns by fumbling and throwing an interception. In the third quarter, he was picked off by linebacker Ken Bordelon, who returned the ball nineteen yards for a TD to give us a twenty-one-point bulge. Stabler had chased after Bordelon and was knocked silly on a block from Barry Bennett.

Later in the third quarter, the Raiders drove sixty-two yards for a touchdown. And in the fourth, Stabler, still feeling woozy, returned to his All-Pro form by throwing three touchdown passes, including two to Cliff Branch.

Having blown a tremendous opportunity to look good in front of the entire nation, we weren't in the best frame of mind to play another game six days later. Thus our 35–0 loss to San Diego in the Superdome, marking the first time the Saints had been held scoreless in two years. We closed the season with a 29–14 triumph over the Rams, who went on to play in Super Bowl XIV and lose to Pittsburgh.

At 8–8, we were home for Christmas.

■   ■   ■

On the morning before I was supposed to leave for my third training camp with the Saints, I sat at the kitchen table of my house in Wyoming and pulled out the sports section of the newspaper.

"Oh, my God, Linda!" I yelled to my wife. "I've been traded."

"Come on," she said. "You haven't been traded anywhere and you know it."

"Just kidding, baby doll."

And I was.

At least, I thought I was.

Less than five minutes later, the phone rang.

"It's Dick Nolan," Linda said, holding out the receiver.

"Sure," I said with a smile. "Very funny."

"No, Connie, it's Dick Nolan. Really."

She was telling the truth. It *was* Nolan.

"Conrad, I just wanted to let you know that we have worked out a trade, and you'll be going to the Buffalo Bills," he said.

I couldn't believe my ears. There I was, fully prepared to report to camp. I had been studying my playbook. I had been working out. I was really looking forward to helping the Saints finally get over the hump, finally become a winner.

And besides all that, we owned a beautiful home in New Orleans. We loved it there. The fabulous restaurants. Bourbon Street. It was my kind of town.

"Traded? To Buffalo?"

"To Buffalo."

Some trade. The Saints had placed me on recallable waivers, something every NFL club does each year to gauge the market for certain players on their roster. They wait to see how many teams put in claims, then recall the players and determine their market value. Since the Bills were the only team to put in a claim for me, the Saints were happy to let me go for a conditional draft choice—an eighth-round pick if I started, an eleventh-rounder if I just made the final roster.

"We truly appreciate all that you've done for us over the past two years," Nolan said. "You really—"

"Save it," I interrupted. "I just want you to know that you're making the biggest mistake of your life. You're not going to win without me."

"Well, Conrad, I'm sorry you feel that way."

"I feel that way because I know you're wrong. Now give me Chuck Knox's phone number."

He gave me the number and I hung up. There were no goodbyes.

My anger subsided as I thought about the situation in Buffalo. The more I thought about it, the better I felt about my chances of finishing my career with a Super Bowl ring on my finger. Knox, known for being a players' coach, had taken the Rams to five playoff appearances—including three NFC championship games—in as many seasons as their head coach. The Bills had shown noticeable improvement in their first two years under his direction; everybody looked for the climb to continue. And, bottom line, Knox was willing to give me a job. That alone made him more astute than any of his twenty-seven peers, who chose to see me only as an old man with ravaged knees. What couldn't be measured with a stopwatch or in a weight room was my heart. My intestinal fortitude. My chutzpah.

Knox showed a lot of respect for me by keeping my practice and playing to a minimum in the preseason. He knew my knees, as well as the rest of my aging body, didn't need pounding above and beyond what they'd get for sixteen weeks during the regular season. Plus, he pretty much knew what I could and couldn't do. The preseason, as far as Knox was concerned, was primarily for evaluating younger players and giving them a taste of the NFL. He expected the veterans to perform when it counted.

There was a slight catch to my marriage to the Bills. On the final day of cuts, I was temporarily exposed to waivers so they could meet the forty-five-man roster deadline while working out a trade that would send the incumbent starter at right guard, Joe DeLamielleure, who had been a training-camp holdout, to Cleveland. They figured there was little chance of anyone else picking me up, and they were right. I was re-signed as soon as the DeLamielleure trade was consummated. The Bills ended up having to give the Saints the eighth-round pick because I would spend the next two seasons as a regular starter.

The good feelings I had about joining the Bills intensified when we opened the 1980 season with a 17–7 victory over the Miami Dolphins. It ended an NFL-record losing streak to the Dolphins that had begun twenty games and ten years earlier. And it touched off a wild postgame celebration, as a large portion of the nearly eighty thousand fans in attendance poured onto the field in Rich Stadium to tear down the goal posts and tear up the artificial turf. In fact, pieces of the goal posts were relayed up through the stands to the private box of Bills owner Ralph Wilson. It was like a rock concert, and we were like Mick Jagger and the Rolling Stones.

Some fans even handed out beers to the players still on the field. I got one. So did my buddy, Phil Villapiano, a linebacker who had joined the Bills from the Oakland Raiders three months before I arrived from New Orleans.

"This is our kind of town," we said, clinking beer cups as we made our way to the dressing room.

The following week, we beat the New York Jets, 20–10, and our defense again was virtually impenetrable. Free safety Jeff Nixon scored on a fifty-yard interception return and it wasn't until the final eight seconds that the Jets got their only touchdown.

My most personally gratifying victory of the season came in week three, when we traveled to New Orleans and defeated the Saints, 35–26. It also was a big day for our outstanding quarterback, Louisiana native Joe Ferguson, who threw three touchdown passes in keying our offense's season-high 410-yard day.

A week before the game, Knox came up to me and asked, "What can you tell us about these guys?" I didn't hesitate one second before giving him everything I knew, right down to what Nolan ate for breakfast each morning. There's no reason not to cooperate in a situation like that. Fuck the team that traded you; someone else is paying for your loyalty. Don Coryell honestly believed the only reason George Allen would ever bring an ex–St. Louis player to Washington was to pump him for information. He was convinced Allen would sit the guy on a chair in the middle of a room, shine a bright light on his face, and say, ''OK, now come clean with everything you know about the Cardinals.'' And I suppose Coryell expected us to divulge nothing more than our name, position, and jersey number.

I had so much material for Knox, he even had me lecture the Bills' defensive linemen about the Saints' offensive line. The players in the meeting room gave me a big hand when I was introduced as Coach Dobler. I made certain, of course, to keep the language as simple as possible so I wouldn't lose any of them.

The biggest thing I looked forward to in the Saints' game was the chance to play for keeps against the defensive linemen I had only practiced against for two years. I wasn't practicing real hard at that point in my career. I would let people get by me all the time in one-on-one drills and they would be very proud of themselves. ''How'd he ever get that reputation for being so tough?'' they wondered. ''I went by him like he wasn't even there.'' What they forgot was that NFL games weren't played on Wednesday or Thursday afternoons.

On the Bills' first offensive play, New Orleans defensive tackle Mike Fultz, who had had his share of practice triumphs over me, came off the ball real hard and knocked me right on my back. I was really embarrassed—first, because I was appearing in the Superdome for the first time since the trade; second, because I knew the guy was a total blockhead who couldn't spell his own name; third, because I had way too much pride not to have been embarrassed. So five plays later, Fultz left the field with a hyperextended elbow. I can honestly say that that was one of the few times in my career I deliberately tried to hurt someone. We were running the ball, Fultz was pursuing, and as he tried to push off of me, he hooked his forearm just under my right armpit. I pinned it by pulling my arm against my rib cage and dropped straight to the ground. Fultz was too dumb to fall down with me; he resisted, and his elbow gave out.

The man should have known better than to try to embarrass someone who invented the technique.

Fultz's replacement was Barry Bennett. On his first play against me he came out swinging, and he pounded me real good the rest of the game. Which was perfectly fine, because he also failed to make a single tackle. That was the primary purpose of my tactics—winning the war, the game, not the battle.

I wound up receiving a game ball for the contributions I made to our victory over the Saints. *Before* and during the game.

Wins over eventual Super Bowl XV champion Oakland (24–7) and San Diego (26–24) pushed our record to 5-0. Funny how players, even those from warm climates, didn't complain about the weather in Buffalo when they were winning.

It wasn't long before my teammates began to recognize me as a leader by example. "A lot of times you can tell Conrad's knees are hurting so bad, but he'll never let you know," said Reggie McKenzie, the Bills' left guard and a holdover from the "Electric Company" line that turned on the juice for O. J. Simpson. "He's been an inspiration to us all, just knowing that he's out there trying to get the job done. And he does. He'll do whatever it takes to do the job. Some guys who might try to take the easy way out won't after seeing what Conrad goes through."

I'd get to the stadium at 8:00 in the morning, about three hours earlier than most of the other players arrived, and begin the process of getting my knees ready for the game. I put everything on them—heat packs, DMSO, Mint Glo. I'd use heat salves other guys couldn't even stand to put on their little fingers, let alone their knees; that's how much they burned. Then I'd do a lot of stretching, get my knees as loose as possible, and by game time, I was ready to go. I almost never made it to the sidelines in time for the national anthem. In fact, I always hoped we would win the coin toss so that, after the kickoff, I could go straight from the trainer's room to the huddle.

"For him to even play is a miracle," said Ray Prochaska, our offensive coordinator and line coach. I considered that mutual respect, because for Ray still to be coaching at sixty-plus years old was no less a miracle.

We hit a little slide after the Chargers game, losing to Baltimore, 17-12, and Miami, 17-14. We were especially frustrated by the Miami defeat, because our defense held the Dolphins to 232 total yards, but we gave the game away with three fumbles.

We rebounded with a victory over New England seven days later, but turned around in week nine and got our asses kicked by Atlanta, 30-14, after taking a 14-0 lead. Then we went on a 3-0 tear, beginning with a 31-24 triumph over the Jets that we won when wide receiver Frank Lewis made a juggling catch of a thirty-one-yard Ferguson touchdown pass six seconds before the final gun. We got our first shutout of the year—and the Bills' first in two seasons—with a 14-0 win over Cincinnati to take sole possession of first place in the AFC East. A 28-13 victory over Pittsburgh gave us a 9-3 record and assured the franchise of its first winning record since 1975.

We blew another 14–0 lead on the way to suffering a four-point loss to the Colts. But we made up for it with a thrilling, 10–7 overtime win against the Rams that sparked a postgame celebration in Rich Stadium that was even more outrageous than the one after our season opener. Despite having sat for three hours through a cold, persistent December drizzle, most of the crowd of seventy-seven thousand refused to leave. They chanted for us to come back onto the field, and we took what was, to the best of anyone's recollection, the first curtain call in NFL history. Placekicker Nick Mike-Mayer, who booted the winning field goal, came out alone, then the rest of us followed. We circled the perimeter of the field, slapping hands and waving, then we joined the dance line of our cheerleaders—the Jills—and high-kicked to the club's theme song, "Talkin' Proud."

I've always felt the primary function of a professional athlete is to entertain, that winning and losing are no less important than putting on a good show. We won that day, but because we put on one hell of a good show in the process, the fans couldn't get enough of us. Fortunately, however, we played better than we danced.

A week later, we headed for Foxboro, Massachusetts, needing only a victory over the Patriots to capture the AFC Eastern Division championship. Instead, we came home with a 24–2 loss and a hobbled quarterback—Ferguson was knocked out of the game in the first quarter with an ankle injury.

But as bad as Fergy was hurting, we were much better off with him playing in our critical season finale at San Francisco rather than his healthy backup, Dan Manucci. If we beat the '49ers, we'd win the division; if we lost, we'd miss the play-offs altogether.

The offensive line had seen enough of Manucci the previous week to be convinced the only function he was qualified to perform in a huddle was distributing water bottles. Then again, I'm not so sure he wouldn't have screwed that up, too. After Manucci entered the Patriots game, we proceeded, through the remaining three quarters, to give up eight sacks. Our total before that day was twelve, fewest in the NFL and a tremendous source of pride for the boys up front. But Manucci was just hanging on to the football too damn long. He had no idea whom to throw to, nor did he have the good sense to throw the ball away when he got into trouble; he just took the sack.

The man simply was unprepared to step in and play, which made you wonder exactly what he was doing in all of those practices and meetings we had had since the start of training camp.

The Monday before the San Francisco game, we, as an offensive line, went up to Prochaska and told him we couldn't block for Manucci. We told him we didn't have any confidence in the guy and that they had to let David Humm, our third-string quarterback, start against the '49ers. But the coaches apparently didn't think Humm was the answer, either, so the pressure was on Ferguson to gut it out.

True professional that he was, Joe came through by completing twelve of twenty passes and guiding us to two first-half touchdowns on the way to an 18–13 triumph in the dense fog and ankle-deep mud of rain-swept Candlestick Park. Actually, it wasn't quite that easy. The '49ers had a chance to win in the final twenty seconds and for each tick of the clock, I don't think any of us on the sidelines took a breath. Not until the last of three consecutive passes by Joe Montana fell incomplete. With an 11–5 record, the Bills had their first division title since 1966 and first playoff berth since 1974.

Afterward, we were like a bunch of kids—hugging, jumping, dancing, singing. We even threw mud at each other. Tom Catlin, our defensive coordinator, was so happy that he managed to put aside his hatred for me for one brief moment and shake my hand. Catlin had been Knox's defensive coordinator with the Rams and had never forgiven me for the way I physically and mentally abused his big old defensive tackle, Merlin Olsen. He just refused to have anything to do with me. Whenever we were in the same room, you could cut the tension with a knife. But after that San Francisco game, Tom came up to me, stuck out his hand, and said, "I'll tell you what, Conrad, you played one helluva game today." That couldn't have been an easy thing for him to do. It's amazing how winning heals old wounds.

Everybody started calling us a Cinderella team. I told a reporter, "They called us a Cinderella team in St. Louis . . . in New Orleans . . . and now in Buffalo. Heck, I'm beginning to think I might be a fairy." Looking back, that probably wasn't a wise thing to say in San Francisco.

■　■　■

Our playoff game was against the Chargers at San Diego. Ferguson's left ankle still was throbbing, but once again he found the courage to play. We built a 14–3 halftime lead, with Fergy throwing mostly short passes because he didn't have to plant both feet—and put more pressure on the ankle—as longer throws require. We controlled the ball and, for the most part, seemed to be controlling the game.

However, in the second half, the pain began to get the better of Ferguson and our offense began to sputter. Don Coryell's Chargers, on the other hand, had a very healthy and very dangerous quarterback in Dan Fouts. He hit Charlie Joiner for a nine-yard touchdown pass to make it 14–10 in the third quarter. A twenty-two-yard Rolf Benirschke field goal cut the margin to 14-13 in the fourth. And, with 2:08 left in the game, Fouts found a seldom-used wide receiver named Ron Smith for a fifty-yard TD to give San Diego a 20-14 victory.

For me, it was one more ill-fated Super Bowl journey—over before it ever really began.

■　　■　　■

I didn't have to check a calendar to see that the 1981 season was my tenth in the NFL—I could feel it in my knees.

But coming off our tremendous success in 1980, I was more excited than ever about our chances of winning a world championship. So was the town. You'd be hard-pressed to find more enthusiastic fans anywhere else in the country. In a blue-collar area like Buffalo, where most season-ticket holders are real people as opposed to big corporations, pro football isn't a diversion. It's a religion.

We opened the year with a 31-0 trouncing of the Jets, dominating them in every respect. In week two, we traveled to Baltimore with a major score to settle with the Colts for beating us twice in 1980. And we settled it, 35-3, behind Ferguson's four touchdown passes. Our combined offense for the first two games was a whopping 848 yards.

Some guys I played with in my career liked to stand up in front of their teammates before a game and boast about the way they were going to handle their opponents. I remember a linebacker with the Bills, Jim Haslett, always vowing that the running back he was about to face wouldn't leave the field in one piece. But like most young players, he was just trying to convince everybody—especially himself—that he was a real badass. Like most young players, he didn't comprehend the magnitude of his words. Vowing to injure someone is serious business—if you say it out loud, you damn well better make good on it. And when you make good on it, it damn well better not hurt your team in the form of a major penalty or your ejection.

I almost never talked about what I was going to do to somebody on the field; I just went out and did it. But I made an exception before we played Baltimore, vowing that Colts defensive end Mike Barnes wouldn't finish the game. This isn't something I recall with a whole lot of pride. It was a situation in which my teammates backed me into a corner. We were in a players-only meeting two days before the game and linebacker Phil Villapiano, one of my closest and craziest friends on the planet, stood behind the podium and asked me to make that vow.

"Forget it, Phil," I said. "I don't do that sort of thing for anybody, including you."

"Conrad, vow to the team," Phil insisted, raising his perpetually hoarse voice. "You ain't shit if Barnes finishes that game. Now vow to the team, Conrad. Vow to the team!"

Soon, all of the other players started chanting, "Vow, Conrad! Vow, Conrad!"

I sat there, glaring at Phil for what he had started and shaking my head as the chant grew louder and louder.

"Vow, Conrad! Vow, Conrad!"

This is so absurd, I thought to myself. So unnecessary. So immature. But the more my teammates persisted, the more pressure I felt to tell them what they wanted to hear. I also began to think about my role on the team. Knox was looking for much more than an experienced offensive guard when he acquired me and my big contract from the Saints; he was looking for a leader, a motivator. He might not have been in that meeting room, but I knew, if everybody wasn't whipped into a frenzy when we came out, he'd hold me at least partly responsible.

"*Vow, Conrad! Vow, Conrad!*"

The next move was mine.

I got up from my chair and walked to the podium. The room became silent. Then, slowly and quietly, I said, "The . . . motherfucker . . . won't . . . finish." And as I headed back to my seat, everybody went absolutely bonkers. They started tearing up the room, picking up desks and chairs and smashing them against walls. They destroyed the blackboard. Just a thoroughly outrageous scene.

At first, I wondered to myself about the sincerity of what I said. I had heard similar promises many times before. Would mine prove just as empty as most of the others? Was I doing what *I* wanted to do or what my teammates wanted me to do?

By the time the game arrived, however, I had no intention whatsoever of rescinding my vow. From our first offensive series, I began legwhipping Barnes with all of the force I could muster. Whap! Whap! Whap!

Judging from the pain I felt in my heels and ankles, I figured I was connecting with some pretty good blows. The wince I saw through Barnes's facemask confirmed as much. And, eventually, he went hobbling to the bench, then to the trainer's room. Diagnosis: hyperextended knee.

Afterward, I went up to Villapiano on the sidelines, stunned him with a forearm to the facemask, and yelled, "OK, Barnes is out of the game. Are you happy now? Don't ever do that to me again. Ever."

We followed our 2–0 start with back-to-back losses—20–14 to Philadelphia and 27–24 to Cincinnati in overtime. Then we won four of our next five games, beating Baltimore (23–17), Miami (31–21), Denver (9–7), and Cleveland (22–13), and losing to the Jets (33–14). Our defense smothered the Broncos, sacking quarterback Craig Morton seven times, while our offense had a season-high 469 yards against the Browns.

My relationship with Knox that season was rocky, at best. And it reached its lowest point in week ten, during a 27–14 *Monday Night Football* loss to the Cowboys at Texas Stadium. I drew two personal-foul penalties for legwhipping defensive tackle John Dutton and was called once for holding. Then I got into a sideline shouting match with Knox when he tried to yank me from the game. I refused to leave at first, but later came to my senses and gave in.

Still, by challenging the head coach's authority—and, even worse, doing so in front of my forty-four teammates, sixty-two thousand fans, and a slew of national TV cameras—I had committed a capital offense. My punishment came the following week, when I was benched for my first return trip to St. Louis since leaving there after the 1977 season. Not coincidentally, our pass protection stank and we wound up losing, 24–0. That the Bills weren't able to win without me was somewhat gratifying, but not enough to make me forget the disappointment of being a spectator for the one game in which I had wanted to play for four years.

I remained on the bench for the start of our next game, a 20–17 victory over the Patriots, at Rich Stadium. But after my replacement, Jim Ritcher, allowed Ferguson to get sacked on the first play, Knox turned to me and said, ''Get your ass in there.'' He did me a tremendous favor on two counts—first, by allowing me to get back into the lineup; second, by allowing me to take part in one of the more incredible games I have ever played in.

With thirty-five seconds left, no time-outs, and New England holding a 17–13 lead, we were in need of a miracle. Ferguson dropped back in shotgun formation from our own twenty-seven yard line and fired a rainbow pass that running back Roland Hooks caught, fully extended, for a thirty-seven-yard gain. We hurried to the line of scrimmage, and Fergy threw the ball out of bounds to stop the clock with twelve seconds remaining. On the next play, we got into our "Big Ben" formation, with three receivers wide to the right side of the line for a desperation bomb that, we hoped, would produce a touchdown or, at least, a defensive pass-interference penalty deep in New England territory. Ferguson took the snap, reared back, and heaved toward the end zone, where a bunch of Patriots had formed a human wall around our receivers. The whole pack jumped at once, the pass ricocheted off linebacker Mike Hawkins and . . . and . . . landed right in the waiting arms of Hooks, who cradled it for the winning points.

We proceeded to win our next three games—21–14 over Washington, 28–27 over San Diego, and 19–10 over New England. That set up, in our season finale against the Dolphins at the Orange Bowl, a showdown for the AFC Eastern Division championship.

Miami, as it almost always does at home, came out on top, 16–6, dropping us to a 10–6 record and a wild-card playoff spot. But not before I wound up climbing back into Knox's doghouse. I did so by picking up a holding penalty that wiped out an eighteen-yard Ferguson to Frank Lewis pass early in the fourth quarter and by publicly wishing harm to the family of John Keck, the official who made the call. I didn't mean that, of course. I just allowed my emotions to get the better of me. In fact, right after I made that stupid remark, I tried to take it back by telling the reporters I was speaking off the record and threatening them with lawsuits.

It was like trying to put out a fire with gasoline. The quotation was on the national wires within minutes.

Norm Schachter, an officiating honcho for the NFL, once told a reporter, "The league doesn't send out a notice saying watch Dobler for biting or anything like that. But when you've been around for a while, you know what to look for and you keep an eye on certain players." Before some games, officials would actually come up to me during warmups and say, "Now remember, Conrad, none of that funny stuff today. Let's have a good, clean game, OK?" I'd just kind of laugh to myself and give them a smile. And if, during the game, I noticed they happened to be watching me more closely than usual, I'd show greater discretion in the tactics I used and play it pretty much by the book—which, of course, was no fun at all.

This was especially true in the early part of my career because for one thing, I still could rely upon some pretty good physical skills to get the job done. For another, I had a lot of football ahead of me and I didn't want my performance to drown in a sea of yellow handkerchiefs before I could establish myself as a top-notch offensive lineman.

But with each season, it became increasingly apparent they were zeroing in on the right side of every offensive line on which I played. Dan Dierdorf, who played right tackle, didn't like that one bit. "If they're watching you," he reminded me on more than one occasion, "then they're watching me, too."

Once, I was called for tripping a guy who never left his feet. Sure, I might have *tried* to trip him. But I've always been under the impression that trying and succeeding are two different things.

In the late stages of my career, it didn't matter what I did—officials were looking to penalize me every chance they got. Pete Rozelle, as part of an overall effort to curb the violence the NFL was bringing to television, clearly wanted me out of his league.

At the time, I joked about being the only offensive lineman in the history of football who was called for holding, tripping, and clipping *before* the snap. But it really was no laughing matter. I felt very uncomfortable, very restricted. It got to the point where I was more worried about avoiding penalties than doing everything possible to block my man. I was being forced to play in a colder, more calculated fashion instead of with all-out emotion, which was essential to my game. I had to pour every ounce of energy I had into the war at the line of scrimmage.

How was I supposed to do that when I was watching the officials out of the corner of my eye?

My worth as a player steadily diminished. I was a constant threat to stop an important drive, wipe out a big play—or both. No coach in his right mind could afford to keep someone like that on his roster, even as a backup. Knox knew he couldn't. He told me, toward the end of the 1981 season, that I had been placed in a fishbowl and that there was no way out.

■　　■　　■

With my having become public enemy number one among NFL officials, Knox felt he had no choice but to bench me for our playoff game against the Jets at Shea Stadium. I figured we were in for an easy day, anyway, when the Jets' Bruce Harper fumbled the opening kickoff and Charley Romes returned it twenty-six yards for a Buffalo touchdown. The play took all of sixteen seconds, making it the second-fastest score in playoff history.

We proceeded to build a 24–0 first-half lead, with Ferguson connecting with Lewis on fifty- and twenty-six-yard TD passes. The Jets came back with thirteen unanswered points before Joe Cribbs ran forty-five yards for a touchdown to give us a 31–13 advantage in the fourth quarter.

But the Jets refused to die, scoring fourteen fourth-quarter points to close the gap to 31–27. Quarterback Richard Todd then drove them to our eleven yard line and, with ten seconds remaining, he fired toward the end zone for Derrick Gaffney. Suddenly, out of nowhere, free safety Bill Simpson appeared to intercept the pass and preserve our advancement to the divisional round, where we'd face the Bengals at Cincinnati.

■　　■　　■

I was back in the starting lineup for what I knew might be the final sixty minutes of my professional football career. After the Bengals took a 14–0 lead in the first quarter, I was almost certain of it.

Hope was restored temporarily when Ferguson hit wide receiver Jerry Butler on a fifty-four-yard pass to set up a one-yard touchdown plunge by Joe Cribbs. A forty-four-yard Cribbs TD run made it 14–14 in the third quarter. The teams traded touchdowns, Cincinnati's Charles Alexander scoring by foot from twenty yards and Ferguson finding Butler from twenty-one. Then the Bengals moved in front, 28–21, on Ken Anderson's sixteen-yard scoring toss to Cris Collinsworth.

We weren't quite dead yet, however, as Fergy moved us to the Bengals' twenty with 2:58 to play. On fourth and three, he hooked up with wide receiver Lou Piccone for an apparent first down, and overtime seemed imminent. But the excitement we felt over Lou's catch suddenly disappeared when we noticed a yellow flag on the ground. The thirty-second clock, the officials ruled, had expired a half-second before Ferguson took the snap, thanks to a couple of late player substitutions (receivers Piccone and Ron Jessie for fullback Curtis Brown and tight end Mark Brammer). The result was a five-yard delay-of-game penalty.

Ferguson then overthrew Hooks in the end zone and that was the ballgame. And my career.

Like many Bills followers, I couldn't, for the life of me, understand how we allowed ourselves to get that killer delay-of-game infraction. Why, when they had called a time-out to set up the play, did it take the coaches so long to send in Piccone and Jessie? How could Knox, with eighteen years of pro coaching experience at that point, with all of those playoff games under his belt, allow such a thing to happen? Indecision on the sidelines—there isn't a hell of a lot the players can do about that.

Going into the game, I knew, with my knees getting worse, the officials watching closer than ever, and younger talent waiting in the wings, there wasn't going to be a next time for me. So I poured everything I had into my performance. I played my heart out. If the coaches had been crazy enough to allow it, I'd have played every position on the field that day. I wanted to run with the ball, throw it, catch it, intercept it, kick it. I wanted to tackle somebody, that is, legally. I wanted to do anything to keep alive the dream of guzzling champagne in the winner's dressing room at the Super Bowl.

But when it was over, it was over. No regrets. No tears. I simply went around the locker room, shook hands with all of my teammates, and said goodbye. Several of them gave me the same "see-you-next-year" they were giving everyone else.

"No, you won't," I said. "I just played my last football game. These guys are done with me now. They won't let me come back."

Nobody really wanted to believe that, but I knew it was

true. And Knox confirmed my hunch when he called me on April 1, 1982, to suggest I retire.

"This wouldn't, by any chance, be an April Fools' joke, would it?" I asked.

"It wouldn't," Knox said.

"Could I have a little time to think it over?"

"Fine."

Knox said he'd be vacationing in Palm Springs, California, and to call him there.

But the call I made four weeks later was to Frank Luksa, a sportswriter for the *Dallas Times-Herald* who had been fair to me during my career and always wrote what I said; not what he *thought* I said. I gave him the following statement: "Due to the difficulty I'm experiencing following a number of injuries, I have determined I will be unable to play football during the 1982 season. I hope to be able to resume my career at a later date. At this time, however, I am physically unable to play."

I wanted to leave the door open, just a crack, even though I knew it really was closed tight. Luksa knew that, too. In printing my statement, he added, "His regrets are minor. Never playing in a Super Bowl. That bum knee likely to bother him the rest of his life. But the scales are over-balanced toward positive memories."

6

Wolfman and Other Friends

Friendships made in football have a lot in common with friendships made in war. Football teammates, like soldiers in the same troop, are bonded by the ever-present uncertainty of whether they'll return from combat in one piece and the belief that those with whom they stand shoulder to shoulder on the battlefield will be there until the bitter end. Too often, the only ones who can really understand the pressure, emotion, fear, and anxiety are those who do the same thing for a living.

In the NFL, the team becomes a second family. For the better part of seven months, you do practically everything together. Eat. Sleep. Meet. Practice. Play. Carouse. Hell, you even take showers next to one another.

The strongest bonding of all can be found among offensive linemen. That's because, with few exceptions, they live in a world of obscurity to which most of their teammates cannot relate. When linemen do gain recognition, it's almost always for the wrong reasons—penalties, sacks, running backs getting stuffed at the line. So they rely heavily on each other for moral support.

I had the good fortune, particularly in St. Louis and Buffalo, to have teammates who shared my motto: Play hard, party hard, but don't party harder than you play. Or at least, try not to.

My closest friends in St. Louis were Dan Dierdorf, our right tackle, and Tom Banks, our center.

People always talk about John Hannah, the behemoth who played guard for the New England Patriots, as the greatest drive-blocker the NFL has ever seen. Most of those people are in the media. From a player's standpoint, my vote for the game's all-time best has to go to Dan Dierdorf. He was a virtual drive-blocking machine. He was a pretty good pass-blocker, too. Not quite as effective as yours truly, of course. But if that sonofagun in the *Monday Night Football* booth doesn't make it into the Pro Football Hall of Fame, there's something seriously wrong with the voting process. Could there be a more appropriate honor for someone who was born in Canton, Ohio?

Wolfman. The nickname said it best about Tom Banks, in terms of both appearance and behavior. His mop of shoulder-length hair and thick, shaggy beard and denim-and-T-shirt-dominated wardrobe set him apart from the rest of our mostly conservative-looking team. And he was as wild and as crazy as he looked—even without a full moon. At six-foot-two and 245 pounds, Tommy was among the league's smaller centers, but he was also one of its quickest and toughest. He had no neck—his head just sort of sat on his shoulders. And he had the skinniest legs I have ever seen on an offensive lineman; they looked as if they had been stolen from the body of a quarter-miler. Of course, given his nickname, they probably were. But the legs and his overall lack of size notwithstanding, Tommy had tremendous upper-body strength and could more than hold his own against defenders who dwarfed him.

I hated Dierdorf and Banks for all the harassment they gave me during my rookie training camp. But after I proved, in my first start that season, that I was a bona fide NFL player, they began to show me a little respect. Five weeks later, after we returned home from an ass-kicking in Miami, they broke down the remaining barriers and invited me to join them for a late-night dinner. Actually, what they invited *me* to do was drive *them* to dinner in my new gold Thunderbird. It was the beginning of a camaraderie that would last throughout our careers.

We hadn't eaten since being served two-day-old submarine sandwiches on our charter flight, so we were seriously hungry. We didn't have the time—or patience—for a fancy restaurant. So we stopped in at the nearest Denny's.

The waitress gave us menus, but she really shouldn't have bothered. Having done our share of drinking on the plane (we were allowed only two beers apiece, but we always brought our own), the three of us barely could see straight enough to walk, let alone read. Besides, Dierdorf and Banks weren't interested in specifics.

Banks told the waitress to bring us one order of everything on the breakfast side of the menu.

"You've got to be kidding," she said.

We were not.

Soon, plate after plate began arriving at the table: eggs, omelets, bacon, sausage, ham, steak, home fries, hot cakes, waffles, biscuits and gravy, bread (toasted and untoasted), all kinds of hot and cold beverages, cereal, oatmeal, and fruits galore.

We sat back and ate. And ate. And we didn't stop eating until every last crumb was gone.

And you wondered how linemen get to be so big that they blot out the sun?

The good times were not limited to the local Denny's, however. We often took our traveling circus on the road. For example, in 1976, the Cardinals traveled to Tokyo for a preseason exhibition against the San Diego Chargers, marking the first time an NFL game was played outside North America. By the end of our ten-day visit, I'm sure some Japanese citizens hoped it would be the last.

NFL teams normally travel on chartered flights, but this time we flew commercial on a 747. There was enough room for the entire team to be seated in the back—and kept a safe distance from the rest of the passengers. For their sake, not ours.

Two-and-a-half hours after we left San Francisco, we had our first crisis on our hands: the plane's supply of alcoholic beverages was exhausted. Such are the consequences of traveling with an NFL franchise. Jackie Smith, our tight end, and Jim Bakken, our placekicker, however, didn't seem perturbed by this discovery. It turned out they had brought a couple of fifths with them. On the other hand, Banks, in desperation, had bought up most of the sake on the plane, taking the plunge into Japanese culture and proving, once again, necessity *is* the mother of invention.

He also got very drunk on the stuff.

"More sake! More sake!" Banks began chanting. "Remember Hawaii! Remember Hiroshima!"

Joe Sullivan, our general manager, quietly suggested we get enough drinks in Tommy to make him pass out. He obviously was beyond the point of reason and the captain wasn't going to tolerate our normal craziness at thirty-five thousand feet. We started feeding Tommy drinks, practically pouring the booze down his throat. He finally passed out and we laid him down in one of the aisles, where he could stretch out.

Tommy awoke just after we landed, but he was still out of it. He had taken off his shirt before he passed out, and his attempts to get it buttoned before we deplaned proved futile. Finally, he just tied it at the waist.

I don't know what the slew of Japanese reporters and photographers thought of American football players when Tommy, half-dressed, wearing jeans, sandals, and that shaggy beard of his, stood swaying at the door of the plane flashing a "victory" sign.

Nor was Tommy through yet. That night, after a few more drinks, he and I went out on the town with Smith, Bakken, backup center Tom Brahaney, and running back Steve Jones. We had dinner at a restaurant with the settings around huge grills so the customers could watch their meals being cooked right in front of them. The waitress came around and put a bowl containing a raw egg, still in the shell, in front of each of us. Because of our inexperience with this sort of dining, none of us was certain what to do.

"I understand it's a Japanese custom to eat a raw egg before your meal," I said with a shrug.

I was joking—the eggs were actually to be used in the preparation of a batter—but Tommy took me seriously.

"I don't care about any damn custom," he said. "I will not eat a raw egg." He downed his last swallow of beer, grabbed his egg out of the bowl, walked around to the inside of the grill, and cracked it open.

"If I'm going to eat this egg," Tommy said, "I'm going to eat it scrambled."

The restaurant broke into laughter at the sight of the "celebrity chef" at work. The cook and waitress, however, did not seem amused. We hid our embarrassment behind several more bottles of beer and sake.

At breakfast the next morning, Banks said to Brahaney and Jones, "Tom, Steve, you've gotta go to this restaurant Connie and I went to last night. The food there is out of this world."

They both looked at him and shook their heads.

"Tom, you dumb sonofabitch," Brahaney said, "you were sitting right between us last night." I guess he was a lot drunker than we thought.

Another night, a bunch of us decided to see what Japan had to offer besides sake and restaurants. So off we went to a geisha house. A few minutes after we gathered together in a waiting room, the geisha girls began to emerge, one by one. Initially, nobody wanted to take the first one, in case a prettier geisha girl happened to come along. Finally, one of the less restrained among us said, "Hell, she's good enough for me," and they left for a private room.

Eventually, we all paired off into private rooms. I was surprised at how healthy and well-developed geisha girls were. And I was even more surprised by their lovemaking techniques. First, my partner covered her entire body with liquid soap. Then, using herself like a washcloth, she slithered all over me, being careful not to miss a single spot. My appreciation was readily apparent. Finally, in a feat of astonishing skill, she slipped a condom over me with her mouth and climbed aboard.

Now that's what I call coming in contact with Japanese culture.

In the days leading up to the game, we were interviewed repeatedly by members of the Japanese press corps. I nearly stuck my cleat in my mouth while trying to explain, with the help of an interpreter, the difference between offense and defense.

"When you came after us at Pearl Harbor, you were on offense and we were on defense," I said. "And when we came after you at Nagasaki, we were on offense and you were on defense. Got it?"

Fortunately, the interpreter suggested a less literal translation for the sake of diplomacy.

Finally, we played the exhibition game. I got the feeling the San Diego Chargers weren't any happier than we were to be on the field that day in Tokyo's Korakuen Stadium for a contest that didn't count. About the only good thing that could be said about the game was that the penalties were announced in Japanese. I'd look at Dierdorf, he'd look at me and, at the same time, we'd say, "It must be on you."

I think we won.

■   ■   ■

Locker-room antics are a part of life in the NFL. We were constantly pulling pranks of one sort or another on each other. Things like filling jockstraps with heating salve, nailing shoes to the floor, swapping helmets, throwing ice water at guys in the sauna, changing shower settings when guys had shampoo in their eyes, wrapping a lower-level assistant coach in athletic tape, stuffing guys' equipment into plastic garbage bags so they thought they'd been cut when they came to work in the morning, giving a rookie a false message the head coach wanted to see him—and to bring his playbook. I usually remained on the sidelines (or tried to), but at least one time I was a victim.

Phyllis George was coming to St. Louis one week to interview me for a feature on CBS's *NFL Today*. I was pretty excited at the thought of meeting the lovely former Miss

America, as well as being seen by millions of viewers coast to coast.

I even bought a brand-new pair of Levi's for the occasion. The interview was scheduled to follow practice. So, after I showered, I spent about an hour sprucing. I shaved twice, got my hair just right—I even went so far as to brush with Pearldrops tooth polish, to make certain my smile would be at its pearly best.

At last, I was ready to slip into my hot new threads. I put on a nice flowered silk shirt (remember when flowered silk shirts were in?) to catch the attention of viewers who'd be watching in color. Then I grabbed the Levi's. The one-legged Levi's.

The one-legged Levi's?

"Awwww!" I yelled, as if mortally wounded, staring in horror at my brand-new pants and the unwanted tailoring that had been performed behind my back.

I was so angry I picked up benches and threw them across the locker room. I tipped over lockers. I ran around like an enraged bull, looking to destroy anything—or anyone—in my path.

Most of the guys scattered, fearing contact with a flying object, if not a flying fist. Some scurried outside with only their jocks on. The equipment manager, Bill Simmons, had the best idea of all—he locked himself inside the equipment cage.

By the time I was finished, my hair was all messed up and my flowered silk shirt was soaked with sweat. And there sat Banks, the only guy who didn't flee to safety, as calm as could be. Tommy slowly shook his head.

"You know, Connie," he said, "I told them not to do it."

"Told who?" I demanded. "Who did this to me? *Who?*"

But Banks wouldn't say. It wasn't until about three years

later that I found out the culprits were Dan Dierdorf and Jackie Smith.

I had my suspicions about Jackie and Dan, though—both were a little too quick to loan me their pants. Dan offered his first, but they were so big I could have gotten another lineman in there with me. The program I was going on was *NFL Today*, not *The Gong Show*. I wound up taking Jackie's jeans. The only catch was that they were about a size-and-a-half too small for me, so when I sat down, I had to keep my legs as straight as possible in order not to bust them wide open. Fortunately, the interview was shot with me seated, inside a jail cell. Phyllis, who was outside the cell, asked, "How do you plead to charges you are the meanest and dirtiest man in pro football?" and I said, "Guilty!"

All you saw was my head and shoulders . . . and pearly white teeth.

Locker-room pranks help to bring players down to earth a little, teach them a little humility. The truth is, it's very easy for a pro athlete to lose touch with the real world. Recognition, and the many perks it brings, can give a player the false notion he is on an endless joy ride, that everything in life comes easy.

And sometimes it does. More than a few women made their way into my arms—and my heart. Not all of them, however, were in the kind of shape I was used to as a professional athlete. I remember one TWA stewardess, after a heavy night of moaning and groaning, suffered a collapsed lung shortly after I left the next morning, and had to be rushed to the hospital. My lungs felt fine.

I guess all of those wind sprints we had to run in practice finally paid off.

Pro football players are always trying to sneak women into

their dormitory rooms to help stay in shape and get them through those long, lonely summer nights at training camp. We didn't do a lot of that in St. Louis, out of respect for Don Coryell. He treated us well and we felt the least we could do was obey the rules. That is, the rule against having women in our *rooms*. He didn't say anything about the back of our cars. It wasn't quite as comfortable as a bed, but I don't recall hearing too many guys complain.

Besides, it was an excellent opportunity to test the shocks.

Jim Hanifan helped make things a little easier on us. When Jim conducted bed-checks, if you told him ahead of time you had a certain lady to see and might be late for curfew, he'd cover for you, as long as you didn't try to take advantage of him by coming in later than the specified hour—which none of us did. You didn't have to sneak around with Hanifan; all you had to do was ask. Jim was one of the boys.

One year, Banks and I spent almost as much time playing the field as playing on the field. I was in the middle of a trial separation from my wife, so she spent the season in Wyoming, while I stayed in St. Louis. If it hadn't been for pretzels and peanuts, I'd have been on a liquid diet that year. As for our romantic endeavors, we were into quantity, not quality. Actually, we tried to maintain some standards as far as the quality of the women was concerned—they had to be willing.

One memorable night that same year, a teammate and I went through an evening of romance together, switching partners throughout the night in one big king-sized bed. But after nearly falling out once or twice, I decided one couple per bed was enough. We weren't practicing for the Olympic gymnastics team, after all.

Or were we?

■   ■   ■

I think my all-time looniest teammate was a defensive back we had in St. Louis named Dale Hackbart. Occasionally, Dale would walk into the locker room before practice fully dressed in a World War II German military outfit. No one really knew why. I'm not certain even Dale knew. I guess Dale took it literally when people called football a war.

One day, a few of us tried to catch Hitler Hackbart off guard. Before he arrived at practice, we removed everything from his dressing cubicle to make room for a commode we had found unattached to plumbing. It wasn't meant to be a comment on his playing abilities. Dale walked into the locker room and up to his cubicle, acting as if everything were perfectly normal.

Without saying a word, he got undressed, placed his clothes neatly on a hanger, sat on the commode, and relieved himself—in front of the entire team. (He later made a door out of cardboard, converting his dressing cubicle into his own private john.)

Another player on the Cardinals, a defensive end named John Zook, had a pet garter snake named Skeezits. Skeezits was sort of our unofficial mascot—he actually lived in the locker room during the season. We liked having him around; he was always a very willing and very effective participant in practical jokes. We put him in shoes, socks, underwear, pants, hats, just about any place you could imagine. And a few places you couldn't. The most popular spot was the lock box in the top of each dressing cubicle where players kept their valuables during practices and games. The reason it was so popular was that for most guys, the box was just low enough to reach but too high to look into. The unsuspecting player would put his hand inside and get a handful of Skeezits.

Dierdorf once enlisted Skeezits's help to play a practical joke on Gary Bender of CBS during the taping of a TV interview. It was about twenty-five degrees outside, so no one questioned the fact Dierdorf kept his beefy arms folded. A couple of minutes into the interview, he nonchalantly opened his hand and out came Skeezits. Suddenly noticing a snake slithering up Dan's arm, Bender let out a yell, dropped his microphone, and set a world's record for the hundred-yard dash. Unfortunately, the first two-thirds of Skeezits's body began to stick straight up in the air; the poor guy was starting to freeze to death. Dierdorf had to rush him back into the locker room and place him inside the sauna to revive him.

One of the stronger individuals I met in my life was Jackie Smith. Jackie was also one of the toughest and fiercest competitors I've ever seen. In one of his final games as a Cardinal, he tipped a pass, caught it, and broke no fewer than seven tackles on the way to scoring the winning touchdown. It's unfortunate that, considering the tremendous hands he had, the play for which Jackie always will be remembered is the third-down pass he dropped in the end zone in Super Bowl XIII in 1979 while playing for the Dallas Cowboys.

The previous season, Jackie had retired from the Cardinals because of a neck condition—a doctor told him he was flirting with paralysis if he continued to play. But the Cowboys were desperate for a backup tight end, and Jackie, desperate for one last shot at a Super Bowl ring, signed after somehow passing their physical examination. Funny thing about physical exams in the NFL—whether you pass or fail depends on how badly the team needs you. The dropped pass resulted in the unforgettable photograph of Jackie lying on his back, banging his legs off the ground in frustration. The Cowboys went on to lose, 35–31, to the Pittsburgh Steelers.

A certain pick for the Hall of Fame, he deserved a more dignified exit from the game.

Someone meeting Jim Hart, our quarterback in St. Louis,

in street clothes would never believe he played professional football (and he played for eighteen years). Talk about a baby face! But, boy, could that baby pass. Hart flourished in Don Coryell's wide-open offense, racking up numbers that give him a healthy portion of the team's record book to this day. His bomb was an absolute thing of beauty—falling straight down, nose-first, as if dropped from an airplane, into the hands of a receiver fifty yards downfield.

Hart is a classic example of how looks can deceive. He was one tough cookie. One week in my third season, we were playing the Cleveland Browns, and I was going up against a very good defensive tackle named Jerry Sherk.

"This guy gets one or two sacks a game," Hart, who was in his seventh season at the time, warned me before kickoff.

"Well, he's not going to get a sack today," I said, in typically cocky fashion.

Sure enough, early in the first quarter, Sherk blew right past me and dumped Hart for a big loss. But I noticed, after he got up off the ground, Sherk was walking with a pronounced limp—he had suffered a twisted ankle on the play and was forced to leave the field for good.

"Dobler," Hart said with a wry smile, "that's why I'm a veteran and you're a rookie."

"Huh?"

"How'd you like the way I put your man out of the game for you?" he said, motioning to Sherk with his thumb. Then he gave me a wink and called the next play.

I developed a new respect for Hart that day. And in the years ahead, I had to remind myself of the incident any time I'd start to worry about going into battle with a quarterback who never shaved.

The wide receiver usually streaking underneath those picture-perfect bombs was Mel Gray. Mel had tremendous speed, which made him one of the more feared deep threats in the league. But every now and then, Coryell felt the need to give him an added step on his opponent. Once, during a game for which Mel had been listed as doubtful with an ankle problem, Coryell had him limp off the field, as if he were hurting. Coryell kept him on the sidelines for a couple of plays, then had him limp back on. After the snap, with Mel still limping, the cornerback was lulled into a false sense of security. Suddenly, *boom*, Mel shot by him as if he were standing still. Hart fired the ball and found Gray all alone for a touchdown.

The Cardinals' first-round pick in 1972, the year I was drafted, was a wide receiver from Oregon named Bobby Moore (who later would change his name to Ahmad Rashad). After the 1973 season, they traded him to the Bills, with whom he spent two years before eventually winding up with Minnesota. I thought Ahmad was a good guy, a real pro, in the short time we were teammates. But he just didn't like it in St. Louis. He became frustrated about constantly being switched in training camp from wide receiver to running back, which he played during his final two years of college. He also didn't think the team's owner, Bill Bidwill, ever would pay him the kind of money he wanted. So he wanted out.

I remember hearing, in conversations with Coryell over the years, that the reason Rashad was traded was that the Cardinals thought he had a "mental imbalance." Which was a total crock. The only reason Don felt that way was that he was convinced his passing game was the world's best; he couldn't believe a sane receiver could walk away from the Great Coryell Offense. Rashad, of course, went on to a spectacular career with the Vikings and now announces for NBC.

I think the greatest running back I've ever blocked for was Terry Metcalf, another prominent name in Cardinal football history. A lot of people complained that Terry fumbled too much—that his five-foot-ten, 180-pound frame didn't allow him to withstand the blows that often jarred the ball loose. And the standard reply of the offensive linemen was, "The way that man runs, we don't care if he fumbles twice a game." Besides, when he fumbled and everybody was scrambling for the ball, that provided a perfect opportunity for me to deliver a bone-rattling shot to the defensive donkey of my choice.

Terry didn't run, he floated. And he was a tremendously hard worker after he got the football. A lot of running backs will hit a pile, decide there is no more room to run, and go down. When Terry hit a pile, he would spin off, his feet churning, and manage to scratch and claw for two or three more yards somehow. There was more than one occasion when two or three guys would appear to have him stopped cold. Then, all of a sudden, Terry would pop free and glide downfield for a big gain. I don't think I played with anyone who had more desire and ambition.

With Metcalf drawing so much attention from opposing defenses, everyone would forget about our big fullback, Jim Otis. Most people took one look at his large, round frame and said, "This guy can't possibly make his living as an athlete." We used to call him Shake, because when he was in motion, his fat ass shook like an agitated bowl of Jell-O. So it was particularly gratifying to the members of the offensive line when he captured the 1975 NFC rushing title and made his first and only trip to the Pro Bowl. If we could do that for Shake, we could do that for anybody. I will admit, however, that Jim got more than a few yards by himself. And in the final seconds of a close game, when you really needed a back to hold on to the ball and keep those chains moving, he would always come through. He had the power and determination to get you those tough, inside yards. Every now and then, he'd even break a long one.

Dierdorf told a revealing story about Otis's standout career at Ohio State. When Dan was at Michigan, his head coach, Bo Schembechler, would tell the team before it faced Ohio State, "Otis is a good fullback, but whatever you do, don't hurt him. Because there's a guy sitting on the bench who's twice as good named John Brockington." For the record, John went on to a brilliant career with Green Bay, winning two NFC rushing titles.

Otis smoked cigarettes, although he went through great pains to hide that fact from his father, who was a physician and had absolutely forbidden his children to smoke. One time, Jim came up to me in the locker room before a game and said, "Conrad, my dad's in town and he's going to be visiting me down here after the game. Now, he doesn't know I smoke. So, whatever you do when he's in here, *don't* come up to me and bum a cigarette. Understand?"

"You bet, Jim."

Of course, immediately afterward, I went around to every guy in the locker room, smokers and nonsmokers alike, and told them, "When you see Otis and his father together after the game, make sure you go up to Jim and ask for a cigarette."

Sure enough, after the game, while Jim and his dad were talking in front of his dressing stall, player after player walked up to our big fullback and asked, "Got a cigarette? Got a cigarette?"

The first few times, Jim cleared his throat, smiled nervously, and said, "Now, come on, you know very well I don't smoke. You'll have to get your cigarette from somebody who does." After several more players came up to him, he said, "All you guys . . . you're just trying to embarrass me in front of my dad."

Finally, I walked up and said, "Come on, Jim. Why don't you just let me look inside that coat pocket of yours? Isn't that a pack of cigarettes in there?"

"Get out of here, Conrad," Jim said, pulling the coat away and still trying to keep that fake smile.

But his father didn't seem terribly amused and I backed off. I wonder if he ever discovered Shake's deep, dark secret. If not, I guess Shake'll just have to buy up every copy of this book to keep it hidden. Not that I'd complain.

■　　■　　■

Considering the reputation of the town, it would make sense that some of my wildest times would have occurred during the years I spent in New Orleans. The truth was, when it came to off-the-field activity, those probably were the quietest two years of my career. We had a fairly tame bunch there. No outrageous characters like Tom Banks or Dale Hackbart. I was about the only hell-raiser on the team. And with nobody else to raise it with, I started becoming pretty mellow myself—a real family man.

I often wonder what it would have been like if Ken Stabler, one of the league's foremost partiers, had played quarterback for the Saints then, instead of between 1982 and 1984, when I was already retired. Kenny tells me now, "Damn, Conrad, if you and I had been running the streets in New Orleans, I'd never have slept." That would have made two of us, Snake.

The quarterback we did have when I was in New Orleans, Archie Manning, was the complete opposite of Stabler. He was a real family man, although that didn't stop us from becoming good friends and cohosting a weekly call-in radio show during the season. We went out to dinner and even hit a few bars. Archie could match me, beer for beer, but never once did I see him get rowdy. He laughed at my jokes, he was a hell of a lot of fun to be around. He just always stayed in control.

Manning, like Hart, didn't have the kind of face you'd expect on a pro football player. In fact, he was commonly referred to as "Huck Finn in shoulder pads." But he was a tremendous talent. He took a hell of a pounding before I got to New Orleans in 1978, and voiced one of the louder complaints when I was shipped to Buffalo in 1980, after the Saints had the second-lowest sack total in the league (seventeen) in 1979. It wasn't fair that Archie had to suffer through all of those years without a winning record. Nor was it fair that he had to stand behind such poor offensive lines. He was getting sacked fifty to sixty times a year. And those were just the times he was tackled for losses. Imagine how often he was getting nailed after he *released* the ball.

I had to laugh when people talked about Archie's sidearm throwing style. That "style" wasn't intentional; he *had* to throw sidearm because his shoulders hurt so bad from the many times they were slammed to the ground.

Manning's backup was a guy named Bobby Scott, who had the palest complexion of any person I've seen this side of a corpse. His skin looked as if it had been shielded from sunlight since birth. The rest of us never hesitated to remind him of that, of course. That and the fact he didn't have a defined muscle in his body; I don't think he ever looked at a weight, let alone lifted one. Besides being a physical curiosity, Bobby was unique in that he was perfectly content with his backup role. Usually, the number two quarterback, even if he refuses to admit as much, is constantly looking for that one big chance to become number one. Not Bobby. He wanted nothing to do with the starting job, wanted nothing to do with all of the pressures and demands that came with it. He was afraid they might interfere with his beer-drinking.

One guy who had a much higher opinion of himself was a rookie wide receiver named Wes Chandler. It's customary in the NFL for rookies to bring doughnuts for the entire team before practice on Saturday morning. But Chandler, the Saints' number one draft pick in 1978, didn't do it when his turn came up. Everybody was pissed off, yet no one wanted to say anything to Chandler's face.

Finally, I volunteered.

"Why the hell didn't you bring in the doughnuts today, Wes?" I asked.

"Because I'm the number one pick," he said. "You guys ought to be bringing them to me."

It wasn't the answer I was looking for. So I grabbed him by the shirt, shoved him against a dressing cubicle, and gave him a quick lesson in pro football etiquette.

"Listen, you rookie sonofabitch, when it's your turn to bring the doughnuts in, you're going to bring them in from here on out. Got that? It's not the damn doughnuts or the five or ten bucks they cost. It's the respect you show by getting them. No matter how good you think you are or how much money you make, you're still a rookie. And the unique thing about this is that you only have to do it for one year. For the rest of your professional football career, you're going to have some other rookie bringing in doughnuts for you. And he isn't going to like it any better than you do. But he has to do it. It's part of being a rookie."

Chandler didn't say a word. The following Saturday morning, he showed up with the doughnuts. In fact, he showed up with them every Saturday morning for the rest of the season.

I didn't know I could be so persuasive.

As it turned out, the other blacks on the team appreciated my setting him straight as much as the white players. I was a little worried about that, because the Saints lived in an area filled with racial tension. You'd walk into redneck bars where they had Saints' team pictures hanging, and written underneath were things like, "Thirty-two whites, fifteen niggers." It doesn't take a hell of a lot, in a situation like that, for black and white players to become divided. And that was just what we had on the Saints: division. An aisle ran down the middle of the main meeting room, with blacks sitting on one side and whites sitting on the other. The head coach, Dick Nolan, was so afraid of starting an incident, he'd just try to appease everybody. But what he should have done was have the chairs set up so that there was no aisle and everyone had to mingle.

I didn't care about any of that white-versus-black stuff. In football, you go to war with your teammates. It doesn't matter whether they're black, white, green, or orange. The only colors that are different are the ones worn by the opposition. During our team meetings in New Orleans, I usually sat on the "black" side, way in the back, next to running back Chuck Muncie. After all, somebody had to wake him up when the films came on.

I liked Chuck, but he tended to be at the center of some of our problems. Somehow, he always managed to get out of practice or the dreaded running we had to do afterward. He'd come up with a hangnail and Nolan would give him the day off. The other black guys would say, "If he doesn't have to practice, why should we?" The white players would say, "If we did something like that, they'd cut our ass." But Muncie could run. He became the first Saint to break the one-thousand-yard barrier, in 1979, gaining 1,198 on his way to the Pro Bowl.

Funny thing about Chuck—he always seemed to have his best games when we played on the West Coast. Never failed. At first, I thought it was only because he played his college ball at the University of California and wanted to show off for those who had watched him during his All-America days with the Golden Bears. But I think what he was really trying to do was impress the NFL teams out there so they'd trade for him. Sure enough, he wound up being shipped to San Diego in 1980, and played in a couple more Pro Bowls with the Chargers.

■   ■   ■

Just as I was starting to settle down in New Orleans, I got traded to Buffalo, where I hooked up with a tough, insane linebacker from northern New Jersey named Phil Villapiano. The Bills had acquired him three months before from the Oakland Raiders.

To put it more accurately, Phil wound up trading himself.

Al Davis, the Raiders' managing general partner, called Phil during the off-season in 1980 to ask his opinion of Bobby Chandler, a wide receiver the Bills were trying to trade.

"Al, if Bobby Chandler's available, grab him, because he'll do nothing but help the Raiders," Phil said. "Do whatever you can to get the guy because, I'm telling you, he's great."

"That good, huh?"

"You bet. What does Buffalo want for him?"

"You."

"Me?"

"That's right. And after the endorsement you just gave me, how can I turn them down?"

Phil Villapiano would proceed, over the next two years, to ruin my life.

Our first official encounter had come the previous season, inside the Louisiana Superdome on a Monday night. I was playing right guard for the Saints; he was playing inside linebacker for the Raiders. I had found out before the game that he'd be playing with a sore rib. So, throughout the first half, I kept hitting him in the rib cage as hard as I could—a simple case of trying to take advantage of an opponent's weakness. He finally doubled over and staggered off the field. I thought I had put him out of the game, but being the great competitor he was, Phil came back for more. And in the third quarter, as I was coming around to block on a sweep, he caught me square in the helmet with a forearm. The blow forced me to leave the game with a pinched nerve in my neck. But I, too, came back for more.

After that, we agreed we were even, that we would stop the cheap stuff and play it straight the rest of the night. It didn't take long for the soreness in my neck to disappear. But Phil, to this day, has a memento from that game—a huge lump on the right side of his rib cage. I like to think of it as my signature, although, I must admit, it was a little awkward for both of us when we found out we'd be roommates during the Bills' training camp at Niagara University.

One of our earliest misadventures came on the final day of that first camp with the Bills. We were set free at noon and didn't have to be back to work until eight the next morning. The coaches figured we needed the time to get ourselves settled in the area for the regular season. So Phil and I began loading our personal belongings into his car. We were very careful and methodical about it—first, we dumped as much stuff as we could into the trunk and forced it shut; then we threw whatever was left into the back seat.

Five minutes later, we were on our way.

Since we stopped at a few local pubs along the route, it took about six hours for us to make the thirty-minute drive from the university to the house Phil was renting in Buffalo. As soon as we arrived, we unloaded the car. Again, we were very careful and methodical—everything was out of the car and into the house in about three minutes. All at once it dawned on Phil he had left his playbook back at Niagara. Losing your playbook is almost always good for a stiff fine and angry words from the coaches, who are forever worrying their team's strategy will wind up in enemy hands. So Phil immediately called the campus. A security guard found the playbook and Phil told him we'd be coming right back to pick it up.

But after hitting those same local pubs along the route, we didn't get there until after midnight. It was time for our evening rounds. After Phil retrieved his playbook, while we were driving through Niagara Falls, New York, he asked if I'd ever been to Canada.

"Can't say that I have."

"Well, it's just over the bridge. And I know of a real nice strip joint there."

"Great, let's go. I wouldn't mind getting a taste of some of that lean Canadian bacon."

After you cross the bridge leading into Canada, you're supposed to stop at customs and answer a bunch of questions about your citizenship, where you're going, why you're going there, and how long you plan to stay. But Phil couldn't be bothered with all of that. He sped right by the Canadian customs officer and through the gate without stopping.

Bells started going off. Lights started flashing. And Phil just kept on driving—he must have been doing ninety miles an hour.

I didn't know very much about customs officers, but I knew a move like that might just prompt them to start shooting. Phil wasn't the least bit concerned. Wearing a silly grin, he pointed out the waterfalls, which were illuminated by colored spotlights, and some of the other sights that we whizzed past.

Fortunately, there was no gunfire. But we figured, since they might have decided to give chase, it wouldn't be wise to hang out in Canada very long. Phil knew a back road that would take us to another bridge back to the United States, so he swung around a bend and headed for it. When we got there, we saw a line in front of American customs about three hundred cars long. No problem. Phil simply put his foot to the floor, screeched his tires, and flew past everybody, driving in the lane that was supposed to be for cars coming in the opposite direction. This time, however, he slowed down when he got to the gate.

"What the hell is going on here?" the American customs officer yelled.

"Hey, man, we're in a hurry," Phil said. "Bye." And he zoomed away, leaving the customs officer speechless.

Still wearing that silly grin, he turned to me and said, "So, Conrad, how did you like Canada?"

That gave me my first inkling of what was to come in the two years ahead.

Early that first season with the Bills, Phil and I were out drinking (what else?) one night when we happened to notice a group of lovely young ladies sitting at a table with no male companions in sight. We walked over and began to chat with them. Naturally, I parked myself next to the best-looking one of the bunch. She really was gorgeous. She said her name was Sandi, she was visiting from Louisiana, and she and her friends had just come from a horse show. Horses were a favorite topic of mine, as I had spent plenty of time around them in Wyoming, so I was well-prepared with small talk. We continued chatting away and, every now and then, she and her friends would look at one another and start to laugh. It seemed odd at the time, but I finally decided Phil and I were just so amusing and clever that they simply enjoyed our company.

Much to our disappointment, the conversation resulted in nothing more than polite goodbyes at the end of the evening from the women, still giggling among themselves on their way out.

The next morning, Phil and I were in the trainer's room, icing down our feet in the whirlpools. Our quarterback, Joe Ferguson, was in there, too. We didn't know him, or any of our new teammates, very well at that point. But our ears perked up when we overheard him talking to someone about his wife being in town from their off-season home in Louisiana and how she and some friends had attended a horse show the night before. Phil and I looked at each other, wide-eyed, as it suddenly dawned on us we had attempted to pick up the quarterback's wife.

And she had reeled us in good—hook, line, and sinker.

"Pardon me, Joe," I said. "Did I hear you say your wife's name was Sandi?"

"That's right."

"Well, I don't know how to tell you this, but . . . uh . . ."

We gave him the whole story, being careful to congratulate Joe for marrying someone with such a tremendous sense of humor. But Joe got really pissed—not at us, but at Sandi for trying to embarrass two of his teammates the way she had. She later apologized to us.

That was a shock. I couldn't imagine anyone apologizing to a couple of scumbags like us, let alone a married woman we had tried to pick up.

But that was the kind of guy Ferguson was—he had a lot of respect for his teammates. And we had a lot of respect for him. The 1980 season proved to be the best of his career, as he guided the Bills to an 11–5 record and their first division title since 1966.

We captured the crown with a victory in San Francisco on the final day of the regular season. Because of the game's importance (a loss would have put us out of the playoffs)—and the heavy snow in Buffalo that time of year—our head coach, Chuck Knox, had us practice in San Francisco the week before.

The Bay Area was Phil's old stomping ground, so he and I did more than our share of partying that week. Two nights before the big game, we went out with Bob Moore, a teammate of Phil's in Oakland who was studying law at Stanford. At the end of the evening, as it was getting close to bedcheck, we decided to head back—we'd put in a good four hours of hard, thirsty work. Down the road, a cop sat in his cruiser, watching as we staggered out to our cars. I got behind the wheel, while Phil stumbled into the passenger seat. Bob somehow managed to get into his car all by himself.

As we drove away, I was afraid it was only a matter of time before one of us would be pulled over. And the one who was pulled over just happened to be yours truly.

"It's ten o'clock at night and you're driving without your lights on," the cop said. "But I could have forgiven you for that. Then, as you pulled away from the curb, you forced the car coming out from behind you [Bob's] into the other lane. I could have forgiven you for that, too. But when you did that illegal U-turn right in front of me, I just had to pull you over.''

Bob got out of his car, figuring, because he was in his first year of law school, he was going to defend me. He was going to defend my ass, all right. He couldn't even stand.

"You can't do this, goddamn it," he told the cop in a loud voice.

Brilliant opening statement, I thought. Then, as he began quoting a lot of traffic laws that I don't think even he understood, I stepped in front of him and said, "Bob, just get back in your car and keep quiet." I didn't want him involved for two reasons—one, he was drunker than I was; two, I knew he had a score to settle with Phil dating back to their days in Oakland. That time, Bob was pulled over for driving erratically. When the cop asked Bob to get out of the car so he could test him for intoxication, Phil, sitting on the passenger side, started laughing and said, "Are you crazy? That guy can't take any tests. He's too drunk!" Bob was arrested, and I figured he just might try to get back at Phil through me.

Paybacks always hurt.

Of course, the way Phil was mouthing off, Bob didn't have to say a thing to get us sent to jail. Phil was taking care of that all by himself.

"Fuck that cop," he said. "He can't do this to us."

"Shut up, Phil," I said.

The cop asked me to count backward from a hundred. I started to count, began to stumble, then stopped.

"Listen, I'm a lot better if I sing it," I said.

"Do it any way you like.''

So I began singing "Ninety-nine Bottles of Beer on the Wall."

"OK, OK," the cop said. I'd barely gotten to ninety-eight when he stopped me. I guess he didn't appreciate my musical gifts.

"Now say your ABCs," he said.

I tried, but I couldn't manage it.

"Can I sing my ABCs, too?" I asked.

"Go ahead," he said, with a pained expression.

I proceeded to breeze through them, using the classic tune to which all kids learn their ABCs. The cop didn't say anything, which, I assumed, was a bad sign. I didn't think there was any point in prolonging the inevitable.

"Look, do whatever you have to do," I said. "Arrest me. Lock me up and throw away the key. But whatever you do, don't let that guy sitting on the passenger side drive."

He turned toward Phil.

"What are you lookin' at, cop?" Phil mumbled, barely able to keep his head up and eyes open.

At that point, I figured the policeman was going to reach for his handcuffs, if not his pistol. But he decided to let us go. Why he would allow Bob and me to drive again that night, I had no idea. Of course, I wasn't going to stick around to talk about it.

We made it back to the hotel before bed-check. The fine for being late was a hundred bucks, but it wasn't the money we were worried about. This was an important game for the Bills organization. It was an important game for Chuck Knox. We were old pros, guys who were supposed to know what it took to win, and we didn't want the head man thinking we would let him down.

We also didn't want to give him any reason to question

whether we should be kept on the roster the following season.

At practice the next morning, Knox looked into our bloodshot eyes and gave us a not-so-subtle warning: "Don't forget, boys, we've got a game tomorrow. You might want to temper your behavior a little bit."

When Game Day arrived, we were ready, having had a good night's rest at last (after five nights of partying). Unfortunately, there were about four inches of mud in Candlestick Park, making the already difficult chore of lifting my aging, arthritic legs that much harder. In addition, the defensive tackle playing across from me was a young man named Archie Reese, who made me feel twice my age when he told me I had been one of his favorite NFL players while he was in high school.

I had to call on every ounce of strength I could muster. Reese was barely working up a sweat. I couldn't believe, in all that mud, how clean his uniform stayed—the two dirtiest spots on his jersey were where I kept grabbing it in desperation to keep him away from Ferguson.

Phil was a backup at kickoff, but entered the game in the first quarter after one of the starters, Shane Nelson, suffered a broken wrist. Despite coming in cold—and having spent an entire week reacquainting himself with all of his Bay Area haunts—Phil finished as the game's leading tackler with nine solo hits, and we won, 18–13. That hardly was a typical performance from someone who had spent most of the previous fifteen weeks on the bench. But the mark of a real pro is his ability to rise to the occasion when the chance to play finally does arrive—especially when that chance comes in a big game.

Villapiano, for all of his off-the-field lunacy, was a pro's pro.

Our triumph over the '49ers put us in the divisional round of the playoffs against the San Diego Chargers. The game was in San Diego and, with the wintry weather in Buffalo, Knox figured we would get more accomplished by moving practice to a warmer climate. So we went down to Vero Beach, Florida, and worked out at Dodgertown, the spring-training facility of the Los Angeles Dodgers. My two Dodgertown training camps with the Saints made me the resident expert on all of the best party spots in town.

Since we were going to be there for an entire week, Phil and I decided we needed our own car. We wanted to travel in style, and ordered a big Lincoln Continental, which we picked up when the team flight landed. While the rest of the players went to the hotel in a bus, Phil and I strutted over to our luxury wheels, put on our sunglasses, honked the horn, and waved to the rest of the boys as we drove away.

They were headed for Dodgertown. We were headed for the Bamboo Room, a favorite Saints' hangout in Vero Beach.

At the bar, Phil and I met a young female bartender who was a real knockout. She had a *very* healthy chest, and a low-cut top that showed her assets to best advantage.

Phil took one look at that chest and, with a wide grin, said, "You know, Connie, I really like this place."

A short while later we met the waitress, who was even better-endowed than her companion. I knew I hadn't seen either one of them when I was with the Saints—because they weren't the kind of girls you could easily forget. I later found out they had started working there during the previous summer's training camp, the one I was about to report to when I learned I had been traded to Buffalo. Talk about lousy timing!

It suddenly dawned on me why the Saints ended up going 1–15 that year.

Phil and I claimed to be star players for the Bills, in town to train for the big playoff game, on our way to the Super Bowl. We laid it on pretty thick, and it seemed to work. Before long we had a dinner date at the finest restaurant in town.

"There's just one thing," I said.

"What's that?" the waitress asked.

"We've got four other friends back at our training facility. Can you rustle up four of your finest-looking girlfriends to come along?" They had just the women in mind, and the evening was set.

We discovered the women were all gorgeous, and dressed to kill. Very chic. Very sexy. One had on a black leather skirt, with slits all the way up to her hips. Another wore a black leather collar around her neck. They were a piece of work.

At the restaurant we started off by ordering several bottles of Dom Perignon—at one hundred dollars a bottle—and it wasn't long before we began to get a little bit tipsy. Nor was it long before the conversation, which deserved an R rating earlier in the evening, became X-rated.

A few of the couples even started making out right there at the table. I could see that one of the young busboys was getting pretty excited about the whole thing. So I told the girls, the next time he came around, they ought to give him a little thrill, something to share with all of his buddies in school. The girls thought it was a great idea, but they wound up getting a little bit carried away. They bent over in front of him far enough so he could look down their blouses. They kissed him, and unbuttoned his shirt down to his navel. One even took off her shoe and began rubbing her foot against his crotch. He didn't know what to think.

But he sure as hell wasn't interested in busing any other tables.

About this time, the date of one team member was sitting on his lap, with her legs straddling his, locked in a long, hot kiss. I was tempted to dump my glass of ice water on them to prevent a nuclear meltdown. The girl had told us earlier she was getting married in two weeks. I guess she wanted one more night of partying before tying the knot. Either that, or her future husband was in for a whole lot of trouble.

The waiters brought us more Dom Perignon, and eventually we stopped pouring it into our glasses and started drinking it straight from the bottle. The people seated at the tables around us weren't terribly appreciative of the entertainment. They obviously weren't used to this sort of behavior at a first-class restaurant.

Before we left, we got something *we* weren't used to—a bill for fifteen hundred dollars. But it was worth it.

And there was another surprise to come. Miss soon-to-be married and the guy she was with couldn't control themselves once they climbed into the back seat of the Lincoln. As I pulled out of the parking lot, I noticed they were out of their clothes and going at it like there was no tomorrow. It was as if they had completely forgotten that my date and I were there. The young lady I was with seemed oblivious, too. I couldn't get over how cool she was. In fact, she suggested we stop for a nightcap before I dropped her off.

I thought of asking the two in the back if they cared to join us, but I could see they already were capping the night off with a bang.

The Hilton Hotel had a quiet little bar, so we stopped there. Our friends were still going at it and, figuring they did not wish to be disturbed, I told the parking attendant, who must have been about eighteen years old, to put the car in the darkest spot he could find.

"Never mind those two in the back," I said. "They're in love."

We had a couple of drinks and laughed about all of the craziness at dinner. We came out about twenty minutes later. I gave my claim check to the same kid who had parked the car and, this time, he was wearing a grin from ear to ear. As he pulled up in front of us, I noticed the back-seat action *still* was as hot and heavy as before. I tried to hand the attendant a twenty-dollar bill, but he refused to take it.

"Keep your money, sir," he said. "I'm going to get plenty of miles out of this story."

The evening ended with us getting back just before bedcheck—no thanks to my teammate. And that was only Day One in Vero Beach.

The game, however, proved to be a letdown. We ended up blowing a 14–3 lead and losing, 20–14.

The following summer, the Bills moved their training camp from Niagara University to Fredonia (New York) State College. Phil and I designated a little bar called Tony's, which was smack in the middle of town, as our official training-camp hangout. We did some of our most strenuous exercise there. It took a lot of work to hoist those beer glasses as often as we did.

Tony, the owner, was the greatest. He was a loyal Bills fan and he loved having a couple of players as regulars. He'd even go to the trouble of having two ice bags waiting for me to put on my aching knees after practice.

Just about all of our off-the-field business in training camp, including media interviews, was conducted at Tony's. If a reporter wanted to talk to us after the second practice of the day, he or she had to meet us there. At our age, it was critical to replace the necessary body fluids we lost in those hot afternoon workouts as quickly as possible.

During one interview, we were interrupted by a cute girl in a tube top who asked Phil and me for our autographs. We had had several cold ones at that point and were both feeling comfortable.

"Sure, you can have our autographs," I told her. "But we'd like to sign something more intimate than just a piece of paper."

Much to our surprise, she immediately dropped her top right there in front of everybody. I grabbed one breast to sign while Phil grabbed the other. She thanked us, picked up her top, and left. And when she did, I started laughing.

"What the hell are you laughing about?" Phil asked.

"I signed *your* name. I figured that if she has a jealous husband or boyfriend, he's going to come after you, not me."

Then Phil started to laugh, too.

"Well, Connie, we're even."

"What do you mean?"

"I signed *your* name."

Each morning, Phil and I would hold court in the trainer's room while getting our ankles taped for practice, telling our latest exploits. The guys loved it, and after all, it was our duty—we were the self-appointed Gurus of Entertainment.

One time we showed up at the trainer's room with our toenails painted purple—thanks to the efforts of a young female artist we'd met at a toga party the night before.

There also were my legendary stories about toe-sucking, complete with ice cream and topping. "I don't suck women's toes," I would explain, "I make love to them."

Another memorable evening, Phil and I found ourselves modeling pajamas in a fashion show. It was a fund-raising event, sponsored by the Bills' wives and held at Salvatore's

Italian Gardens, a very swank restaurant outside Buffalo. We were supposed to model tuxedos, but the organizers didn't have them for us because we had intentionally missed all of the fittings beforehand.

Phil and I insisted on being the last models of the evening. That way, during the show, we could sit with our wives and harass the other players up on stage. Finally, it was our turn. Or so we thought. We headed backstage and changed into our pajamas and bathrobes. We were all set to go . . . until one of the coordinators told us we still had twenty minutes.

"Let's get a drink," I said to Phil.

"Good idea."

And so we made our way to the cocktail lounge of this very swank restaurant—wearing our pajamas and bathrobes. All around us were men in suits and ties and women in long gowns and furs. They looked at us as if we were some sort of alien species. We explained that we had just dropped in for a nightcap.

We received another cue that it was our turn to perform—and this time it was the real thing. I came out with my pajama top opened to the waist, dragging the bathrobe behind me as if I were gay. Phil came out with a cigarette in his mouth and his bathrobe wrapped around his neck, Mr. Macho Man. The audience, including my wife, Linda, and Phil's wife, Pattie, kept yelling, "Take it off! Take it all off!"

Not only did we wind up stealing the show, but there was a photograph of our performance in the newspaper the next day. And we didn't even have to go to one of those borrr-inggg fittings.

■   ■   ■

Knox was concerned about the bad influence some of the older veterans might have on his younger players, especially the born-again Christians. So, at our Fredonia training camp, he gave five of us—me, Phil, linebacker Isiah Robertson, defensive end Sherman White, and cornerback Mario Clark— our own dormitory wing, away from everyone else. With all of the freedom and independence it gave us, we nicknamed it Fantasy Island.

Isiah (Butch) Robertson had joined the Bills from the Los Angeles Rams in a 1979 trade. He made Pro Bowl appearances in six of his eight seasons with L.A., and his experience and savvy, particularly in pass defense, made him a valuable member of our two playoff teams. But Butch had a tendency to rub people the wrong way and, as a result, he didn't have very many friends among his teammates.

In fact, Rich Saul, a hulking center for the Rams, physically attacked Robertson when they played together in Los Angeles. It all started, believe it or not, with Isiah's scrotum. He had developed a rash there that he was treating with a salve. One day in the locker room, he removed some of the salve with his finger and ran it down Saul's naked back. Rich turned around, grabbed Isiah by the throat, lifted him off the floor, and began to squeeze. He squeezed so hard, Robertson started to urinate. Jim Youngblood, a linebacker for the Rams, sat nearby but did nothing. It seemed old Butch had criticized several of his Rams teammates in an article in *Sport* magazine, and the one he criticized the most was Youngblood.

Though Robertson was born in Louisiana, went to high school in Kentucky, and went to college at Southern University, everything about Butch was Hollywood-slick. He was the kind of guy who would go to a restaurant and have himself paged, just so people would know he was there. He also was the kind of guy who would trip over an honest dollar in order to cheat somebody out of a dime. Just to see if he could get away with it. Just for the action.

Case in point. We were having a friendly golf game one day, Isiah and Matt Robinson, our backup quarterback, against Phil and me. Phil brought along his video camera, which we took turns using between shots. On the first hole, I sent the ball flying toward a drain pipe to the side of the green. Incredibly, the ball bounced off the pipe, over a fence, and onto the green.

"That's it, I give up," Isiah said, dropping his club in disgust. "If you're going to make shots like that all day, we haven't got a chance."

He was standing on the green, having already chipped on. As Phil walked toward him to see just how close my shot was to the hole, Isiah asked him to go back to his bag and grab his putter. When Phil turned around, Robertson looked up in the sky, started to whistle, and gave my ball a kick that sent it rolling about thirty feet. Little did Butch realize I had been standing behind some trees the whole time, watching him through the zoom lens of Phil's camera—with the power on.

"I saw you kick that ball," I yelled.

Isiah was startled. However, being the gambler he was, he tried to deny the accusation. He figured there was no way I could prove it, that it was my word against his.

"I saw you do it," I said. "In fact, I've even got you doing it on tape."

"I'm telling you, man, I didn't kick your ball," he insisted. "That's where your shot landed. I saw it land there myself. Besides, I'll bet you didn't even have the recorder on."

"OK, fine. I'll play it where it is. But I know you're a goddamn cheat and I can prove it."

We finished the match with Isiah still denying he had done

anything wrong. The next day, word of the incident spread through the locker room like wildfire—pro football players are the world's biggest gossips—and whenever somebody asked him about it, Isiah called me a liar. Meanwhile, Phil and I looked at the videotape. The evidence backed me up one hundred percent.

This was one call even an NFL replay official couldn't screw up.

Two weeks later, we were at a Halloween party—me and my wife, Phil and his wife, Butch and his wife. We all dressed as *Wizard of Oz* characters, and I just happened to have the controversial tape tucked inside my Tin Man suit.

"I have a special treat for you tonight, folks," I said. And I proceeded to pull out the tape, pop it into a recorder, and show Isiah's dastardly deed. Back and forth. Back and forth.

And in slow motion.

Mr. and Mrs. Robertson left the party in shame. That was one gamble that didn't pay off.

■　　■　　■

Our antics often, I felt, helped pull the team together. Perhaps my favorite such memory is of what happened on the way to a regular-season game at San Diego. The team charter was approaching the airport and the pilot couldn't get the wheels down automatically because of a malfunction in the hydraulics. He then tried to crank them down by hand, but the light that was supposed to indicate they were, in fact, down wouldn't come on. He kept trying and trying, but it was no use—we would have to make an emergency landing.

There was, however, one other problem: the runway wasn't long enough. So we were diverted to Los Angeles International, from where we would bus to San Diego. That is, if there were any of us still around to be bused. Naturally, everybody on the plane started to panic—everybody, that is, except me. I just sat there reading a book, *The World According to Garp*. I was at the part where the boyfriend of Garp's wife loses his manhood, literally, and I just couldn't put it down.

Some guys went absolutely crazy. They were screaming and yelling and running up and down the aisle. I've seen less sweat in a sauna. And Isiah's face was the sweatiest of them all. He didn't like flying to begin with, and that we were in some serious trouble was just too much for him to handle. He was so certain he was going to die, he wanted the team chaplain, Father John Manion, to hear his confession.

"Isiah," I said, looking up from my book, "there isn't enough time for you to confess all your sins. There wouldn't be enough time if we were flying to Europe . . . and back."

Isiah then walked over to Phil, who was sitting next to me and was just as frightened as everyone else.

"It was great knowing you, Phil," Butch said, his eyes welling with tears. "We've been in the league together for eleven years. You're a great teammate and a good friend and I love you, man."

"I love you, too, Isiah," Phil said. "It's been great knowing you, too."

Phil is Catholic, and I had to remind him that he shouldn't tell lies when he was so close to death.

Fred Smerlas, our standout nose tackle, walked up to his position coach, Willie Zapalac, and handed him a twenty-dollar bill. "There, now I feel better," Smerlas said. "I just didn't want to die owing you money."

As cheap as Freddie was, I'm surprised he didn't write Zapalac a check. That way, if we lived, he could still call the bank and put a stop on it.

Before making our final approach to LAX, the pilot flew

close enough to the tower to determine if, in fact, the landing gear was down and the problem was in the light. Sure enough, the people in the tower said they could see the wheels. But there was no way of telling if they were locked in place. Thus, the emergency landing continued. The runway was covered with foam and we all were instructed to lean forward and put our heads between our knees. I had always wondered why they had you do that.

Then it suddenly dawned on me: It makes it easier to kiss your ass goodbye.

"Why the hell are you so calm, Conrad?" Phil asked, holding Isiah's hand.

"What do you want me to do?" I said. "Jump out of the plane and hold the wing up? If we land safely, we land safely. If we don't . . . pffft! That's it. We're history."

Phil paused, looked away for a moment, then looked back at me.

"Well, Conrad," he said in a low voice, "even though it's only been a couple of years, I've really appreciated knowing you." What a nice thing for him to say in the face of disaster.

"The feeling's mutual, Phil," I said. "It's been a lot of fun."

"And there's something else I'd like to tell you, Conrad," he said, smiling.

"What's that, ol' buddy?"

"You are, by far, the worst scumbag I have ever met in my entire life. And if we end up dying, I know I'm going to go straight to hell just for knowing you. And the best thing that's going to come out of this crash is that I'll never have to lay eyes on you again."

"Maybe so, Phil. Maybe so," I answered. "But while we're being so honest with each other, I have something I'd like to share with you."

"What's that?"

"You know that child your lovely wife is about to deliver?"

"Yeah?" he answered nervously.

"Well, ol' buddy, it's mine."

Suddenly, Phil forgot all about the emergency landing, about being scared to death, and started dog-cussing me at the top of his lungs.

"Why you sonofabitch!" he said, fighting back a smile. "I ought to get up right now and knock your goddamn head off."

"Wait a few minutes, Phil," I said. "This crash might do it for you."

"I refuse to die next to a scumbag like you. Hey, stewardess, I want another seat. Right now!"

Thanks to the two of us, the dead silence that had come over the plane was shattered. Just by being the scumbags that we were, we eased the tension and fear as everyone contemplated our fate.

Needless to say, the plane landed safely. And as we rolled to a stop at the terminal, Phil started laughing. Then I started laughing. Then everybody started laughing.

The self-appointed Gurus of Entertainment had done it again.

7

Coaches Are Coachable, Too

I've never understood why most pro football players walk on eggshells around their head coaches. I mean, if you're going to war together, you have to work together as a team—from the guy who owns the club to the kid who collects the dirty jocks. Nobody should feel more or less important than the rest of the people in the organization.

If I had something to say to any of the head or assistant coaches I played for, I said it. My remarks weren't always appreciated, of course, but I made damn certain they were heard. Especially when I knew the information we were getting was wrong. I mean, the coaches never hesitated to tell us when we messed up. I just felt it was my responsibility to be the one who said, "Hey, you guys mess up, too."

Bob Hollway, my first head coach with the Cardinals, is among the worst NFL coaches I ever met. He had absolutely no rapport with his team. You'd ask him a question in practice like, "What exactly do you want done on this play,

Bob?'' And he'd give you a scowl and say, "Hell, I don't know. Go ask your position coach.''

He stacked our roster with so many guys from the University of Michigan, I was beginning to think we should have been called the St. Louis Wolverines. Hollway had played and coached for several championship squads at Michigan, and thought it was the only school in the country that produced good football players. In fact, when he was coaching the Minnesota Vikings' great defensive line, known throughout the league as the Purple People Eaters, and they were preparing for the Super Bowl, he showed the players a highlight film of one of Michigan's Rose Bowl appearances. And when he shut the projector off, he told guys like Alan Page, Carl Eller, and Jim Marshall, "That's how defense should be played,'' trying to motivate them by explaining the Super Bowl was "even bigger" than the Rose Bowl.

Before our training-camp workouts, he would have us do twenty minutes of ups and downs—that means that you run in place, collapse on your stomach, bounce right back to your feet, and repeat the sequence. Hollway was like a Japanese commander leading the Bataan Death March through Illinois. Later, he couldn't figure out why, when we finally did start practice, everyone looked sluggish and our timing was off. After all of those ups and downs, we barely had enough strength in our legs to walk, let alone run. A lot of guys wouldn't even make it past the ups and downs. They'd just drop on the field.

We wound up having a whole bunch of injuries that year. Hollway, in his wisdom, called us together one day to explain why: "The problem with you guys is that you just don't know how to fall. You've got to learn how to fall in such a way that you don't hurt yourselves.'' We all looked at each other with puzzlement.

"Did he say what I thought he said?" I asked the guy sitting next to me.

"I'm afraid so."

Sure enough, we spent the first twenty-five minutes of practice working on our falling technique. I couldn't believe it. I always thought the trick was learning how to stay on your feet.

After Hollway's second 4-9-1 record in as many seasons as the Cardinals' head coach, he was fired. The Cardinals let him know by changing the locks on his office door while he was on the field during the final game of the year. I wonder if he got the hint.

His replacement was Don Coryell, who joined the Cardinals after compiling a 104-19-2 record, including three undefeated seasons, at San Diego State. Don was the head coach through the balance of my six-year career in St. Louis. I wish he could have been the head coach for all ten seasons I spent in the NFL. The man's approach was refreshing compared to everything else I had been exposed to up to that point. He was the first coach I ever had, on any level, who tried to make the game fun for his players. In practice, if you weren't involved in a particular drill, he'd let you sit on your helmet. Now that might sound like a small thing, but most coaches make it mandatory that helmets be worn, with chinstraps buckled, at all times. As if that had anything to do with making you a better football player. Coryell's practice rules were simple. On the field, concentrate at all times; off the field, relax and enjoy yourself—just as long as you weren't disruptive.

A lot of us came out of our shells after he arrived.

Coryell was easily the most intense man I have ever seen during a game. He didn't just watch the action; he was totally involved in it. He would bend over, put his hands on his knees, and wear an expression of sheer agony. It didn't matter if we were winning or losing, he'd still have the look of a man who had had something awful crawl down into his stomach and die. When he was dressed in Cardinal red and scurrying up and down the sidelines, he reminded me of a Tasmanian devil. And that intensity was infectious. You couldn't help but play hard for him—even several notches above your skill level. You were convinced that, despite his being as small as he was, he truly wanted to be out there doing battle right next to you.

But there was one time Coryell's intensity really got the best of him. We had a Foosball machine in our locker room, courtesy of the NFL Players Association, which distributed one to each club in the league. At halftime of a game in which we trailed badly, Coryell launched into a tirade about how we were allowing ourselves to be distracted by such things as "that goddamn Foosball machine over there." With that, he took a running start and charged the thing, determined to knock it over. Instead, it was a classic case of an irresistible force meeting an immovable object—and poor Don wound up flat on his back.

We all nearly bit holes through our lips trying not to laugh.

Air Coryell. This pass-happy offensive approach received its greatest publicity when Don was coaching Dan Fouts and the San Diego Chargers. But its foundation was built in St. Louis, with Jim Hart at the controls. Coryell always loved the big play. He believed you had to pass to set up the run, not the other way around. And I couldn't have agreed more. By connecting on the bomb early, you break the back of a defense for the rest of the game. You have opponents so worried about the threat of the pass, they forget about stopping the run. So while we ranked at or near the top of league statistics in passing, nobody noticed that we also ranked at or near the top in rushing.

The pass is a far better weapon for setting up the run than the run is for setting up the pass.

Teams that depend on their running attacks to develop their passing games run into serious problems when they find themselves on the wrong end of the scoreboard late in the fourth quarter. Because when you're behind at that point, you *must* throw the ball in order to make a comeback. So why not make the passing attack your strongest suit from the beginning?

We didn't really have a choice in St. Louis, because our defense was horrible. In fact, it was so bad, when the opposing offense had a third and ten, we didn't even bother to stand and stretch when we were sitting on the bench. We were pretty confident they would have first and ten in a moment. But with Coryell's offense, we could be down two touchdowns at halftime and still be smiling and laughing in the dressing room. "That's not too bad," we'd say to each other. "Two quarters is plenty of time to get those points back." That's how much confidence we had in Coryell's philosophy.

On the negative side, Don did suffer from excessive paranoia—especially when we faced the Washington Redskins. He felt the same mistrust and hatred for George Allen, the Redskins' head coach, that most people in the NFL now feel for Al Davis, the managing general partner of the Los Angeles Raiders. And as a result, we rarely beat the Redskins. Because of Allen's reputation for being a cheater, Coryell spent so much time trying not to lose the ballgame that he never left enough time to figure out how to win it.

How paranoid did Allen make Coryell? Before each practice, the shades were drawn in the windows of the Busch Stadium club restaurant, which was open for business during the week. One day, Coryell noticed a window was open, with the shade up, and the person inside appeared to be watching our workout through a camera lens. Practice was stopped and, within minutes, security guards were up there wrestling the guy to the ground. He turned out to be just a maintenance man cleaning the window.

How paranoid did Allen make Coryell? During practice, our injured players sat in the upper deck of the stadium with binoculars focused on the parking garage next door, looking for spies.

How paranoid did Allen make Coryell? The day before any other game, we could pretty much do whatever we pleased with our game plans—leave them in our lockers, throw them into the trash, make paper airplanes out of them. But the day before we played the Redskins, the assistant coaches not only would come around to collect all the real game plans, they'd leave fake ones lying around in their place.

One year we were getting ready to play a home game against the Redskins when St. Louis was in the midst of a terrible cold snap. The temperature never climbed above zero all week. Having already spent much of his coaching career in Southern California, Coryell hated being out in the cold as much as anyone else on the team—maybe more. But that didn't stop him from having us practice outside the entire week rather than using a nearby gym for one or two days.

During his speech the night before the game, he explained why.

"Men, when the Alaskan Pipeline was being built," he began, "it was discovered the Eskimo workers could put in longer hours than those who came up from the lower forty-eight states. The guys from the lower forty-eight states would only work forty-five-minute shifts, then they'd have to go inside for forty-five minutes to thaw. The Eskimos never stopped. In fact, some of them would be out there operating heavy machinery in their T-shirts.

"Now all kinds of tests were conducted to determine if there were any physiological reasons the Eskimos were better able to handle the climate. None was found. Eventually, it was concluded that it was just a psychological thing—a simple case of mind over matter. The Alaskans accepted the climate as part of everyday life. The workers from the lower forty-eight states, on the other hand, had read and heard all about how cold it would be in Alaska, so they had psyched themselves out long before they ever got there.

"It's the same with the Redskins. They've been reading and hearing all about how cold it is here. And when they come running out of that tunnel tomorrow and that wind hits them right in the face, they're going to be psyched out, too. But you guys have been practicing in it all week, so you know exactly what to expect. You're used to it. And that's why we're going to kick their ass."

Dan Dierdorf, who was sitting next to me in the front row (we always had front-row seats for Coryell's speeches because he was always so much fun to listen to), raised his hand.

"Yes, Dan," Coryell said.

"What you just told us sounds pretty logical. But what happens if, the first time I get in my stance tomorrow, I look into the facemask of the defensive end across from me—and I see an Eskimo?"

Everybody in the room burst out laughing.

Everybody, that is, except Coryell.

"You know," he said, looking more worried than ever, "I wouldn't put it past George Allen, that cheatin' sonofabitch."

But I guess I could understand where Coryell was coming from. I once heard an incredible story about how far Allen had gone to win a game at California's Whittier College, where Coryell followed him as head coach. One of Allen's graduate assistant coaches still had a year of eligibility as a player. So Allen sent the guy up to Santa Barbara, Whittier's biggest rival, to practice with the football team there. Not only did he wind up making the squad, he became its starting quarterback.

Two days before the opening game, he suddenly and mysteriously disappeared. Then, the day Santa Barbara played Whittier, the guy turned up again . . . wearing his coaching togs . . . standing next to Allen on the Whittier sideline. There wasn't a play Santa Barbara's offense ran that day that Whittier's defense wasn't ready for. And there were few plays Whittier's offense ran that Santa Barbara's defense was able to stop.

And people accused *me* of going to extremes to gain an edge? Of course, I suppose that sort of thing had to be expected from a school whose most famous graduate is Richard Nixon.

Another example of Coryell's paranoia was the way in which he guarded his secret plays. There were several he had us work on in practice, week after week, but we never seemed to get around to using on Sunday. I remember one game we were leading and the situation was just right for one of those secret plays, a double-reverse pass. I suggested to Coryell that we use it.

"You're right, Connie, this is the perfect situation for it," he said.

"It sure is."

"And we set them up beautifully for it, didn't we?"

"We sure did."

"But there's just one problem."

"What's that?"

"If we use it, then they will know we have it and it won't be a secret anymore."

That's logic for you—I guess.

Coryell hated one-on-one blocking drills in practice because we, on the offensive line, would always humiliate the defensive linemen. There wasn't one of those guys who could beat us, or our backups, for that matter.

I, of course, got into quite a few practice fights during my early days with the Cardinals. There were times when Coryell really got pissed off at me for brawling with a defensive teammate. Or two.

During one workout, I was going at it pretty good with a defensive tackle named Charlie Davis. Coryell came up behind me to grab my shoulders and pull me away. As he did, Davis wound up to throw a punch with the hand on which he was wearing a cast. I ducked and, *pow*, Coryell was doubled over with a broken nose. I swear, there wasn't a single word spoken through the balance of the practice. And we all struggled hard to keep from laughing when Coryell returned to the field with cotton hanging from each nostril.

"Now, come on, guys, we've got to calm down a little bit out here," he told us in a nasal voice and Daffy Duck lisp. "Otherwise, someone's going to get seriously hurt."

It's hard to believe, given the man's intensity, that football wasn't Coryell's first love. We were having a friendly little chat in the locker room one day, just the two of us, when he told me his lifelong dream was to become a forest ranger. That way, he explained, he could have a lot of time to himself. Privacy was extremely important to Coryell. Despite the high profile that goes with coaching, he really didn't like being around people all that much.

Still, I couldn't help but smile while listening to the speech he gave in 1986, after announcing his retirement as the Chargers' head coach. He talked about looking forward to the days he could spend sitting in a little rowboat on quiet Lake Elsinore outside San Diego. All I could picture was Coryell, with that look of pain he always wore on the sidelines, furiously churning his stubby arms and the boat bouncing across the water like a hydroplane.

■　　■　　■

As far as pure coaches go, there are few in the business more dedicated to their craft than Jim Hanifan. That's because he's a teacher first, a coach second. The man just loves to see people learn. Unlike most position coaches, he'll take the time in training camp to work with every single one of his players, including those at the very bottom of the depth chart. Most position coaches feel their responsibility begins and ends with the starters. To them, the other guys are just bodies—human fodder for training-camp drills. They don't care about improving their talent. They don't care about developing their techniques.

But I saw Hanifan take someone he knew was practicing for the last time before being cut and try everything possible to make him better than he was the day before. Jim always felt his responsibility was to the game. His thinking was that the guy just might take the knowledge he received and someday pass it on as a high-school or college coach. And the players he coaches would be better for it. And the overall quality of the game, from the scholastic level all the way up to the NFL, would benefit in the long run.

Hanifan was a major part of the tremendous camaraderie we had on that offensive line in St. Louis. He was the glue that kept us together. Why, he'd even socialize with us, something a majority of his peers—past and present—would consider in strict violation of proper coaching etiquette. Just about every Friday night during the season, Jim and his wife, Mary, would join me and my wife, Linda, and Dierdorf and his wife, Tammy, for dinner and a movie. There also were times when Jim would go out drinking with the boys. He's the only person I know who can down fifty beers without having to stop once to take a leak. Incredible. And if, while we were at a bar, some loudmouth happened to make a derogatory remark to me or anyone else on the line, Hanifan was ready to punch his lights out.

"If anyone's going to curse at these guys, I'll be the one to curse at them," he'd say. "I'll be goddamned if I'm going to let you do it, because you've never gone to war with them. I have."

Jim taught us to think of our unit as a family. He told us it was OK to love one another, that we should never feel ashamed to say "I love you" to our linemates. He wanted us to love him, too. And when grading our performances from film review, he took the approach of a parent who understands his children all have different personalities and must be handled accordingly. For instance, Dierdorf would get real upset over minus grades, so Hanifan made certain to give him as few as possible just to keep him in a good frame of mind. Then, when any of us would complain that he was catering too much to Dan, Hanifan would say, "Calm down, calm down. These grades don't mean shit, anyway." He also catered to me, trying not to discourage my highly aggressive style of play. Nonetheless, he wrote on my grade sheet after a 1974 victory over Dallas: "Be careful downfield! You know teams will bitch to officials about late hits. Keep it up—but watch yourself.''

Once, when I was giving Jim a hard time about making us run after practice, he said, ''Conrad, you have got to run these ten wind sprints if you want to be a great football player.''

I asked, ''How many do I have to run if I only want to be pretty good?''

For added incentive, Hanifan would put twenty-five dollars (five for each offensive lineman) into our kitty any time we went through an entire game without allowing a sack. That proved to be quite expensive for him in 1975, when we set an NFL record for fewest sacks given up in a season with eight. We usually took all of the money in the kitty and gave ourselves a party, but that year we decided to buy Hanifan a gift to commemorate our remarkable feat. He was really touched, though it was mostly *his* money that paid for the gold watch we gave him.

But I can still say, to this day, that I love Jim Hanifan—a great coach, a great man, and a great friend.

Hanifan was one of three assistants on Coryell's staff who went on to become a head coach, holding the position in St. Louis from 1980 to 1985. The others were our quarterbacks-receivers coach, Rod Dowhower, who coached Indianapolis from 1985 to 1986, and our running backs coach, Joe Gibbs (now head coach of the Washington Redskins).

Gibbs has had great success with the Redskins, but I was responsible for some humbling moments early in his NFL coaching career, which began with the Cardinals in 1973. Gibbs was in charge of holding the blocking dummies when we practiced our trap blocks. When it was my turn, I'd come firing out of my stance and knock him ass-over-teakettle. This happened about five times in a row. Then, as I was about to make it an even six, Gibbs moved the dummy out of the way at the last second—the way Lucy does with the football on every field-goal attempt by Charlie Brown. I went skidding, face-first, and cut open my chin.

That's when I learned coaches were coachable, too.

■   ■   ■

Bob Hollway was the only killjoy I ever played for . . . until I got to the Saints and met Dick Nolan. He tried to do things the way Tom Landry did them in Dallas and he wasn't successful, because he wasn't Tom Landry. He refused to believe that part of his job was to motivate players. You never heard him give anything that even remotely resembled a Knute Rockne–type speech. Instead, he'd say, "You guys know what you have to do, you're all professional football players. So go out there and do it." That's the kind of thing you were supposed to say to a team like the Raiders—a veteran group with a long tradition of winning. You weren't supposed to say that to a club like the one we had in New Orleans—a club filled with young players who had no idea what it took to be successful in the NFL, who needed someone they could look up to and believe in and follow into battle.

Everyone seemed to fall asleep when Nolan stood at the podium. And the few times he tried to light a fire under your ass—for instance, by telling you on the sidelines, "OK, now get in there and go! Go! Go!"—it was obvious it wasn't coming from the heart, that he was simply mouthing words the coach's manual said were appropriate for that particular situation. We could have gotten a wall to coach us and it would have been just as effective.

The man had the personality of a grapefruit.

So, in my first year with the Saints, I took it upon myself

to be their chief motivator. I tried to get things started during one-on-one blocking drills in practice, just as I had done so many times in St. Louis. I'd get the offensive and defensive linemen talking back and forth, calling each other names, really getting pissed off. I'd bring some life to an otherwise boring workout, which, I always assumed, was the kind of thing coaches wanted their veteran players to do.

But Nolan, perhaps because he had heard about Coryell's broken nose, didn't like it one bit. He pulled aside Dick Stanfel, our offensive line coach, one day and said, "Hey, I don't want any more of that chatter from your guys. There's no need for that stuff." Stanfel relayed the message and that was the end of it.

But I got my way with Stanfel in training camp once. It happened the very first time I saw an offensive lineman try to restrain another offensive lineman who was fighting with a defensive guy.

"What the hell's going on here?" I yelled. "Goddamn it, Dick, you've got to talk to these people in our meeting tonight and tell them they should never grab another offensive lineman in a fight. You know as well as I do the guy they should be grabbing is that defensive lineman, so the offensive lineman can get a few extra licks in."

I figured I could appeal to the leather-tough approach he had taken while establishing himself as one of the game's all-time great offensive guards in Detroit. Sure enough, at the meeting that night, Stanfel said, "If you grab somebody, make sure he's one of the bad guys. Now don't ever let me see that shit again."

The best compliment I ever received from the man was when he told me one day, "You know, Conrad, you could have played on those great teams we had back in the 1950s, with Bobby Layne and Doak Walker and Fum McGraw." Guys who played in that era don't say that very often to modern-day players.

In 1979, my second year with the Saints, we went through a five-game stretch where we were averaging around thirty points and close to five hundred yards in total offense. The only problem was, we wound up losing three of those games because our defense played so poorly. After the fifth game, Ed Hughes, our offensive coordinator, walked into the meeting room, looked at the entire offensive unit, and with a perfectly straight face said, "We have got to get a little bit more offense."

Naturally, I spoke up.

"Listen, Ed, I'm not going to say anything about the defense, but what you've been getting from the offense these last five games is downright astronomical. How we've been able to do it this long is beyond me. And you're looking for more? There aren't enough minutes in a game to give you more offense than that."

Hughes looked down and slowly nodded his head. Then he looked up, took a deep breath and said, "I just want you guys to know that I was told to say that."

He didn't have to mention who told him. We all knew only one person was dumb enough to send such a message, and his name was Dick Nolan.

■ ■ ■

Like Coryell and unlike Hollway and Nolan, Chuck Knox is a players' coach. He has always preached that the greatest assets of a football franchise are its players. And he has always practiced what he preached by making every effort to keep his players as happy as possible. That was no easy task with a general manager like Stew Barber, who was disliked by just about every player on the team for his hard-line negotiating tactics and the arrogance he showed whenever he was around any of us. Stew had been a standout offensive tackle for the Bills in the 1960s, and he carried himself as if he were tougher and stronger and a better player than any of us could ever hope to be. Knox wasn't too crazy about him, either.

I guess the thing I liked most about Chuck was how much he respected and valued the experience and leadership of the older pros. One time, we were on a return flight from a game when, in the rear of the aircraft, an argument erupted between linebackers Isiah Robertson and Chris Keating. Isiah, staying true to his unpopular form, had begun to rib Keating about the fact he was starting and Keating wasn't. It kept getting louder and louder, and everyone knew it wouldn't be long before Keating threw the punch Isiah had coming to him. Knox got up from his seat and, without even looking in the direction of Robertson and Keating, walked over to where Phil Villapiano and I were sitting. Speaking in a quiet voice, he said, "You guys are the veterans on this team. I don't know what's going on, but I want you to get back there and straighten it out. And do it now!"

Ordinarily, we didn't appreciate being disturbed while relaxing in our seats with glasses of Jack Daniels or whatever the bourbon was we happened to sneak on board that week. This, of course, was an exception: The head coach had a problem and he came to us for the solution. There were any number of bigger and stronger guys he could have sent back there to pull them apart if things got physical. But he was counting on two old pros to see to it that it never reached that point.

"OK, Phil, which one do you want?" I asked.

"I'll take Isiah, you take Keating."

Keating was just about ready to haul off when I put my

arm around his shoulders and walked him into the bathroom. Having joined the Bills only a year or two earlier as a rookie free agent, Chris was in need of a lesson in the politics of pro football.

"You're right, but you're wrong," I told him. "You're right to feel the way you do, because it's frustrating to be a backup and Isiah should keep his fucking mouth shut. But you're wrong to argue with him, because, number one, he's a starter and you're a backup and if it ever comes down to where they have to choose between you and him, you're gone. Number two, it just ain't worth it. Just ignore him because he'll hang himself someday."

Keating took my advice and the matter was dropped. And the best part for Knox was, after we landed and the reporters traveling with us asked him about the fight on the plane, he could say, in all honesty, "Fight? What fight?"

Knox always scheduled a special-teams meeting an hour before our regular morning group session. I wasn't on special teams, so I never had to attend. Phil was. One Saturday morning before we were to leave for a game at San Diego, he came to pick me up at my house and found I was still in the bathroom blow-drying my hair.

"Come on!" he yelled. "You're going to make me late for the meeting. You're going to get me fined."

"Will you calm down," I said. "I'm not going to make you late and I'm not going to get you fined."

Phil was late. Phil was fined fifty dollars.

"Don't worry," I told him. "I'll talk to Chuck and straighten the whole thing out."

That night in San Diego, I ran into Knox at the door to our hotel meeting room. He had just returned from dinner and was puffing on a big cigar. It was obvious the cigar wasn't all that was lit—he had that "special" glow that no doubt resulted from a few well-mixed martinis. It seemed like a perfect time to approach him about Villapiano.

"Look, Chuck, it was my fault Phil was late for the special-teams meeting this morning," I said, pulling out a wad of cash. "So here's the fifty bucks for his fine."

I figured he would tell me to keep my money and forget the fine. In fact, I was so certain of that, I peeled off another fifty and said, "Here's an extra one from me to you. Go have a good time."

Much to my surprise, Chuck took both fifties out of my hand.

"That's really nice of you, Conrad," he said, pulling out an even larger wad than mine and tucking the hundred bucks inside. "Thanks a lot."

Knox taught me a valuable lesson that night: Never trust a coach when he has that "special" glow.

Ray Prochaska, our offensive line coach in Buffalo, was on in years and there were times when understanding him could be difficult. He had coached me in a couple of Pro Bowls when he was with the Rams so I was somewhat familiar with the way he spoke, fast and sort of in rhyme. For instance, when explaining our blocking assignments, he'd say we had to *bing! bang! bong!* our opponents.

"What do you mean?" someone invariably would ask.

"Just what I said. You go *bing!* over here, *bang!* over there, and *bong!* over here." And he'd point to the corresponding spots on the chalkboard.

"Oh."

Ray never could remember the numbering system of our offense. The even numbers were supposed to be for the holes on the right side of the line and the odds were supposed to be for the holes on the left. When he was coaching college ball back in the 1940s, the odds were on the right and the evens were on the left—and that was what he followed when he diagramed our blocking schemes. We constantly corrected him, but it was no use. He couldn't break the habit. Finally, we just began to flip-flop the numbers in our heads.

The rookies weren't aware of our little adjustment because we never really talked about it; we just did it. They assumed the information Prochaska was giving them was accurate, when, in fact, he was telling them to do the exact opposite.

At the end of a meeting early in my second training camp with the Bills, Ray asked, "Does everyone understand what we're doing here?"

The rookies moved their heads up and down.

"Any questions?"

The rookies moved their heads from side to side.

"OK, then, that's all for tonight. See you on the field tomorrow morning."

Ray left the room, but Reggie McKenzie, our other offensive guard, and I told the rookies to stay put. We then explained how they were supposed to read the blocking schemes, that the numbers had to be mentally flip-flopped. It took a while before we finally had them convinced we were telling the truth and not laying the groundwork for a prank.

But it wasn't their best interests we had in mind; it was our own. Because if they kept screwing up at practice the next day, we all would have to stay on the field an extra half-hour. And that meant a half-hour less we could spend at Tony's, our official training-camp watering hole.

Being a former offensive line coach, Knox had a special place in his heart for offensive linemen. In fact, blocking drills were about the only phase of practice in which he would offer hands-on instruction. He liked to twist his baseball cap around, roll up his sleeves, and hunker down right next to us.

I enjoyed playing for Knox, although there were times our relationship experienced some turbulence. Like during the 27–14 *Monday Night Football* loss to the Cowboys at Texas Stadium in 1981. I had launched an all-out assault on defensive tackle John Dutton because he made some unkind remarks about me in the newspapers before the game and because he began to mouth off at me during the game. He didn't say a word as we were building a 14–7 halftime lead, which might have been 21–7 if the Cowboys hadn't intercepted at their own nine yard line late in the second quarter. But when the game began to turn around, with Dallas's twenty-point third quarter, Dutton, who had yet to make a single tackle, started talking.

"You're a piece of shit, Dobler," he said. "Just a no-good, cheap-shotting piece of shit."

After I picked up two personal fouls and a holding penalty, Knox sent second-year man Jim Ritcher in to take my place. But I waved him off. Ritcher then went back to the sidelines, shrugged, and told Knox, "Coach, he won't come out." I didn't leave the field until the end of the series. And when I did, Knox told me I was being removed from the game.

I didn't take the news very well.

"You can't do this to me!" I cried. "There are thirty-five million people watching this game on TV and sixty thousand people in the stands. You're not man enough to take me out of there. The game's bigger than you."

Knox stepped back, with the look of a man who had been ambushed.

"You don't take a warrior out of a war!" I continued. "You

let him fight to the finish. You just can't take me out of this game. I'm not going to leave.''

I was completely out of control. What Knox should have done was grab me by the shirt and say, "Listen, I'm running this team, not you. Now you're going to sit down and you're going to shut up. Understand?'' But he didn't. Maybe he was afraid I was going to deck him. Who knows? Maybe I would have. But shortly thereafter, with Villapiano pulling me toward the bench, I found the good sense to comply with his order and remain on the sidelines for the rest of the night.

I found out the game was bigger than me, too.

Meanwhile, Dutton wound up leaving the field with a badly bruised thigh from all of my legwhips. As a result, the Cowboys would blame me for their failure to make the Super Bowl, for a record sixth time, after that season. They insisted they'd have gone all the way if Dutton had been able to play in their NFC championship game against San Francisco, which they lost, 28–27, in the last minute. There was actually a line in Dutton's biography in the Dallas media brochure that said: "Dutton's absence from the NFC championship game in San Francisco because of a bruised thigh was considered a major blow to Dallas.''

The next day Knox called me into his office. And the moment he did, you could hear a towel hit the carpeted floor of our locker room. My teammates knew I was in serious trouble. Some figured I was going to get, at the very least, a stiff fine; at the very most, a one-way ticket to the waiver wire. Chuck got right to the point: I was being benched for my personal homecoming that week at St. Louis.

He knew that would hurt the most and it did. Badly.

"You've got three options,'' Knox said. "One, accept the benching like a man and be ready to contribute as a backup.

Two, retire. Three, if you don't want to accept it like a man and you don't want to retire, I'll put your ass right out there." He pointed to the street outside his window.

"But, Chuck, I thought you wanted me to act like that to fire up the rest of the team," I said, making a last-ditch effort to justify my actions.

He pondered that for a moment, and I really thought I had him. Then he slowly shook his head.

"Nice try, Connie, but it won't work this time."

"Well," I said, clearing my throat, "if those are my only options, then I guess I'll take number one."

As soon as I returned to the locker room, the first question out of everyone's mouth was, "What did he say?" I looked at them and, with a faint smile, said, "Guys, I learned one thing today. Pride is a hard thing to swallow. But it will go down . . . it will go down."

My teammates gave me a consolation prize—and kind of thumbed their noses at Knox in the process—by making me one of the cocaptains for the St. Louis game.

The Cardinals, with a far better pass rush than they ever had when I was with them, immediatley began to apply heat to our quarterback, Joe Ferguson, and would continue to do so throughout the game. At one point, Knox looked over at me as I stood on the sidelines, conspicuously champing at the bit. I looked at him, hoping he was going to give me my cue to take the field. But then he suddenly turned away and would never look in my direction the rest of the game. We got our ass beat, 24–0.

I realized something about Chuck Knox that day. He was always talking about the team concept, about how players and coaches should never put themselves ahead of the team. But he showed me that day his personal feelings and his need to prove to me and everybody else that he was right and I was wrong were far more important than having me in there to help us win. Make no mistake: I consider Chuck among the greatest coaches in the game. But what he did that day only proved that even a great coach is capable of allowing his ego to get in the way of the good of the team sometimes.

My punishment finally ended in the first quarter of our next game, against New England, and I remained in the lineup through the balance of the regular season. I knew after our playoff loss to Cincinnati I had hung up my cleats for good, although Chuck and I wouldn't discuss my impending retirement for another three months.

Knox has had a lot of success as a head coach. He was a winner with the Rams. He was a winner with the Bills. He has been a winner with the Seahawks. But the one thing he hasn't won, or for that matter reached, is the Super Bowl. He has come close, taking the Rams to three conference championship games, the Seahawks to one, and all three clubs to a total of ten playoff appearances in the last sixteen years. In fact, Knox is the only coach in NFL history to lead three different teams to the playoffs.

In my opinion, the reason he can't go the distance is simple: He pays far too much attention to statistics and far too little to his instincts. Statistics tell you what has the highest percentage for success. Such as, when you're up by two touchdowns, it's time to go to a ball-control offense. Knox went to it so often, it became known as Ground Chuck (which, not coincidentally, is the worst kind of meat you can buy). Stats are great for the regular season. Let them be your guide through a sixteen-game schedule, and you'll probably come out with more wins than losses.

But when you get to the playoffs, stats aren't worth the computer paper they're printed on.

In the playoffs, you either win or you go home. Each game

is a separate entity and requires decisions based on what happens moment to moment rather than over a sixteen-week period. That's where instincts come in. You can't go to ball control just because the numbers say it's the right thing to do. And if your opponent has a good enough passing game, it's the wrong thing because a two-touchdown lead isn't enough. Go for another TD. And another. And another. Keep going until the clock says you can't go anymore. Make the other coach worry about keeping the ball away from you, not vice versa.

It's too bad. I'd really like to see Chuck reach and win the Super Bowl once and for all. He deserves it.

■   ■   ■

I wasn't any less comfortable around the owners of the teams I played for than I was around the coaches. Most of the other players would try to avoid having any direct contact with the big bosses, but not me. I was always kidding around with them, putting them in headlocks—all kinds of playful stuff. When other guys saw me doing that, they'd start laughing. It kept everybody loose.

Of course, I never worked for Al Davis, managing general partner of the Raiders. Phil did. And from what he has told me, I'm not so certain I'd have been quite as comfortable around him as I was around Bill Bidwill in St. Louis, John Mecom in New Orleans, and Ralph Wilson in Buffalo.

Phil swears, to this day, that Davis bugged all of his player's telephones during training camp.

"I first became a little suspicious when, a minute or two after I hung up, I heard a clicking sound coming from the phone," Phil told me. "Then, one night during the middle of contract negotiations, I was on a long-distance call with my agent. And I said, 'You know, sometimes I'd like to just punch Al Davis right in the mouth.'

"At practice the next day, I happened to walk past Davis, who was leaning against a goal post. He called me over. 'What's up?' I asked. 'I understand you'd like to punch me in the mouth, Phil.' He gave me a wink and walked away."

Davis likes to generate among his players a certain amount of the same fear and mistrust that exists among his competitors in the NFL. He wants them to know that he'll go to any length to maintain the Raiders' winning tradition—that anything he can find out about their personal lives just might allow him to make sure it doesn't interfere with their performance on the field.

Bidwill bugged me in many ways during my six years with the Cardinals, but never electronically. At one time, he had the distinction of being one of the fatter men ever to control an NFL franchise. Former Redskins owner Edward Bennett Williams once joked that Bidwill would have been the greatest defensive end in the world "if two ham sandwiches were painted on the helmets of all opposing quarterbacks." I was always inviting Bill to come out to my off-season home in Wyoming. "Don't worry," I'd say, "we'll knock out a couple of walls so you'll be able to move around." He and I and Dan Dierdorf were all set to have our picture taken together one time when, suddenly, the photographer walked away and left us standing there.

"He'll be right back, Bill," I said. "He just had to go get his extra-wide-angle lens."

But I respect Bidwill, because he lives his life the way all of us would like to live ours. He does what he wants to do and he doesn't care what anyone thinks about him. Billy made money the old-fashioned way: He inherited it. What's more, he was an orphan who had the great fortune of being adopted by the late Charles Bidwill, the millionaire who owned the Cardinals from the time they were in Chicago.

I basically liked Bill, but his cheapness could be downright maddening. He once was quoted as saying, "A Super Bowl would be a disaster for the Cardinals because the players would demand higher salaries." We used to joke about the reason he wouldn't allow the already stale leftover submarine sandwiches from our chartered flights to be thrown away: because he took them home to his family.

Then again, with that waistline of his, he probably ate them all by himself.

■   ■   ▓

I got along pretty well—albeit from a distance—with John Mecom, the Saints' owner when I was in New Orleans. There wasn't a sharper-dressed executive in the NFL, and there certainly wasn't one with longer hair. I guess John still saw himself as the twenty-seven-year-old kid who, thirteen years before my arrival in New Orleans, had become the youngest owner in league history when his Texas-rich parents gave him the Saints as a birthday present.

I could just hear Mom and Dad telling him, "Son, we shopped and we shopped, but we just couldn't find a thing. So here's a twenty-eight-million-dollar pro football franchise. Hope you enjoy it!"

My relationship with Steve Rosenbloom, New Orleans' second general manager when I was there, was over before it ever really had a chance to begin. Steve, son of late Colts' and Rams' owner Carroll Rosenbloom, joined the Saints' front office after his stepmother, Georgia Frontiere, fired him as executive vice-president of the Rams. Not only didn't he have the kind of administrative talent even a stepmother could love, he also didn't have much of a sense of humor.

Unfortunately, I would find that out as Steve went around the locker room to meet the players during our minicamp in the spring of 1980.

I was sitting in front of my dressing stall, smoking a cigarette and shooting the breeze with Archie Manning and a couple of other guys, when Rosenbloom finally came up to me. I figured I'd do the respectful thing and stand to shake his hand.

"That's OK, that's OK, you don't have to get up," he insisted. "Sit down, sit down."

After noticing I was a good foot-and-a-half taller than he was, I joked, "Oh, you want me to sit so you can talk down to me, is that it?"

Rosenbloom was absolutely stunned. Then, out from behind him emerged his even shorter assistant, Harold Guiver.

"Well, I guess you don't have to talk down to me after all, Steve," I said. "That's why you have this guy around."

The other players responded with nervous laughter. The air was thick with tension.

"Well, uh, glad to have met you," Rosenbloom said, and he and Guiver quickly moved on to meet someone else. It was clear I had made a major mistake.

Twice.

A few months later, I was traded to the Bills.

■　　■　　■

The owner I probably had the most fun with was the one I played for in Buffalo, Ralph Wilson. He did much more interacting with his players in the postgame locker room than Bidwill and Mecom ever did. Most guys were uncomfortable when Ralph came around to shake hands and chat, but I thought it was great.

Ralph had a big, gaudy rainbow tie and I noticed he kept wearing it to several of our games. He called it his lucky tie, because it seemed, every time he wore it, we'd win.

Naturally, that wasn't enough to stop me from making a wisecrack about it after one game.

"Listen, Ralph, if you need some cash for a new tie, I'll be happy to loan it to you," I said. "Just do me a favor and get rid of that ugly thing."

Ralph's comeback was great: He bought everybody on the team that same rainbow tie for Christmas. I still have mine. Who knows? I might need it if I ever get a job selling used cars.

Once, I stuck Ralph with a restaurant bill without his ever knowing it. We were in New Orleans to play the Saints, and the night before the game, I got seven of my teammates together for dinner at Brennan's, one of the top restaurants in the country. Louis, the maitre d', was a friend of mine from when I played in New Orleans, so he put us at the best table in the place.

Then, as we were finishing our meal, he came over to tell us Ralph and his wife were seated nearby at a table for two.

"Listen, Louis," I said, "he doesn't know it, but I've got a feeling Ralph would really like to pay our bill tonight. Will you help me see to it that he does?"

"Consider it done, Mr. Dobler," Louis said.

Without my even asking, he brought a bottle of champagne to Ralph's table and told him it was from us. We had champagne, too, and as Louis did the pouring at Ralph's table, we all stood, glasses in hand, to toast our great owner and his lovely young wife. He was so proud that eight of his players would do something as thoughtful as that, he wouldn't *allow* us to pay our bill.

After games, Ralph always made a point of introducing me to the friends he happened to bring into the dressing room.

"I want you to meet the toughest sonofagun I have ever seen in my life," he would say. "Look at that man's knees. Look at all those scars. He's as courageous as they come."

The introductions were flattering, but they also could be a little bit embarrassing as well. I mean, here was this multimillionaire putting *me* on a pedestal. Hell, I was the one who should have been in awe of him. All that wealth . . . and not a single scar on his knees.

Inside Sports did a real offbeat article on me that appeared in its September 1981 issue. The headline read, TALKING DIRTY. The subheadline said, "When Conrad Dobler is the subject, it's hard to clean up the conversation." Dave Kindred, who wrote the piece, interviewed Phil and me on the final day of training camp at Fredonia State College. Like all Fredonia interviews, it was conducted at our table at Tony's. And as the night wore on and more and more beers were consumed, the conversation grew crazier and crazier. The next day, Phil and I began to wonder how our words would look once they wound up in print.

The article—written in dialogue form with comments from several players and coaches I played with, against, and for during my career—actually wasn't quite as incriminating as we expected. But it did contain its share of outrageous material, including Phil saying: "Conrad Dobler, the prince of Wyoming, where the men are men, and the women are glad of it—and sheep are a little nervous."

I was amazed, after a victory the week the magazine came out, when Ralph walked up to me with a big smile and said,

"That was a great article, Conrad. Best I've ever read!" How could you not like an owner who was as open-minded as that?

After my retirement, I sent all three owners I played for a letter. I thanked them for the opportunity they gave me to play in the NFL and told them I had had ten great years in the league and so forth.

The only one to reply was Bidwill. He sent my letter back to me with a stamp on it that said "BULLSHIT!"

8

My "Tough Guy" Hall of Fame

Believe it or not, there was a time when most players in the NFL actually *looked* as if they'd been in a football game after the final gun. When it wasn't a criminal offense for them to be covered with mud and grass stains. Or to wear their jerseys on the outside of their pants. Or to allow their socks to droop to the ankles.

There was a time when the game was literally dirty.

Television changed all of that. More specifically, the millions of dollars the networks began paying for broadcast rights in the 1970s gave them the clout to pressure the league into cleaning up its act. The game stopped being a game and turned into a TV production. As I entered the NFL in 1972, I witnessed the transition firsthand.

Why do you think artificial turf was installed in so many stadiums around the league? Because, among other things, it would help keep the players' numbers and names free of obstruction for those watching on the tube (unless, of course, some charitable defensive lineman happened to allow an offensive lineman, like yours truly, to take the shirt right off his back).

When the game was still a game, the people who sat in the stands, the dedicated followers who showed up regardless of the weather, didn't need numbers or names to identify their heroes. Back then, players made the same kind of money as a majority of those who watched them, so they often traveled in the same social circles. There weren't very many players who even knew what a five-star restaurant was, let alone its location. And when the players were on the field, the fans knew them by their positions, their shapes, their sizes.

Paying customers weren't the least bit offended by the sight of grown men rolling around in what often took the form of a giant bog. They considered it part of the game's appeal.

In the good old days of the NFL, there were no rules stating jerseys had to be tucked in and socks had to be pulled all the way up to the knees (and that if you used tape to hold them up, it had to match the color of the socks). I thought I was only wearing a football uniform, not making a fashion statement. But, again for the sake of the television cameras, neatness became a priority and that's why such nitpicking found its way into the rule book. Referees are always on the lookout for uniform violations and constantly walk up to players to warn them when they're flirting with a fine.

I'll never forget one game when I was with the Cardinals. I had just gotten kicked in the balls and was doubled over with both hands between my legs. The referee walked by, noticed my socks had fallen a little bit below my knees, and said, "Pull those socks up, 66, or you'll have to leave the game."

"Ref," I responded in a strained voice, "right now, I've

got my hands where I believe they'll do me the most good. But just give me a minute to toss my cookies, and I'll be more than happy to pull up my socks.''

The rule change that had its greatest impact on cold-weather teams was the one that made it illegal for players to stick their hands in their pants. Not only did it take away the most convenient method of keeping your hands warm during a game, it also eliminated the chance to check your manhood after taking a hit to the crotch. Did NFL and network executives believe we'd have our hands down there for some *other* reason?

Come to think of it, I wonder if TV had anything to do with so many teams employing the shotgun formation on offense. Maybe they frowned on the quarterback being seen so often with his hands underneath the center's nice, warm behind.

I realize the networks' money—which, in 1982, went from millions to billions—is largely responsible for player salaries increasing significantly over what they were in the old days. I realize the exposure provided by TV is mostly responsible for the tremendous popularity of the sport and its participants. At the same time, however, I think it's a shame that greed and selfishness, resulting from money-making opportunities on and off the field, have taken away a lot of the game's heart and soul. Most players today seem far too businesslike. They show up at the stadium in three-piece suits, carrying briefcases as if they're about to spend a day on Wall Street.

Even the sweaty, musty, Ben-Gay-like smell is disappearing from the locker room. The Dallas Cowboys' training complex is a case in point. Soon each player will have a private, officelike cubicle, complete with a telephone and a computer terminal. I can see why the players would love such a setup; it allows them to be in constant touch with their accountants and stockbrokers.

I just can't relate to the cold, mechanical approach that is prevalent in today's NFL. I played with a great deal of emotion, because I felt that's what we were paid to do and that's what the fans paid to see. Nobody wants to watch picture-perfect execution by a bunch of robots. They want the excitement and drama that go with one group of eleven men trying to outperform another group of eleven men.

The final score isn't always indicative of which team was bigger, stronger, faster, or smarter. More often than not, it's indicative of which team was hungrier—which players were willing to do whatever it took, even if it wasn't so pretty, to come out on top. There's nothing wrong with striving for picture-perfect execution. That's why coaches have minicamps and training camps and an entire week of practices and meetings before each game. But picture-perfect execution, by itself, isn't enough. You have to have heart and soul.

Otherwise, the league might as well computerize everything and stage contests between squads of Max Headrooms.

One of the more disturbing trends I've noticed is the number of players who listen when their agents tell them, "Whatever you do, don't play hurt. Don't do anything to jeopardize your career and your future earning power. The key to success in this game is to play as many years as you possibly can. And the key to playing as many years as you possibly can is staying healthy." What agents really are saying is, "If *you* can stay healthy, *I* can continue to support my family in the manner they're accustomed to. Do you have any idea what insurance on a Mercedes costs?" Consider this: There are something like fifteen hundred professional football players and twenty-two hundred registered agents. Given that kind of ratio, agents soon will be looking for clients in maternity wards. "Excuse me, sir, is that your son in the third bassinet from the left? I've been watching the way he's been kicking his feet and tugging at his blanket. With that sort of aggressiveness, there's no doubt in my mind he'll be a first-round linebacker about twenty-one years from now. So if you'll just sign right here . . .''

From an economic standpoint, the players are absolutely correct. The longer you play, the more money you make. The more money you make, the less you have to worry about life after retirement, providing you've been reasonably intelligent with your investments. And in all fairness, once players no longer perform up to a certain level, they're scrapped like pieces of old machinery. NFL owners have been able to disassociate themselves from the human element of the game. In fact, at one time they were allowed to claim depreciation on their players. Toward the end of my career, I knew which side of the balance sheet I was on—the liability side.

But from the standpoint of good football, players who follow the protect-yourself-at-all-costs advice of their agents have lost all perspective. They've forgotten everything it took for them to get where they are and what it takes to get where every NFL player should want to go—the Super Bowl. They've put themselves ahead of their teammates, which, for any club, is an open invitation to disaster. Morale problems can destroy the most talented of units.

If you can't play hurt, you can't play, because pain is a constant companion—especially late in the season, when weeks and weeks of pounding begin to take their toll. It seems most players today have a hard time distinguishing between pain and injury. When they have a little pain, they think they're injured. And that makes me laugh. An injury is a ravaged knee or a broken bone or anything else that truly prevents you from leaving the field under your own power. Bumps and bruises—and the soreness and stiffness they create from head to toe—are not injuries. You're supposed to be bumped, bruised, and sore as hell. There were times when I was so bumped, bruised, and sore that the coaches needed a calendar to clock me in the forty-yard dash. On most Mondays after a game, practice sounded like a MASH unit with all of the collective moaning and groaning.

The fact is, if you aren't a little banged up, then you haven't been doing very much on the field.

Talent alone is never enough in pro football. It takes talent plus toughness. If you're a quarterback, what good is it to have a tremendous throwing arm if you can't withstand the punishment you receive before, while, and after you release the ball? If you're a running back, what good is it to have great quickness and cutting ability if you can't hold up under the constant pounding that goes with the position? If you're a wide receiver, the softest hands and fastest feet in the world won't help if one teeth-rattling, over-the-middle lick intimidates you and throws off your game.

Players who have been blue-chip athletes all their lives are susceptible to contact just like everyone else. In fact, if they've been drafted high enough, they can count on getting hit a little bit harder than those drafted on the lower rounds or signed as free agents. As a fifth-round choice, I know I always saved my best shots for the number one and two picks. That's because I was always trying to prove I was every bit as good as they were, if not better.

There are two basic kinds of toughness—physical and mental. Physical toughness is something certain players are just born with; they have that mean streak that automatically takes over in the heat of battle, regardless of their off-the-field personalities. Mental toughness is something players must develop—and quickly—in order to survive in the violent world of the NFL.

I know there are a lot of ingredients that go into making an outstanding football player. I'm sure I weigh toughness far too strongly. But because of my approach to the game, because I wasn't the most gifted athlete ever to play professional football myself, because I needed something extra to become a longtime starter and three-time Pro Bowler, toughness is the one ingredient that has always mattered the most to me.

You're supposed to have the raw skills; if you didn't, you wouldn't be in the league in the first place. What we're talking about is the thing that, more often than not, separates those who become champions from those who don't.

My *Tough Guy Hall of Fame*, chosen from among those I played with and against during my NFL career:

QUARTERBACKS

There are few quarterbacks in league history who have been subjected to the physical abuse Archie Manning took when the Saints were fielding some of the worst offensive lines ever assembled (that is, before I arrived in New Orleans). With all of the time Archie spent on his back, counting the rafters in the Superdome, it's a wonder he didn't become an architect after his retirement. It takes a special kind of courage to keep picking up your crumpled body after a sack and returning to the huddle—especially when you know damn well the same thing is going to happen again and continue happening throughout the game. But no matter how hard he was hit on a play, Archie always came back for more. His shoulders had sustained so much damage from repeated contact with the ground that he started throwing sidearm. The man may have looked like Huck Finn, but he played like the Terminator.

Joe Ferguson, my Buffalo teammate for two years, was just a farm kid from Louisiana who happened to be an NFL quarterback. He didn't know the meaning of the word glamorous. His personality probably was more appropriate for an offensive lineman than a glamour boy, which may explain why he was so much tougher than the average guy at his position. He also was a hell of a lot stronger than the average quarterback—he had to be strong to throw the ball as hard as he did in the face of those gale-force winds whipping off Lake Erie. Joe demonstrated the kind of character he had when, despite being severely hobbled by an ankle injury, he led us to a victory over San Francisco for the 1980 AFC Eastern Division championship, completing twelve of twenty passes and guiding us to a pair of touchdowns in the first half. Two weeks later, we nearly rode that powerful arm of his to a playoff triumph over San Diego, until the pain in his ankle became unbearable. One of my fondest memories of Ferguson is the game in which he retaliated against a defender who had started a fight with Joe's longtime teammate, left guard Reggie McKenzie, after a touchdown. Fergy pulled the guy off Reggie, jumped on his chest, and started punching him in the face. That may not have been the world's brightest move, but it certainly made everyone else on the field and in the stands take notice. Those of us on the offensive line were especially appreciative that the man for whom we took the lumps was willing to deliver a few on behalf of one of our own. Besides, quarterbacks aren't supposed to be *that* nasty. I can honestly say I'd feel comfortable if, while sitting in a bar filled with Hell's Angels, the only friendly face I saw was Fergy's.

These career statistics say it best about Fran Tarkenton's

toughness: 674 carries for 3,674 yards and thirty-two touch-downs, and an NFL-record 483 sacks. I don't know of any other quarterback in the game who could run as much as he did, get hit as much as he got hit, and still function as a top-flight passer (he's the NFL's all-time leader for passing yards with 47,003, attempts with 6,467, and completions with 3,686). And play in the league for eighteen years (with Min-nesota and the New York Giants)! And make the Hall of Fame! Obviously, it was poor pass protection that forced Tar-kenton to flee for his life. But the constant threat posed by scrambling and his ability to throw on the run only enhanced his overall effectiveness. Bobby Douglass also ran quite a bit for Chicago between 1969 and 1975, even setting an NFL record. Of course, Douglass didn't run out of desperation as much as stupidity—he usually didn't know when or where to throw the ball.

As much as it hurts to do this, I must include Roger Stau-bach on my list of all-time tough quarterbacks. It hurts, first, because he's an ex–Dallas Cowboy; second, because he has always been so damned squeaky clean. He just doesn't fit what I consider the image of a hard-nosed pro football player. But he withstood a great deal of pounding, seldom missing a game during his eleven-year career. He must have had about twenty concussions, dating back to his days at Navy, and played the entire second half of a game against Washington with fractured ribs. In training camp before the 1976 season, Roger actually got into a fistfight with his backup, Clint Long-ley, and wound up on top. A short time later, Longley was waived. But before he left camp, he sucker-punched Stau-bach in the eye as Roger had both arms raised while putting on his shoulder pads. Longley fled the scene and has not crossed Roger's path since. After the season, Staubach and I wound up sitting next to each other on the flight to the Pro

Bowl. We got into an argument about something, and I couldn't believe my eyes when, all of a sudden, he stood up like he wanted to fight me. I said, "Hey, Rog, you'd better sit down. This is no backup quarterback you're messing with here." He sat down, but I had to respect him for his courage. Or was it temporary insanity?

The thing that made Kenny Stabler so tough wasn't his ability to cope with the physical abuse others gave him; it was his ability to cope with the physical abuse he gave himself. He's the only guy I knew who, on Game Day, looked worse in person than he did in the photograph on his driver's license. He was the only player in the league who had to wear a seat belt while sitting on the bench. But Kenny was a lot like Bobby Layne in that, no matter how much drinking and carousing he did the night before, he'd always give his best effort on Sunday. Look at what he accomplished in ten years with the Oakland Raiders: a Super Bowl victory, 1976 NFL Player of the Year, and three Pro Bowls. Having experienced the sheer agony of a Game Day hangover, I can truly appreciate the magnitude of performing well under those conditions.

Joe Namath's toughness began with his mouth. He said a lot of things that wound up in big newspaper headlines and, in turn, all over his opponents' locker-room bulletin boards. People criticized him for being too brash and cocky, but to me, those were the qualities that made Namath the great quarterback he was for the New York Jets. He always created a situation in which he had to put his talent where his mouth was. And he usually did. He was absolutely fearless in the pocket, no matter how badly it collapsed around him. Many quarterbacks begin dancing up a storm when that happens, and usually, when the music stops, there is no gain. Not Namath. His cleats would stay riveted to the ground as he looked for an open target. Seven days after suffering a fractured cheekbone from the flying elbow of Raider defensive lineman Ike Lassiter, Namath donned a special mask and threw for 343 yards against San Diego. But perhaps the most daring thing Broadway Joe ever did was pose in a pair of panty hose for a Beautymist commerical. A lot of people were outraged, and those who envied him for his booze-and-broads lifestyle were very disappointed—especially since Namath's shaved legs looked almost *too* good as the camera panned its way up from his toes. But if the truth be known, before the use of thermal underwear became widespread, we all wore panty hose under our football pants to help us stay warm. Equipment men throughout the league were more than a little embarrassed about having to walk into lingerie departments and buy panty hose for ''full-figure girls'' by the case.

I consider almost anybody who played for any length of time in the 1950s and 1960s tough. I always considered myself a throwback to those eras. But there were a few quarterbacks who played back then who had the toughness to still be around during my first few years in the league. Among those are George Blanda, whose career began in the late 1940s with the Bears and ended in 1975 with the Raiders; Johnny Unitas, who broke in with Baltimore in 1955 and retired with San Diego in 1973; Earl Morrall, Sonny Jurgensen, Len Dawson, and Billy Kilmer.

Blanda is the only NFL player who, on the day he retired, collected both his final paycheck and his first pension check.

How tough was Kilmer? Early in his career, he was in a car accident and nearly had to have his leg amputated. The doctors told him, ''Sorry, son, but you'll never play football again.'' Billy said, ''Wanna bet?''

Jim Hart also had tremendous longevity. He joined the Cardinals six years before I came along, and didn't leave until 1983, a year after my retirement (he finished his career with Washington in 1984). Jim was as tough as they come, but with the kind of pass protection we gave him, he hardly got touched through most of the 1970s.

Other quarterbacks I'd put in the all-toughness category are Terry Bradshaw, Jim Plunkett, Joe Montana, and Bert Jones. I remember hearing stories about Jones kicking defenders who were a little too aggressive when they knocked him out of bounds. I liked that.

Bob Griese had tremendous talent, but I can't classify him as a particularly tough individual. He was too much of a pretty boy. I'll never forget that, during the bench-clearing donnybrook between the Cardinals and Dolphins on Thanksgiving Day in 1977, one of the few players who never left the sidelines was Griese. I always thought attendance at team brawls in the NFL was mandatory.

RUNNING BACKS

From what I saw and heard, trying to tackle Larry Csonka was a lot like trying to tackle a manhole cover. One look at that human battering ram on film was enough to cure me of any desire to switch to defense. He was among the few running backs in the league who never ran around defenders, just over them. I'm sure his offensive linemen loved blocking for Zonk, because there were some defenders who really didn't have to be blocked—they simply stepped out of Larry's way. When he ran, it wasn't always easy to tell the hunters from the hunted.

O. J. Simpson was so graceful, his rushing was an art form. But make no mistake—Juice had to be tough to gain all of the yards he did on those pathetic Buffalo teams of the early 1970s. I mean, who wasn't keying on him week after week?

By taking him out of the game, a team would eliminate the only chance the Bills had for victory. And here was a guy out of the sun and fun of USC who was able to establish himself as one of the game's all-time greats in the snow and the ice and the cold that are a part of playing football in Buffalo, New York.

I had the pleasure of being Walter Payton's teammate in a couple of Pro Bowls. The first time I opened a hole for the guy, I literally felt the shock waves as he ran past me. Walter's position during his thirteen seasons with the Bears was halfback, but he played more like a small fullback. You rarely saw him run for the sidelines to avoid contact, as Franco Harris tended to do. He would just barrel ahead, taking as many hits as necessary to gain that extra inch. It's saying quite a bit that the league's all-time rushing leader (with 16,726 yards) was also known for being a very willing blocker. There have been more than a few halfbacks in the NFL who felt blocking was beneath them.

Terry Metcalf was one of the scrappier football players I've ever seen. He didn't take any guff from anybody. When we were teammates in St. Louis, I actually saw him throw punches at defenders who tried to get an extra shot or two at him. That's risky business for any running back— especially one who stands only five-foot-ten and weighs 185 pounds. But inch for inch and pound for pound, you'd be hard-pressed to find a tougher guy at any position in the NFL. Seeing all that toughness in such a small package was quite an inspiration to those of us with whom Terry looked eye-to-navel.

You might say John Riggins was the Bobby Layne/Kenny Stabler of running backs, a guy who liked to party hard before and after a game. When he wasn't overcoming the aftereffects of partying, big John was often recovering from the aftereffects of the extreme punishment he took as a plodding, straight-ahead runner. They didn't call him "The Diesel" for nothing. But he wasn't stopped very often, especially near the goal line—he ranks second on the NFL's all-time list for rushing touchdowns with 104—where even fractional gains are difficult. A chronic back problem caused him to miss quite a few practices and spend more than a few nights sleeping on hardwood floors late in his career. Of course, Riggo never was a great believer in practicing even when he was healthy. As for sleeping on floors, that's how he finished the night at a 1985 black-tie dinner in Washington, D.C. He got drunk, passed out on the foot of the wife of Senator John Glenn, and snored through a speech by George Bush (not that there weren't more sober members of the audience doing the same). But it was earlier in the evening that John *really* made a spectacle of himself, asking Supreme Court Justice Sandra Day O'Connor when she would pose for a pinup poster. Her failure to see the humor in the remark prompted Riggins to say, "Loosen up, Sandy, baby. You're too tight."

Larry Brown, who played for the Redskins, and John Brockington, who played for the Packers, also were bruising rushers. And when it came to guys you'd want next to you in a foxhole, Rocky Bleier would have to be at the top of the list. On top of being a productive little runner for Pittsburgh, the man also was a Vietnam veteran.

Tony Dorsett has had an outstanding career in Dallas. But if he had the heart of a Csonka or a Metcalf, he'd have been gaining three hundred yards a game in his prime.

Another notable Cowboy, Duane Thomas, was a pretty good and tough runner in the brief time he played. But as bizarre a person as he was, the only all-anything team I'd put him on is an all-flake team. In fact, I'd make him the captain—providing Jim Brown, the legendary fullback for Cleveland in the 1950s and sixties, would agree to relinquish the title.

WIDE RECEIVERS

Fred Biletnikoff and I were in the Superstars competition in Sarasota, Florida, one year and had a little time to kill between events. Freddy was puffing on a cigarette and down by his feet were the butts of about twenty cigarettes he already had smoked. I asked him what his next event was. "The mile run," he said, matter-of-factly. I had to bite down hard on my lip so I wouldn't burst out laughing. But sure enough, that little smokestack went out there and took third. Now *that's* what I call tough! Rumor also has it that, during his fourteen-year career with Oakland, Freddy would smoke ten cigarettes at halftime of every game. That was in addition to the two packs he smoked before the opening kickoff. Biletnikoff was hardly a speed-burner, but he had great hands—even when not all the bones were intact—and he finished his career with 589 receptions for 8,974 yards and seventy-six touchdowns. Another thing that helped Freddy quite a bit was stickum. He wore so much of the stuff that the ball would cling anywhere from the elbows down.

Frank Lewis, with whom I played in Buffalo, had a quiet mental toughness that probably was more visible to teammates and coaches than outsiders. Late in his thirteen-year career, he'd come out of a game so banged up it seemed impossible for him to be ready to play the following week. But each day, little by little, he'd put himself back together and, when Game Day arrived, he was there. Frank was always the last one out of the trainer's room, spending whatever time was necessary to get the treatment he needed. But you never heard him gripe, privately or publicly, about the pain or the considerable effort it took to keep himself on the active roster. Frank may not have been in the same class as Lynn Swann or Paul Warfield in terms of pure talent, but he made the most out of everything he did have. Which is something I can closely identify with. Another thing about Frank: He had the most deceptive speed of any player I've ever seen. He'd sort of glide along, opening hardly any distance between himself and the defensive back. Then, *boom*, he'd be wide open for a deep pass. Small wonder he set two Bills records in 1981 with seventy receptions for 1,244 yards.

Of the 178 regular-season games the Seattle Seahawks have played in Steve Largent's twelve NFL seasons, he has missed only three. He was sidelined once in 1983 with a knee problem, once in 1982 with knee trouble, and once in 1979 with a broken wrist. You want tough? The wrist was broken *before* he caught two touchdown passes in a game against Denver, the second TD coming late in the fourth quarter and giving the Seahawks their first victory over the Broncos. I admire Steve's willingness to play hurt, but even more impressive is his willingness to practice hurt. I can't count the number of guys I've heard try to weasel their way out of practice, using every lame excuse from a hangnail to their wife's period. But Largent has taken part in practically every regular-season workout in Seattle since 1976. Besides longevity, the other reason he is the NFL's all-time reception leader with 752 is that there isn't anyone in the league who runs more precise pass routes. The guy amazes me with the way he's able to put a different wrinkle into each pattern and keep defensive backs guessing. And he's one of the best blocking receivers in the league, even with the crack-back block outlawed. Receivers used to love to block when they could use the crack-back, because it allowed them to blind-side defenders. But ever since they've been required to take them on face to face, receivers have become less and less willing to sacrifice their bodies for the running back. Largent is a noticeable exception.

Lynn Swann may have been as graceful as his name, but that didn't mean he didn't sacrifice his body at every turn to make the most difficult of catches. I'm sure there were more than a few defensive backs who were out to do a little *bird-hunting* whenever they played the Steelers.

Paul Warfield and Otis Taylor, too, withstood their fair share of pops and became dominant performers for Miami and Kansas City.

TIGHT ENDS

Jackie Smith was the proverbial old-style tight end—six-foot-four and 230 pounds, strong like a bull, a crushing blocker, and a reliable receiver. He also was big on revenge. My former Cardinal teammate would always look to even the score with someone who gave him a cheap shot. In fact, I think he actually preferred blocking to receiving, because it gave him the opportunity to go downfield and put out the lights of the defensive donkey who'd made the mistake of hitting him late or diving at his knees. He was one of the few tight ends I ever played with who was accepted as a full-fledged member of the offensive line.

There almost wasn't a pass thrown that was too hard for Dave Casper to catch. He'd dive for the ball. Leap for it. Twist, turn, and do a cartwheel for it. And no matter how tight the coverage, he'd usually come up with the reception. There were few, if any, defensive backs in the league who could outmuscle his six-foot-four, 230-pound frame. Plus, as a standout offensive tackle during his junior year at Notre

Dame, he had the knowhow to deliver blocks that left a number of defenders temporarily unable to remember their names. Casper was an intellectual, and that made him a bit of an outcast with the Oakland Raiders. But in case anyone doubted his toughness off the field, he'd occasionally kick chairs across a meeting room or turn over a water cooler.

I heard stories that Mike Ditka, during his days as a tight end, would actually growl before the snap and warn defenders lined up across from him, "I am going to kick your ass all day today." And he usually did. Mike doesn't seem to have lost any of that aggressiveness as head coach of the Chicago Bears, for whom he played before going to Philadelphia and Dallas. He was so frustrated after one game, he punched an equipment locker hard enough to break his hand.

Bob Trumpy had his share of wars with linebackers while playing for Cincinnati. Defenders used to say that Tom Mitchell—who played for Oakland, Baltimore, and San Francisco—was so nasty, he even smelled bad.

The Chargers' Kellen Winslow, who redefined the tight end position with his multidimensional athletic ability, displayed his toughness by rebounding from a career-threatening knee injury.

OFFENSIVE LINEMEN

My teammate Tom Banks had a lot of skill and knowledge of the game, but it was his toughness that allowed him to survive ten years in the NFL. As a six-foot-two, 245-pound center, he found that most of those lined up across from him were larger and stronger. But they often wound up losing the one-on-one duel. Tommy had great upper-body strength, and used every bit of it, along with a relentless, streetfighting approach to the game, to establish himself as a Pro

Bowler. He was nicknamed Wolfman because of his shaggy appearance, but it also accurately described his style of play. I used to get a little nervous myself when Tommy would start to howl when we were at the line of scrimmage.

Dan Dierdorf was born to be an offensive tackle. Not only did he have the height (six-foot-three) and the weight (280 pounds), but he also had a great deal of strength. Trying to move Dan was like trying to move the Gateway Arch in St. Louis. He had enough power to drive-block like a giant snowplow, great footwork, and superior intelligence. But of all of his many All-World attributes, the most important, in my opinion, was his toughness. In his thirteen years in the NFL, Dan could get every bit as dirty as yours truly. I'm sure more than a few defenders around the league had to think twice about screwing with him after they witnessed, during a Monday-night game in 1977, Dan lift New York Giants linebacker Brian Kelley off the ground and ram him, headfirst, into a goal post.

Like Dierdorf, the Raiders' Gene Upshaw was huge—six-foot-five and 265 pounds—and he was as nasty as they come. The thing I liked best about Gene was that he shared my protect-the-quarterback-at-all-costs philosophy. Ken Stabler loved him for it, of course, because it was Snake's ass he was so bent on protecting. During one game between Oakland and Cleveland, Joe "Turkey" Jones, the Browns' homicidal defensive end, blind-sided Stabler long after he released a pass. Upshaw plotted his revenge in the huddle, and on the very next play, Jones wound up on his knees. Gene then gave him a taste of his own cheap-shot medicine and the "Turkey" was cooked, leaving the field on a cart and never returning the rest of the day. Upshaw also subscribed to the hate-building ritual I followed the week before a game. One time, as Oakland was preparing to face Washington, he caught wind of some uncomplimentary remarks Redskins defensive tackle Diron Talbert had made about the Raiders in the press. Gene saw to it that Talbert had a very quiet afternoon and publicly blasted him after Oakland won in overtime. His selection to the Hall of Fame says it all about the talent Gene displayed during his sixteen-year career. And he commanded a great deal of league-wide respect, which was why he replaced Ed Garvey as executive director of the NFL Players Association. But judging from the difficulties in the 1987 collective-bargaining talks between the union and management, I'd say Gene was a much better offensive guard than labor negotiator.

Ed White, too, was tough—he had to be tough, and talented, to survive for fifteen seasons as a guard with Minnesota and San Diego, then play two more years as a tackle with the Chargers. He also was a little bit strange—his idea of a good time was tearing a Los Angeles telephone directory in half with his bare hands. To no one's surprise, White was the NFL's wrist-wrestling champion in 1975. Now that he's out of football, Big Ed's able to devote most of his attention to the thing he loves best: making figurines out of brass. Somehow, it isn't easy picturing a barrel-chested, six-foot-two, 285-pounder doing something as delicate and intricate as that.

A few other all-time tough offensive linemen are Jim Otto, who spent fifteen seasons playing center for the Raiders; Art Shell, a tackle for the Raiders; Jeff Van Note, who survived for eighteen years as a center for the Atlanta Falcons, and guard Reggie McKenzie, O. J. Simpson's main man in Buffalo.

Despite being six-foot-five and weighing 300 pounds, Shell was extremely light on his feet, thanks to his basketball-playing days in college. On the other hand, the footwork of John Hannah, widely considered the greatest offensive guard of all time, left an awful lot to be desired, especially when it came to pass protection. True, he had great speed to pull out and make blocks on the run. But when it came to shuffling to stay with a pass-rusher, when he had to rely more on finesse than his awesome strength, he usually had two left feet. The man wouldn't have made it past his first lesson in an Arthur Murray dance studio.

Another overrated offensive lineman is Pittsburgh center Mike Webster. He is a creature of the 3–4 defensive alignment, which positions a tackle right in his face. With his great upper-body strength, Webster is able to win a majority of his battles at the line. But against a four-man line, he isn't nearly as effective.

I don't know how Tom Mack established himself as one of the game's foremost guards while playing for the Rams. He's one of the few guys at my position who did more holding than I did. On the other hand, maybe that wasn't such a bad technique, after all.

DEFENSIVE LINEMEN

The Mean in Mean Joe Greene was firmly established during his rookie season with the Steelers. Besides being tossed out of two games that year, he KO'd a quarterback, Fran Tarkenton, with a late hit, and punched out an offensive guard, the Vikings' Jim Vellone. Later in his career, he got away with spitting on the toughest of tough guys, Dick Butkus, and stomping on Cleveland guard Bob McKay, kicking him in the nuts and legs, before a bunch of Browns came to the rescue. I thought I had reached an all-time low point in my career when I publicly wished harm to the family of a referee who had called a phantom holding penalty on me when I was with Buffalo. But consider this comment from Greene on referees in general: "I wish a bolt of lightning would come down and strike one of their hearts out." If you were an opposing quarterback or running back, that bolt of lightning usually was Greene.

The Cowboys' Randy White is a classic example of what I call a football warrior. He'll just never quit when he's locked in a battle with an offensive lineman. He's going to keep fighting you and fighting you until he makes the tackle or hears the whistle. Randy's one of those guys who's extremely talented and physically gifted—with quickness and tremendous upper-body strength in his six-foot-four, 265-pound frame—and has a mean streak to boot. He'll pick guys up and toss them around like rag dolls. No wonder he made nine trips to the Pro Bowl and already has a spot awaiting him in Canton, Ohio.

The thing that concerned me the most about going up against Herb Orvis, who played for the Lions and Colts, was that he was even meaner and nastier than I was. In one game between Detroit and St. Louis, I legwhipped him so hard in the thigh, I actually turned his steel thigh pad inside out. He went down, holding his leg in agony. Then, for good measure, Dierdorf jabbed a knee into his rib cage. As the trainers got him onto a stretcher and carried him off the field, Orvis was cursing and threatening us at the top of his lungs: "I'm gonna kill you guys! You got that? I'm gonna kill you!" We were just thankful they had him strapped down tight.

Any time the Cardinals appeared on the Bears' schedule during my St. Louis years, tackle Jim Osborne was always ready for me—more so than almost any other defensive lineman I faced in my career. He would ignore everything else going on around us and spend the whole game fighting me. It wasn't a case of his trying to conquer me so he could pursue the quarterback or the running back. He just wanted to whup me for the sake of whupping me. It wasn't the Bears versus the Cardinals when we played; it was Jim Osborne versus Conrad Dobler. And no matter what methods I used against him, he'd always come back harder the next time, forcing me to do the same. For sixty minutes, we were totally absorbed in each other. Of course, I always considered it a victory whenever a defensive donkey spent more time pounding on me than on those I was paid to block for.

Lyle Alzado, a defensive end who toiled with Denver and Cleveland before winding up where he truly belonged—with the Raiders—incorporated street toughness into his game. He'd fight you at the drop of a hat. Hell, he even had the courage to step into the ring with Muhammad Ali for an exhibition boxing match. But I suppose anyone who isn't afraid to admit that Yankton College is his alma mater has to be pretty tough.

Jack Youngblood, a defensive end for the Rams, hobbled through two-and-a-half games on a fractured fibula. Now if *that* isn't tough, I don't know what is. As unfriendly as our rivalry was, I'd be remiss if I didn't include another L.A. defensive lineman, Merlin Olsen, on my all-toughness list. I'm sure, if we had met in his younger days, I'd have had a lot more trouble handling him. The Vikings' Carl Eller and Kansas City's Curley Culp, pro football's first and best nose tackle, also have to be included.

San Francisco had an ornery defensive end named Cedrick Hardman. And the Browns and Chiefs had one of the league's scariest-looking players in Gene Upshaw's brother, Marvin, who played defensive end. Marvin had the biggest, widest eyes I'd ever seen, and they always seemed bloodshot. Looking into those menacing peepers, you didn't know whether he was going to try to beat you with football skills, or pull out a knife and just stab you to death.

LINEBACKERS

Dick Butkus's orneriness is legendary. There was no tactic too dirty for this killer Bear. MacArthur Lane, a running back for Green Bay, watched in horror once as Butkus grabbed one of his ankles and tried, unsuccessfully, to break it in two over his knee like a piece of kindling. He also attempted to claw the eyes out of Charlie Sanders, a tight end for Detroit, and left countless others bruised, battered, or unconscious. If he wasn't elbowing somebody in the ribs, he was kneeing him in the groin. I was a big biter, but Butkus left at least as many teeth marks in his wake, if not more. He even bit the fingers of an official, something I'd never dream of doing. Doug Plank, former head-hunting defensive back for Chicago, once said: "On the sound track of Bears' films, Butkus . . . sounds like a lion chewing on a big hunk of meat." What a lot of people might not realize is that he didn't put very many licks, or bites, on offensive linemen during his career. In fact, he'd work to get around them with minimal contact. Then he'd make the ball-carrier wish he had never been born. Though people thought of Butkus as a Neanderthal whose vocabulary started and stopped with "Kill," he really was pretty intelligent. He knew that offensive linemen never got the football—by avoiding us, he could pack the maximum wallop when it really counted. I also think he made a special effort to stay away from me, because when we met late in his career, he knew I wouldn't be afraid to go after his deteriorating knees.

My one and only encounter with Packer great Ray Nitschke came in a preseason game in 1972, the year his NFL career ended and mine began. As brash and cocky as I might have been, I couldn't help but feel a bit intimidated to be sharing the field with this bald, toothless middle linebacker who'd been terrorizing pro football since 1958 and was on his way to the Hall of Fame. When I noticed we were wearing the same number, 66, I was tempted to ask if he wanted me to change to a different one. Despite the fact Nitschke was nearing the end of the line, everything I saw him do that day through my twenty-one-year-old eyes seemed tough. Sometimes, as I would find out firsthand over the years, the most effective weapon of all is your reputation and mystique.

The nickname Ted Hendricks was given while playing outside linebacker for the Raiders said it best about his style of play. He was known as "Kick-'em," which is short for "Kick-'em-in-the-Head Ted." He also is among the freest of the free spirits ever to play in the NFL.

Besides Butkus and Nitschke, other middle linebackers I regard as among the toughest of the tough are former Kansas City Chief Willie Lanier and Mike Curtis of the Colts. Curtis was known as "The Animal," and with good reason. Perhaps the most damaging hit he ever made occurred when he forearmed a fan who tried to run away with the ball with three minutes left in a game between Baltimore and Miami. The guy not only dropped the ball, but also fell unconscious and took two weeks to recover from the shot to his neck.

Pittsburgh's Jack Lambert shared the natural mean streak that Curtis and other linebackers possessed, but he also had something that others at his position didn't—the great "Steel Curtain" defensive line with Mean Joe Greene, L. C. Greenwood, Ernie Holmes, and Dwight White. Those guys could make any linebacker look good.

John Madden, head coach of the Oakland Raiders, put Phil Villapiano in the same class as Butkus as far as being a guy who just loved to hit. And I couldn't agree more. There wasn't another player on those great Raider teams who embodied the franchise's rough-and-rowdy spirit, on and off the field, more than Villapiano. When we became teammates in

Buffalo in 1980, he still had the Raider spirit, even as a reserve inside linebacker.

DEFENSIVE BACKS

Larry Wilson and I were teammates only for my rookie season in St. Louis, after which he retired. But it didn't take long for me to find out there wasn't a tougher player in the NFL than old Larry. Not only did the man play a 1965 game against Pittsburgh with two broken and heavily bandaged hands, he intercepted a Bill Nelsen pass with them and returned it thirty-five yards. This Hall-of-Famer also has the distinction of being the first safety in league history to blitz. The only guys who blitzed in the early 1960s were linebackers. But the Cardinals' defensive strategists changed all that when they instructed Larry to rush the quarterback from his regular free safety position. Soon, every team in the league followed suit. Although he stood only six feet and weighed 190 pounds, Larry proved that a safety, with enough heart and soul, could be every bit as effective in that situation as a linebacker.

Jack Tatum didn't merely like contact; he lived for it. He got a genuine thrill out of delivering all of those snot-bubblers during his nine-year career with the Raiders and Oilers. Some defensive backs covered wide receivers. Jack buried them. There were even times, in the course of hitting a receiver, when he'd knock out some of his own teammates who were in on the coverage. And, no, he shouldn't be viewed as a cold, ruthless villain for his crippling hit on New England's Darryl Stingley in 1978. What happened to Stingley was very unfortunate and I'm sure he'll never be able to forgive Tatum for putting him into a wheelchair. But there was absolutely nothing illegal about the play. Stingley slanted inside and jumped to make the catch, and Jack gave him a good, clean shot—very hard, but clean. There isn't a coach around who wouldn't want his free safety to be as hard-hitting as Tatum, although he was a rare find. As I've said over and over, it's a violent game; accidents happen.

Pat Fischer was a little guy (five-foot-nine, 179 pounds), but managed to survive in the league for sixteen years—with St. Louis and Washington—at a position that involved him in a lot of collisions with bigger and stronger bodies. That alone shows Pat was a tough cornerback. I found out just how tough during a game when I was with the Cardinals and he was with the Redskins. I was coming around to block on a screen, and Pat came to a stop so he could slip underneath me. But as I went by, I stuck out my arm and clotheslined him. He hit the ground and, having lost my balance in the process, I fell, too. The next thing I knew, Pat was already on his feet, kicking me in retaliation. The best players never give an inch.

I had a similar experience with Ken Houston, when he was playing safety for Washington. On a sweep in another Cardinals-Redskins game, I was coming around and just as I was about to throw a block at old Kenny, he swung a forearm up as hard as he could right into my facemask. I mean, he brought that thing up from his shoes and hit me so hard, my head hit the ground first. The only consolation was that he knocked himself down at the same time and was unable to make the tackle. As we watched the play on film the next morning, Jim Hanifan laughed and said, "Well, Conrad, I'm happy to see you got your man. But there's got to be an easier way to do it, don't you think?" Unfortunately, that hit drew a lot of attention throughout the league, which was something I discovered soon after I was traded to New Orleans. Within minutes after I met several of my new Saints teammates, a couple of them said, "Hey, we saw the film of that Washington game when Ken Houston just about took your head off." Gee, thanks for reminding me, guys. Kenny also intimidated quite a few quarterbacks during his Hall-of-Fame career—he returned nine interceptions for touchdowns, a league record.

At six-foot-three and 200 pounds, Pittsburgh's Mel Blount was one of the largest cornerbacks ever to play the game. He also was one of the strongest and toughest. Besides reaching over and around receivers to intercept and knock down passes, Blount's octopus arms also were good for wrapping around pass-catchers and throwing them down. With or without the ball in their hands. Although not nearly as tall, the Steelers' Donnie Shell brings the same aggressiveness to strong safety that Blount brought to cornerback.

They didn't call him "Torpedo" Shell for nothing.

KICKERS

It's hard to imagine a placekicker appearing on anyone's all-toughness team, but Jim Bakken is an exception. He was a natural athlete first and a placekicker second. He played quarterback and safety at Wisconsin and was our third-string QB in St. Louis. Most placekickers aren't really part of the clubs they're on, at least as far as those of us who fought the wars were concerned. They just don't fit into the mainstream. They stand around in practice, scratching their hemorrhoids, so they won't tire their legs out. But Jim's background as a quarterback and his athletic prowess gave him the skills to run the scout-team offense that serviced the defense in practice, and he was the guy who would get the call during a game if Jim Hart and his backup went down with injuries. He also had enough baseball talent to take batting practice with the other Cardinal team that occupied Busch Stadium without embarrassing himself. He would actually knock the stuffing out of Bob Gibson's pitches. He also was a great handball and racquetball player—one of the best in Missouri. Oh, and he was one hell of a placekicker, too, setting all kinds of Cardinal records for field goals and point-after attempts in his seventeen seasons.

It took a lot of courage for Tom Dempsey, holder of the record for the longest field goal in NFL history, to play with half a foot and a deformed arm. George Blanda was another placekicker with a lot of courage. But George didn't like to be called a placekicker. He always told people he was a quarterback who kicked on the side.

The toughest punter around was another Raider, Ray Guy. His first love was safety, where he played in college, but Oakland made him a first-round draft pick because of his All-Pro punting ability. At six-foot-three and 190 pounds, and blessed with outstanding athletic ability, Ray was as rare as they come. In high school, he played quarterback and attracted interest from major-league baseball teams for his pitching arm.

■　　■　　■

Genuine toughness can't be taught and it can't be learned. It's a personality trait, something you're born with. You either have it or you don't.

Sure, you can act the part, and even be very good at it. A number of former NFL players did. A number of those currently in the league do, for the benefit of their opponents, their teammates, their coaches, their fans, and most of all, themselves. But deep down inside, they put limitations on just how far they'll go to make a play—how much they're willing to sacrifice themselves, how much they're willing to punish themselves to punish the opposition.

That's not to say I think everyone who only played the part of a tough guy was a bad football player. For instance, I respected the hell out of Philadelphia Eagles linebacker Bill Bergey. He was a great player, better than most others at his position in the middle to late 1970s. But, in the final analysis, he wasn't what I'd call genuinely tough. Not like Dick Butkus or Ray Nitschke or even Larry Stallings, my former Cardinal teammate who moonlighted as a top executive at a steel company. Bergey acted and sounded tough and mean on the field, but you never believed it was coming from the heart. You just knew he felt, as a highly regarded player at a highly aggressive position, he had a reputation to uphold, an image to maintain.

The truth was, Bill relied much more on his skills and knowledge of the game than he ever did on toughness. And his skills were legendary. He played in a lot of Pro Bowls.

I just feel that being a truly tough individual, physically or mentally, can only enhance your chances for success in the NFL. It prepares you for the game's violent nature. It helps you to avoid intimidation. It gives you the ammunition to be an intimidator. And it makes you more tolerant of pain than someone who is neither physically nor mentally tough. True, if you're blessed with all of the natural talent in the world, you have a better-than-even chance of making somebody's roster and performing well. But if you have toughness in addition to those other qualities, you're likely to reach the heights.

It's no coincidence so many of the players I've listed in this chapter are present or future Hall-of-Famers.

I don't see very many players of that type in today's NFL,

at least not among the players who entered the league in the 1980s. And I think that is a reflection of how the game has changed from a strategic standpoint. The roles of players on both sides of the ball, particularly linemen and linebackers, have been altered in such a way that one-on-one matchups aren't as prevalent as they were in the 1950s, sixties, and seventies. Most teams today play the 3–4 defense, with three linemen and four linebackers. For an offensive guard, that usually means blocking a linebacker. If a linebacker doesn't come your way, then you slide over to help the center with the nose tackle, the man in the middle of the defensive line. And with so much substitution on defense—different personnel for running downs, passing downs, short yardage, and so forth—and all the flip-flopping that goes on across the line, you can wind up blocking four or five different guys through the course of a game.

It's just not the same as when a majority of defensive lines were composed of two tackles and two ends and you knew you were going to go head to head with a certain guy for most of the day. Now, you can't really spend an entire week focusing the brunt of your attention on one man, building up that hatred for him from Monday to Sunday. There are just too many people and too many assignments to worry about. Even with teams that play each other twice a year, you don't see nearly as many you-and-me-and-forget-about-everybody-else showdowns as before. You don't have the grudges, the constant verbal exchanges across the line of scrimmage that carried over from game to game and season to season.

I actually liked it when opponents called me names. That was fun. In today's approach to verbal warfare, players spend most of the time trying to kill each other with kindness. Sometimes, it's hard to tell whether they want to do battle or date.

The 3–4 defense forced teams to change their thinking in the scouting and drafting of centers. They turned away from small, quick guys like Tom Banks and began looking for big, hulking monsters. Small, quick guys no longer could match up against the ever-increasing size of the nose tackles. Ultimately, the 3–4 drove Tommy out of football. On the other hand, Dan Dierdorf got an extra season out of his career when the Cardinals moved him from tackle to center.

Today, the average size for linemen, offensively and defensively, is six-foot-five and 280 pounds. Whatever happened to those short, dumpy "Poppin' Fresh" bodies that used to occupy the trenches? Whatever happened to the offensive linemen who needed thumbtacks to hold up their socks because they had no calf muscles?

Maybe there's something to be said for better football through chemistry.

From a defensive standpoint, the 3–4 has had its greatest impact on the linebacker position. Linebackers today possess as much strength as those who played in the 1950s and sixties and seventies, if not more. But they also must have great speed and quickness. Rather than brawling toe to toe with offensive linemen and stuffing the hole, they try to win their battles with finesse. This is especially true with outside linebackers. If they don't have a lot of sacks, they aren't viewed as productive.

They have to be able to blitz. They have to be able to make plays from sideline to sideline. They have to be able to cover the pass.

More and more, football is turning into a giant chess game between coaches. Offensive and defensive players aren't responsible for each other so much as for areas of the field. There is much greater emphasis on the mental aspect of the game than on the physical aspect. And you have to wonder if this approach is having a dehumanizing effect on the players, if it is forcing them to put less emotion into their performances. You have to wonder if it's making the game too antiseptic.

I seriously doubt a player like me would emerge in the eighties. With the way the game's structured, my concentration would be spread out in too many different places for me to zero in on a target and get myself emotionally worked up. And I just wouldn't be placed into enough situations in which I could piss off guys like Merlin Olsen or Doug Sutherland or Lee Roy Jordan. And if I didn't piss them off, they wouldn't go complaining to the press about me. And if they didn't go complaining to the press about me, nobody would label me the "dirtiest and meanest player in professional football."

The NFL, as a whole, doesn't have as many colorful characters as it did at one time. There's Jim McMahon, the head-butting, headband-wearing, pants-dropping quarterback for the Bears. A definite tough guy, although he does seem to have a problem staying in one piece. But after McMahon, who else is there? It takes more than one guy to shake things up. As it stands now, the game, in terms of off-the-field behavior, is just too damn sophisticated. Too tame. Too boring.

It needs a "Broadway" Joe Namath with a girl (or two) on each arm, partying into the wee hours at his own bar, The Bachelor's Three. It needs a Kenny "Snake" Stabler getting drunk the night before a game and then giving the opposing secondary a hangover the next day. It needs a Ted "Kick-'em" Hendricks arriving for practice, in uniform, on a horse. It needs a John "The Tooz" Matuszak going on an all-night "cruise" a few days before playing in the Super Bowl. It needs a Tom "Wolfman" Banks acting, well, like his nickname suggests.

Of course, I'm sure the characters from the 1950s, like

Bobby Layne and Art Donovan, said the same thing about us. Layne left us all with these words to live by: "My only request is that I draw my last dollar and my last breath at precisely the same instant." Stabler may have tipped a few on the eve of a game, but Layne's the only player I ever heard of who did his drinking at halftime. In his book, *Fatso*, Donovan tells a story about how, in the third quarter of one game, he sacked Layne and nearly passed out from the fumes on his breath.

I'm sure there's a feeling among players from each era that the players from the next era have too much sophistication and not enough toughness. And I think it all goes back to money. We made a hell of a lot more in the seventies and early eighties than the guys who played in the fifties and sixties. Because of that, they saw us as a bunch of fat cats who weren't hungry enough to go all-out every Sunday the way they did. And those playing today are making a hell of a lot more than we did, with much larger portions of their salaries guaranteed and paid up front. And, yes, I have to question whether they have the motivation to go out and break their asses week after week for sixteen weeks.

With so much at stake financially, my not-so-wild guess is that many of them wouldn't want to break a thing.

Picture this: A $300,000-a-year offensive lineman blocking for a $500,000-a-year running back who has just taken the handoff from a $1-million-a-year quarterback. Not to mention the $800,000-a-year defender waiting to make the tackle. On November 30, 1987, a *Monday Night Football* audience witnessed an $18.4-million collision when a pair of rookies, Raiders running back Bo Jackson and Seahawks linebacker Brian Bosworth, met head-on in the end zone of the Kingdome.

Early in my career, that would have bought you an entire *franchise*.

I have to believe astronomical figures like those have an enormous impact on the outlook of the players and coaches. I mean, if you're making $1 million a year, you're likely to think of yourself as a know-it-all superstar, even if, in reality, you have a few things to learn, a little more developing to do.

"I make almost as much money in a week as the coach makes in a year," the player might say to himself. "I'm already set for life. Why do I need to listen to his crap?"

Meanwhile, the coaches, in most cases making considerably less money, take a look at your salary and, perhaps, assume you must be good enough to step right in and produce with minimal instruction. Or they'll at least feel a certain amount of pressure from the owner, the man who has spent all of those bucks, to get you into the starting lineup as quickly as possible, regardless of what you know or don't know.

None would ever admit as much, of course, but coaches have got to be somewhat intimidated by those salaries. Wouldn't anyone in their shoes?

The truth is, no matter how large a player's paycheck is or how good he thinks he is, he needs coaching. The game may look fairly simple and may often come down to physical superiority. But it does require an education process, even for the occasional M.B.A. or Ph.D. who dons a helmet and shoulder pads. In fact, with coaching strategy becoming increasingly complicated year after year, it is more important than ever for a player to listen and learn and study. Again, with so much emphasis on being responsible for an area of the field rather than a warm body, mental mistakes can spell far greater disaster than they did, say, ten years ago.

And they usually do.

If my man got the better of me, if he really kicked my ass

for sixty minutes, I saw it as utter humiliation. It wasn't Conrad Dobler, right offensive guard, losing to another football player. It was Conrad Dobler, the man, being stripped of his pride in front of everybody on the field and the sidelines, as well as the thousands of people in the stands and the millions watching on television.

That isn't an easy feeling to cope with, even if, in the end, we wound up with more points than the other guys. Donny Anderson, a halfback for the Cardinals, came up to me one day early in my career and offered the following advice: "You know, Conrad, you can't continue to play as aggressively as you do and have total disregard for your body. If you want to last a long time in this league, think about your body first. Same thing with Terry Metcalf. If he keeps trying to break all of those tackles and doesn't start hitting the ground quicker, he's not going to last very long."

At the time, I listened and I wondered: Was I right or wrong in playing the way I did? Looking back, I can honestly say I wouldn't have done it any differently. I couldn't.

I know my approach had a lot to do with whatever success I enjoyed as an individual and as part of one of the best offensive lines in NFL history. For me, it was important to know that I could look myself in the mirror each day and say, "Hey, I'm playing the game the way it was meant to be played."

9

Taking It "Lite" in Retirement

Of the few regrets I had upon retiring from the NFL in 1982, the biggest was not having a Super Bowl ring. No ring, and never really getting the opportunity to receive one.

I played for some great teams. I played for the St. Louis Cardinals, and we made the playoffs. I played for the Buffalo Bills, and we made the playoffs. I played for the New Orleans Saints, and we came pretty close to making the playoffs one year.

But in ten seasons in the league, the teams I played on made not one trip to the Super Bowl. That hurts.

The team that I thought had the best chance of making it was the last one I played for—the Bills. We reached the play-offs by winning the AFC East in the final week of the 1980 season, but then blew an eleven-point lead and got bounced by San Diego. Although we sort of backed into the tourna-ment the following year, making it as a wild-card entry, I felt we were as strong as any team in the AFC. Beating the

Jets in New York in the first round made us feel that much stronger.

But then came our heartbreaking loss to Cincinnati, followed by the even larger frustration of watching the Bengals go on to face San Francisco in Super Bowl XVI. We knew that should have been us.

It's very hard for me not to feel a little bit envious when I notice a Super Bowl ring on the finger of another ex-player. It's even harder for me to swallow the fact there are former and current players who received Super Bowl rings without playing a lick before or during the game—they just happened to be in the right place at the right time. I look at those bent and twisted fingers of mine, and I look at all the other deformities that eighteen years of organized football brought me. And I think about all the pain and all the sacrifice—the long, hot July and August afternoons at training camp, the cold November and December practices, the endless film sessions.

And I ask myself, Was it worth it?

The answer is always the same: Hell, yes.

Never reaching the Super Bowl is a big disappointment, sure. But the way I look at it, it's only about twenty-five percent of what I wanted to achieve as a pro football player. I'm very satisfied with everything else I did.

Just making an NFL roster as a rookie was a tremendous accomplishment, especially when you consider that most who try fail, and it took me two tries to succeed. I also helped two teams make a combined four playoff appearances. I was part of some of the best offensive lines the NFL has ever seen. I was regarded, at one time, as among the very best at my position, being selected to three consecutive Pro Bowls.

And I got a lot of publicity.

There have been a number of pretty good offensive linemen who toiled in obscurity their entire careers. It's the nature of the position to be unrecognized and unappreciated. But I was an exception, receiving as much national exposure as players at the so-called glamour positions—sometimes more. Granted, not all of the exposure was flattering, but when you're an offensive lineman, you really can't afford to be choosy.

The reason I say the Super Bowl was only twenty-five percent of what I wanted to accomplish as a player is that, as an individual, you have only so much control over the process of getting there. Everybody on the team has to play well enough and stay healthy enough to make it happen. For instance, we had tremendous offensive lines in St. Louis, but our defensive lines were hardly world-championship caliber. No one unit or individual or game or play determines the outcome of a season. Everything has to mesh, and when you think about it, it usually doesn't for most teams.

That's what makes the opportunity to play for the world championship of professional football so special.

■   ■   ■

Several months after announcing my retirement, I was given an opportunity to suit up again—this time, in the now-defunct United States Football League. The opportunity came from the Arizona Wranglers. Bill Baker, my offensive line coach at the University of Wyoming, was the Wranglers' player-personnel director. He called and asked if I'd be interested in joining his team if the Wranglers could acquire my territorial rights from the Denver Gold (which owned them because I played at Wyoming). I said I was, and he made the deal.

The next step, of course, was agreeing to a contract. And that's where the problems began. The Wranglers offered me

$50,000, and there was no way I was going to come out of retirement for that. It was going to take at least $150,000 to get me even to consider exposing my already battered body to another year of punishment. So Bill went back to his superiors to try to sweeten the offer.

Then, all of a sudden, they said, "You know, with those bad knees of his, he just isn't worth signing at any price." But that was fine. I hadn't gone to them; they came to me. Nothing gained. Nothing lost.

Late in the 1983 USFL season, my agent, Richard Bennett, received an offer for my services from the Washington Federals. The Federals were willing to pay me $100,000 if I would play in the final seven games for them. That was all I had to do—play seven games, collect my money, and go back into retirement.

"I'll take it," I told Richard.

But there was one big catch—the Wranglers still owned my rights. They told the Federals, "Sure, you can have Dobler. But it'll cost you two first-round draft picks." No way the Federals, or any team for that matter, were going to give up that much for a thirty-two-year-old offensive guard with two bad knees. But the Wranglers refused to budge, preventing me from making an easy $100,000.

The irony of the whole thing was, the Wranglers didn't consider me worth two cents to them, yet when someone else wanted to sign me, I suddenly commanded two first-round choices.

Believe it or not, one of the first things I did after putting my professional athletic career behind me was to enroll in weekly aerobics classes.

But I still had that instinct of wanting to hit someone, especially when July rolled around. July's when a pro football player begins gearing himself up for training camp—his first taste of contact in seven months. Football contact, that is. So, for most of that first year away from the game, I tried my best to stay out of the bars and off the streets. When you've been used to hitting people in practice and games every year for eighteen years, it's not something you can just turn off like a light switch. I was afraid, if some guy did or said the wrong thing to me, I might start playing football with his head.

And the officials who came to break it up wouldn't be wearing zebra stripes; they'd have badges.

Watching NFL games on TV that year was very difficult. Being the emotionally charged player I was, I couldn't even stand to watch from the sidelines, let alone my living room. I wanted to be out there doing battle again. And I'd look at certain guys and say, "I know I could do a better job than him. Look at that guy miss his block! Look at him blow his assignment!" Looking back on it now, with the way my knees were at that point, I probably wouldn't have done much better and I might have done a lot worse.

Fortunately, I gradually was able to let go of those feelings.

In 1983, Hoffmann-La Roche, Inc., which manufactures Valium, assembled a panel of celebrities to share their experiences with arthritis as part of a program to help physicians better understand the psychological effects of the disease. Having developed degenerative arthritis in my knees early in my career, I was an obvious choice from the world of pro football. The other distinguished panelists were Eric Sevareid, Virginia Graham, Dr. Christiaan Barnard, and Lynn Adams, a world champion women's racquetball player.

Basically, our message to the physicians was to do a little bit more for their patients than say, "You've got arthritis; you'll just have to learn to live with it." You *do* have to learn to live with it. But I think doctors should help their patients understand exactly what they have to learn to live with. They must explain to the expert skier that he or she has got to settle for being an intermediate skier. Not *stop* skiing, but accept that you'll never be as good as you once were. If you lecture standing up all day and you have arthritis, you'd better learn how to lecture sitting in a chair. If you are a marathoner, you'll find that you can't jog as long or as frequently as you want.

I lived with arthritis as a player. I'm living with it now—the only time I don't experience pain is when I'm asleep. There's nothing you can take to make it go away. The best treatment for me is swallowing about eight aspirin a day—four in the morning, four at night. That keeps the pain at a tolerable level for basic activities, like moving around the house or sleeping (although I can't sleep on my side with one leg on top of the other because the weight of the top knee bothers the bottom knee, and there are many nights when I sleep with ice bags on both knees). When I do other things, like ski or play racquetball or walk around a golf course, I'll take aspirin plus Indocin to reduce the swelling in my joints temporarily.

But my definition of living with the pain is not living *without* everything else. That's not me. I always like to be where the action is.

After my retirement, there was plenty of nonfootball activity awaiting me in the many business ventures with which I got involved during my playing career. At one time, I had interests in a bank, a bar, a radio station, a racquetball facility, a construction company, office buildings, apartments and warehouses in Wyoming, oil-drilling rigs in Louisiana, and a farm in Iowa.

I still own some of that property. I'm a partner in a real estate firm in Fort Collins, Colorado (where I now live with my lovely second wife, Joy, and our children), I'm a celebrity host for the El Dorado Hotel in Reno, and I do some work for a U.S. shipping company.

However, when people ask what I do for a living, I always tell them I work for the Miller Brewing Company. To me, making public appearances throughout the country as a Miller Lite All-Star is the greatest occupation in the world. It pays well, I get first-class treatment, and the exposure helps my other businesses. In fact, I tell my business partners that I can give them only an average of three days a week because the rest of the time is spent traveling for Miller. It behooves them to want me to approach it that way because all of those public appearances and the contacts they produce add up to a ton of free advertising.

My association with Miller officially began with the making of my "Famous Troublemaker" TV commercial for Miller Lite. It took three years, three auditions, and three scripts before I finally landed that spot.

And I thought breaking into the NFL was tough!

Marty Blackman, talent coordinator for the Miller Lite commercials, contacted me in 1983 to set up my first audition in New York. I had worked with him during my playing career on a TV ad, called "The Ten Toughest Beards," for Bic razor blades.

The audition tape is the first critical step in getting hired; because it is sent to corporate headquarters in Milwaukee, where the decision is made whether to go ahead—not with the *airing* of the commercial; just the making of it. There's no guarantee, even after the commercial's made, that it will ever see the light of day. Needless to say, the Miller executives weren't impressed with my first two offerings. I wasn't too crazy about them, either. In both cases, I was dealing with terrible scripts.

The first one had me standing on the sideline for the playing of the National Anthem. Before the song ends, I suddenly run over to tackle a player from the other team. It didn't work. I just wasn't comfortable with the concept because, reputation notwithstanding, I was an offensive lineman—a blocker, not a tackler. The second script had me starting a "Tastes great! Less filling!" fight in a bar, and a referee suddenly emerging to throw a yellow flag.

Then, in 1986, they came to me with the "Famous Troublemaker" idea. I fell in love with it immediately. It has me taking a seat between two fans at a game, introducing myself to the audience as a troublemaker, but confessing I'm really "just a nice guy who likes to watch a game with a Miller Lite."

I proceed to get the two fans into a "Tastes great! Less filling!" argument, with both sides of the section joining in. A few seconds later, I reappear in another section of the stadium, find another guy drinking Miller Lite because it "tastes great" and get another argument started.

Unlike the previous two auditions, for which I went in stone-cold, for this one I was sent a copy of the script in advance. That gave me ample time to study before I arrived in New York for the taping.

Miller put me up at the Grand Hyatt Hotel. And on the eve of the audition, Phil Villapiano drove up from his home in New Jersey—along with a few other guys I had met through him down there—to help me rehearse. We spent about four hours going over the whole scene in my room, with members of the Jersey gang playing the other parts as I recited my lines. I'll bet we went through an entire case of Miller Lite before we were finished. Just for the sake of keeping it as realistic as possible, of course.

I felt sorry for anyone who might have been staying in the rooms next to mine, because we had gotten fairly loud—at least as loud as the extras who shout "Tastes great! Less filling!" at each other in the commercial. OK, maybe louder.

We talked about the facial expressions Miller's corporate people would be looking for, and about how I might use some real-life experiences to help create those expressions. Pretty heavy philosophy from a bunch of drunks.

But they really wanted me to get that commercial. They were my friends, and that's what friends are for.

My buddies had asked if they could accompany me to the audition the next day. They wanted to play the parts of the other fans—after four hours of rehearsing and drinking, I guess we all thought we were the greatest actors in the world. But I figured, since Miller never said anything about me bringing my own talent and I was in no position to be pushy, it would be best if I went by myself.

Most Miller Lite commercials are filmed on location, rather than in a studio. That's just the way people at the advertising agency of Backer & Spielvogel prefer to do them. They've rented softball diamonds, bowling alleys, taverns, you name it. They even rented a train for John Madden, the only man I know who hates to fly more than my ex-Buffalo teammate Isiah Robertson.

For my spot, they went to all the cost and trouble of renting Giants Stadium, just to use a small area of seats in one of the end zones.

The shooting took about five hours. Although there probably were thirty or forty takes, I thought things went rather smoothly. The biggest problem we had all day was keeping a head on each plastic cup of beer we were holding. Periodically, someone would come around with a little battery-powered mixer, stick it in your cup and, *presto*, you had a fresh head.

Bob Giraldi, who directs the commercials, was great to work with—especially for someone like me, who really didn't have much acting experience (that is, if you exclude the times I pretended to look interested during Dick Nolan's pregame speeches in New Orleans).

The only acting technique I'd acquired was to tighten the muscles in my ass before I spoke so it would make me sound angry. I only wish I had known about that little tactic when I was playing. Maybe, if my voice had been more intimidating, I wouldn't have had to put my body through so much punishment.

I decided that day that if I ever did pursue a career as an actor, the first thing I'd do was take lessons. I wouldn't want to embarrass myself, like so many athletes-turned-actors have. Take O. J. Simpson. He was terrible when he started out in the movies because he went about it as if he knew what he was doing when he really didn't.

As with anything else, if you take the time and get the instruction, you're only going to be better for it.

My second TV appearance for Miller Lite came in the 1987 reunion commercial. That's the one where a bunch of us are dressed like cowboys sitting around a campfire in the middle of a desert, when all of a sudden a flying saucer lands and we flee in terror as an army of Rodney Dangerfield clones gets off. What made it so much fun was that just about every member of the All-Star team took part in the filming, which took three-and-a-half days. The Culver City, California, studio was filled with sporting legends clowning around, telling jokes, and trading war stories.

Giraldi's handling of the group made him sound more like

a head coach than a director. He even gave us a "pregame" speech the first day we arrived about not drinking and staying out late. We complied with those orders the same way we complied when our coaches gave them to us.

Which is to say we didn't.

But, like true pro's pros, everyone answered the bell each day at 6:00 A.M.

The public response to my first Miller Lite commercial was phenomenal. In all of my ten years in the NFL, a visit to my hometown of Twentynine Palms, California, barely generated enthusiasm among my own family and friends, let alone strangers. But when I visited there after the reunion taping, about three months after "Famous Troublemaker" came out, everyone who saw me wanted an autograph.

Men bought me beers. Women offered me sexual favors.

I had to laugh. I mean, you go through what you think is a pretty illustrious pro football career. You beat up your body and receive a lot of recognition from your peers, the media, the fans. Then you go and do one beer commercial, five hours' worth of work, and suddenly you're an American hero. If I had known then what I know now, I'd have headed straight for Hollywood.

I don't mind my celebrity status. I thought it was great when I was playing, and I'm even more fond of it now that I've been out of the game for six seasons. When a professional athlete retires, when he stops hearing the roar of the crowd, there's a tendency for him to feel forgotten. No matter how popular he was when he was playing, he no longer has that regular opportunity to perform. Nobody is monitoring his every action and reaction, on and off the field, on a daily, weekly, monthly, or yearly basis anymore.

So it's especially gratifying to walk down the street or be sitting in a restaurant and have people come up to you and say, "I know you. You're Conrad Dobler. You're the trouble-maker." Or have them yell, "Tastes great!" encouraging me to yell back, "Less filling!" Or bring over their empty bottles of Miller Lite and have me sign the labels.

Since then, I've become a part of the Miller Lite All-Stars. In that capacity, I travel all over the country to appear or speak at a wide variety of functions. Another job of an All-Star is to go around to several bars in a town and mingle with the customers.

Imagine getting paid to barhop. And to think of all those years I did it for free.

I still want to be the very best at anything I do. My All-Star career is no exception. I may not always have succeeded at being the very best offensive guard during my ten years in the NFL. But I always tried, causing quite a bit of commotion along the way.

Enough to fill a book. Or two?